The Cemeteries of Westchester County

Volume III

...k · Mount Vernon · New Rochelle

...ye Town · Scarsdale · Yonkers

...k Raftery

...nty Historical Society

2011

ISBN 0-915585-15-4

Published by the Westchester County Historical Society
2199 Saw Mill River Road, Elmsford, NY 10523

Front Cover, Outside: This early 20th-century color postcard depicts Saint Paul's Episcopal Church Cemetery in Mount Vernon.

Front Cover, Inside, Top Left: The fieldstone which was placed at the grave of Richard Shute is the oldest identifiable tombstone in Westchester County. Shute was a leading citizen of the Town of Eastchester, which at the time included the present City of Mount Vernon, and served as Eastchester Town Clerk for 38 years.[1] Shute died on December 14, 1704, and was interred within sight of his home lot, which was located on the west side of South Third Avenue between South Columbus Avenue and East Seventh Street. The fact that Shute had an inscribed grave marker is indicative of his prominence in the community.

R S · D
DECEM
BER
14 · 1704

Front Cover, Inside, Top Right: This tombstone, which stood in the Nelson Family Burial Ground in Mamaroneck for more than 100 years, is now located in the Rhinebeck Cemetery, Dutchess County.

PALYCARPES
NELSON
WAS   BORN
IVLY · 21 · ABOT · 4 ·
A · CLOCK · IN · THE · MO
RNING · IN · THE · YEAR ·
1688 · I · FINNIST · MY · CORS
AND · QVIT · THE · LAND · IN ·
WITNES · HERE · OF · MY · HART · MY ·
HAND · DESESED · DESEMBER · 19
1738

Front Cover, Inside, Bottom Left: Michael Keirns' tombstone is located on a hillside in Saint Mary's Cemetery, Yonkers, only a few yards away from the New York State Thruway. The marble monument is carved in the shape of a Celtic cross and contains the depiction of a harp, which is Ireland's heraldic emblem.

MICHAEL KEIRNS
A NATIVE OF
CO. MAYO,
IRELAND.
DIED
OCT. 26, 1871,
AGED
32 YEARS.

MAY HIS SOUL REST
IN PEACE AMEN.

ERECTED BY
HIS BELOVED WIFE,
BRIDGET KEIRNS.

Front Cover, Inside, Bottom Right: The tombstone of Bella Levine in Sherwood Park Cemetery, Yonkers. In Jewish cemeteries, images of candles or candelabra often appear on tombstones of women. Many early Jewish graves in Westchester County also contain photographs of the deceased.

Beloved Wife
And Dear Mother
Bella Levine
Died July 2, 1922
Aged 46 Years

MOTHER

Above: The tombstone of Moses Clark (1732-1806) in the Christ Methodist Church Cemetery.

In
Memory of
MOSES CLARK,
who departed this Life
the 2nd July 1806,
Aged 74 Years 2 Months
& 24 Days.

Remember man as you pass by,
As you are now so once was I;
As I am now so you must be,
Prepare for death and follow me.

Contents

Foreword	vi
Preface	viii
Acknowledgments	ix
Introduction	x
Eastchester	1
Mamaroneck	11
Mount Vernon	43
New Rochelle	59
Pelham	121
Rye City	123
Rye Town	151
Scarsdale	169
Yonkers	175
Appendix	207
Notes	213
Sources	229
Index	233

Foreword
By Gray Williams

Above: A portion of the Huguenot Burying Ground in New Rochelle, December 3, 1911.

The graveyards and cemeteries of Westchester are rich repositories of our county's history. The sites themselves reflect the evolution of the county from pioneer Colonial settlements to modern suburbs. The gravestones and other monuments contained within them not only record the deaths of our forebears, but also provide insight into their lives, their communities, their culture and their values.

Patrick Raftery has made an enormous contribution to the history of Westchester with this definitive catalog of all its known churchyards, family graveyards and public cemeteries, including both those that still exist and those that have disappeared. He has combined exhaustive documentary research with painstaking observation and photography to provide what will unquestionably prove to be an enduring reference. But from his detailed descriptions there also emerges a revealing account of how the commemoration of the dead has evolved over the centuries and of how this evolution reflects changes in society itself.

The earliest grave markers in Westchester, dating back to the beginning of the 18th century, are fieldstones, sometimes roughly shaped like traditional gravestones but often just upright slabs, and crudely lettered by family members or by semiprofessionals like blacksmiths or sign painters. Not until the 1750s did professional monuments start to appear, carved in reddish-brown sandstone by artist-craftsmen in New Jersey and New York City, and reflecting the growing stability and prosperity of Westchester communities in the decades leading to the Revolution.

After the war, professional gravestones became prevalent, except among the plain-living Quakers, some of whom continued to mark graves with fieldstones well into the 1800s. About the turn of 19th century, when Americans found a spiritual kinship between their young republic and ancient Greece and Rome, the makers of grave monuments shifted from sandstone to Classical marble. New shapes were introduced based on Classical architecture, and new decorative motifs such as the weeping willow and funerary urn became popular. Epitaphs also changed, from dire warnings of death and damnation ("As I am now, so shall you be, / Prepare for death and follow me.") to promises of heavenly resurrection ("Man dies to live, / And lives to die no more."). In the 1830s and 1840s, parklike rural cemeteries began to supplant traditional churchyards and private burying grounds. And in the decades leading to the Civil War, elaborate memorials to the wealthy, such as crypts and mausoleums, started to appear, a trend that would become even more pronounced later.

In the 1880s monument makers began to shift once again, this time from marble to more durable granite, which largely remains the material of choice to this day. Up until the Great Depression, the monuments and mausoleums of the wealthy, like their extensive estates and opulent houses, became even larger and more extravagant. The leveling effects of the Crash are reflected in the simpler and more modest grave markers that became prevalent in the latter decades of the 20th century. They remain so still, with the possible exception of the increasingly popular personalized monuments of the last 20 years or so, which have been made possible by new etching technology, and commemorate the deceased with detailed illustrations of their favorite landscapes and activities in life.

One rather surprising aspect of Westchester funerary history is the great number of private graveyards that exist—or used to exist—around the county. They reflect the fact that through most of the 19th century, Westchester remained largely rural, and burial on the family farm was an easy option. But they also represent the religious and cultural diversity of New York State, from Colonial times on. For example, Westchester has almost no community burying grounds or large churchyards like those that are common in New England, partly because so many farm families evidently preferred the greater privacy and flexibility of burial at home.

But the privacy of family graveyards proved their undoing. Most of them have been long abandoned by the families that created them, and many have disappeared entirely. Typically, when a farm was sold or bequeathed out of the family, the family graveyard was specifically excluded from the deed to the property, with the expectation that descendants would always be ready and willing to care for it. Such hopes almost always proved vain, as later generations scattered or died out. Only a few such private graveyards are still maintained. Of those that still exist, most are in a state of neglect. Many more have vanished, usually as victims to the all-devouring bulldozers of suburban development.

Nowadays, virtually all Westchester burials are in free-standing cemeteries, some religious, the majority secular. But the cemeteries are running out of space, and no new ones are being established. Open land is generally considered too

valuable to the living to be used for the dead. Within existing cemeteries, communal mausoleums have become an increasingly popular alternative to earth burial. Cremation has also become more common. Cemetery columbaria and church memory gardens offer a space-saving option, and some families elect to scatter the ashes and dispense with any monument at all–a choice that would have been all but inconceivable to our forebears.

All these traditions are meticulously described and copiously illustrated in this comprehensive, community-by-community survey. It will provide a rich feast for those (like myself) who are interested in graveyards and grave monuments for their own sake. But for those who are interested in the history of our county in general, this book offers a valuable insight into one of its most important cultural elements. Graveyards not only record our history, they embody our history.

Right: This marble tombstone in the Disbrow Family Burial Ground in Mamaroneck reads:

IN MEMORY OF
EDWARD MERRITT.
who died Sept. 16th, 1831,
Aged 40 years & 6 months.

When the last trumpet shall bid thee rise
We'll haste to meet thee in the skies
Where smiles of love eternal glow
And parting tears will never flow

Preface

"Cemeteries?" remarked one of the Society's board members when I proposed this book. "That's a strange topic for a young man to be interested in." I prefer the term "novel," but I suppose it might be a little strange. Growing up in lower Westchester, I had occasionally taken note of the county's old burial grounds. I can well remember hearing my grandmother recounting the removal of an old Huguenot cemetery for the construction of the New England Thruway, as well as my father telling a story that he heard from his father regarding the discovery of Revolutionary War soldiers in Eastchester. There was also the graveyard with dilapidated white stones that my family passed along Palmer Avenue in Mamaroneck on the way to Walter's Hot Dog Stand, as well as the ancient tombstones that leaned over Route 9A just up from West Rumbrook Park. When I played at the Quaker Ridge Country Club with my high school golf team, I wondered how many golfers saw their errant shots land in the overgrown burial ground on the right side of one of the fairways.

In the summer of 2004 I had an internship at Saint Paul's National Historic Site in Mount Vernon. Much of my time there was spent in the churchyard plotting a map of the late 19th-century family lots. While spending the summer days out in the old cemetery, I was fascinated by the stories that were told by the tombstones and monuments. An old sandstone marking the burial of a slave named Thomas stood not far from the elaborate marble memorials at graves of Mount Vernon's wealthy families from the late 1800s. The bones believed to be those of patriot soldiers were interred a few yards from a sandpit that served as the final resting place for their Hessian adversaries.

One day after work, I decided to finally have a look at the old tombstones that were just up the street from Walter's. "That's James Fenimore Cooper's father-in-law," a man shouted to me as I tried to decipher the worn words on a tall marble headstone. I became curious—what other stories could be found in these historic places? When the time came for me to choose a topic for my senior paper at Concordia College, I already had an idea in mind—I would research the burial grounds that I had always been curious about.

I was fortunate enough to have my senior paper published in the Summer 2006 issue of *The Westchester Historian*. Afterward, I was approached by a number of people who were curious about burial grounds located in northern Westchester. Although I had originally planned on writing a second article for *The Westchester Historian*, I soon realized that the topic deserved book-length treatment. I hope that this work is useful not only to researchers, but also to those who are interested in preserving the county's burial grounds.

This book is dedicated to the memory of my grandparents

William Joseph Raftery II (1914-1961)
Mary Margaret Sullivan Raftery (1913-1995)
Joseph Thomas DeLigio (1913-2000)
Agnes Patricia Keaveney DeLigio (1922-1977)

and my great-uncle

John Edward "Jack" Sullivan (1907-1991)

Funding for this publication was generously provided by

Jane and Robert Keiter

Acknowledgements

As I've learned over the past few years, no book is ever truly the work of one person. Since I began researching the cemeteries of Westchester County in 2004, a number of individuals have assisted me with information, photos, proofreading, wisdom and encouragement. First and foremost, I am grateful for the assistance of my fellow staff at the Westchester County Historical Society. Executive Director Katie Hite and "Librarian Emeritus" Elizabeth Fuller were receptive when I first suggested a cemetery book in 2007. Both Katie and Elizabeth painstakingly read my manuscript several times for style and grammar. Librarian Diana Deichert and Trustee Bill Ketchum also read my manuscript, and their comments and suggestions helped improve the quality of the final product.

New Castle Town Historian Gray Williams, the county's foremost expert in all things cemetery-related, read the manuscript and offered several corrections and additions as well as photos from his personal collection. Without his knowledge, guidance and time, this project would never have reached such a high standard of quality. Gray's tremendous efforts in chronicling the county's cemeteries have included research and documentation as well as physical preservation.

In the spring of 2008 I contacted Bedford Town Historian John Stockbridge, who coincidentally had just become part of a fledgling committee that was established to restore the burial grounds in his town. With John's help, I was able to visit 10 of Bedford's family burial grounds that are surrounded by private property.

Mount Pleasant Town Historian George Waterbury and his wife Claudine shared their knowledge regarding the various burial grounds in their town. Claudine was gracious enough to copy all of the Mount Pleasant Historical Society's cemetery information for me. For 20 years, George personally maintained the Banks Cemetery in Pleasantville, and it is largely due to his efforts that the three cemeteries at Broadway and Church Street are kept in excellent condition.

Four members of the North Castle Historical Society provided invaluable information regarding their town's cemeteries: Barbara and Lewis Massi, Tony Godino and George Pouder. George and the Massis graciously shared their cemetery photos as well as the information they had gathered during a survey they conducted of North Castle's burial places. Barbara and Tony's investigative research uncovered a long-forgotten cemetery in the Mianus River Gorge Preserve.

The following staff members and volunteers at the Westchester County Archives and Records Center never failed to assist me during the seven years I was conducting research for this project, both as a student at Concordia College and as an employee at the historical society: Larry Auerbach, Melanie Brocklehurst, Larry Brotmann, Patty Dohrenwend, Courtney Fallon, Trish Foy, Jackie Graziano, Christine Hogan, Marilyn Littman, Nell Macdonald, Elaine Massena, Bill Prusak, Cindy Sauer, Walter Schwartz and Muriel Weiss.

The following individuals also provided me with invaluable assistance:

Wint Aldrich	Peter Eschweiler	David Osborn
Jack Archer	Ryan Herchenroether	Gloria P. Pritts
Terry Ariano	Miguel Hernandez	Janice Rabinowitz
Nancy Augustowski	Jim Hoch	Rick Rogers
Steve Basch	Rob Hoch	Sister Maryann Ronneburger
Alison Beall	Frank Jazzo	Christopher Ross
Lucas Buresch	Maureen Koehl	Stanley Telega
Barbara Davis	Jean Ann Orser Lupinetti	Susan Thompson
Monica Doherty	Norman MacDonald	Doris Finch Watson
Ken Eldon	Florence Oliver	Harvey Wolchan

Last, but certainly not least, I am thankful for all of the encouragement and support that my parents Dan and Nancy and my brother Brian have always provided me.

Introduction

Each town and city in Westchester County has a chapter which contains entries for most burial places in that municipality. Incorporated villages are listed within the towns that contain them. A listing of the burial places may be found on the first page of each chapter. Additionally, the end of each chapter contains a listing of miscellaneous burial places for which there is no separate entry. Generally, each burial place entry contains the following information:

-Location.

-Dates of use.

-A mailing address for active cemeteries.

-Other names by which the burial place is known.

-For cemeteries that are no longer in existence, the burial ground or grounds to which removals were made.

-Where a list of inscriptions may be found for the cemetery within the collection of the Westchester County Historical Society. Note that the Society's lists generally predate 1925, and, with few exceptions, are for cemeteries founded before 1850.

-A brief history of the cemetery.

-A guide to useful sources that are not listed in the bibliography.

Types of Cemeteries

Municipal and **community** cemeteries and burial grounds are places of interment that are owned by a municipality and are open to all its residents. The idea of the village burying ground comes from New England, where each community had a public cemetery. The Blind Brook Burial Ground in Rye, which was settled by New Englanders, served as a community burial ground for nearly 200 years. The Town of Mamaroneck established a municipal cemetery in 1829, while the City of Mount Vernon used a section of Saint Paul's Episcopal Church Cemetery as a public burial ground from 1892 to the 1940s.

Churchyards were the most widely used places of interment in communities that were not settled by New Englanders. It was customary for congregations to set apart a portion of the property on which their houses of worship stood as a "God's Acre." The county's first churchyard, the Old Dutch Burying Ground in Mount Pleasant, is also its oldest surviving cemetery. The popularity of churchyards as places of interment began to decline toward the mid-19th century, partly because many churchyards were running out of space, and partly because non-sectarian rural cemeteries were coming into fashion.

A number of **family burial grounds** were established throughout Westchester County. These burial grounds were generally established by landowners on their farms and estates. The oldest surviving family cemetery in Westchester is the 17th century Richbell Cemetery in Mamaroneck, while the last family burial ground established in the county is the 1936 Norman-Weil Family Cemetery in Bedford. Unfortunately, as time progressed and the owners of these cemeteries sold their estates and moved away, these burial places were often neglected and forgotten. For example, the Flandreau Family Burial Ground in New Rochelle was nearly destroyed when the land surrounding it was subdivided and developed in the 1930s and nearly all of the tombstones in this burial ground have disappeared over the past 80 years. The majority of Westchester's family burial grounds are located in the northern part of the county.

The **rural cemetery** movement began in the United States when Mount Auburn Cemetery in Massachusetts was opened in 1831. Rural Cemeteries are intended to be "burial parks" which feature winding paths and unique landscaping. On April 27, 1847, the New York State Legislature passed the Rural Cemetery Act, which established guidelines for independent cemeteries. On April 15, 1854, this act was amended, and mandated that no land in Westchester could be dedicated for burial purposes "without the consent of the [county] board of supervisors."[2] Westchester's first rural cemetery, the Sleepy Hollow Cemetery in Mount Pleasant, was established in 1849. There are three rural cemeteries located in the municipalities that are covered by this volume: Beechwood Cemetery in New Rochelle (1854), Greenwood Union Cemetery in the City of Rye (1855) and Oakland Cemetery in Yonkers (1867).

Sectarian cemeteries began to develop after the Civil War, as religious groups sought to create proper burial places for the deceased members. Nearly all of the sectarian cemeteries in Westchester are for those of the Roman Catholic and Jewish faiths, both of which generally did not establish burial grounds adjacent to their churches and synagogues. Instead, these congregations purchased large pieces of land in an undeveloped area not far from their houses of worship. For example, the

Church of Our Lady of Mercy in Port Chester acquired a tract which became Saint Mary's Cemetery outside of the village boundaries in 1870. The oldest sectarian cemetery within the municipalities covered by this volume is Saint John's Cemetery, an Episcopal burial place in Yonkers.

Recently, a new kind of interment place has become popular in Westchester County: the **columbarium**, which contains niches for the placement of cremated remains. In some cases, columbaria are located adjacent to houses of worship. Such is the case, for example, with Christ Episcopal Church in Bronxville. Although cremation is permitted in the Roman Catholic Church, the ashes must be buried or placed in a proper enclosure. Blessed Sacrament Church in New Rochelle has recently constructed a columbarium for its parishioners in Saint Joseph's Cemetery.

 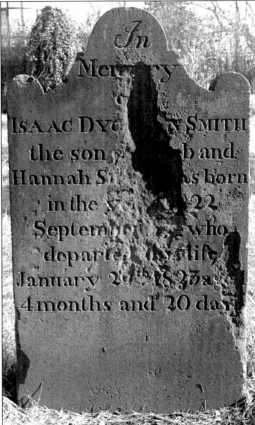

Types of Gravestones

There are several kinds of gravestones that are discussed in this book:

-**Headstones** were used to mark the head of a grave, while **footstones** were used to mark the foot of a grave. Generally, footstones were only inscribed with the initials of the deceased. While footstones are usually found behind their headstones, they may occasionally be found in front of them. The use of footstones began in the late 18th century, and declined at the end of the 19th century, when the more careful mapping of burial plots made them unnecessary. Many have disappeared since, often removed by maintenance workers to facilitate mowing.

-**Fieldstones** (top left) were the first grave markers used by residents of Westchester County to mark graves. Occasionally, these stones included the initials of the deceased and the year of death, while a few even had lengthier (albeit crudely carved) inscriptions. This fieldstone is located in the Richbell Cemetery, Mamaroneck.

-**Sandstones** (top right) were the most commonly used kind of grave markers in Westchester County from the late 1750s to the early 1800s. This sandstone marks the grave of Isaac Dyckman Smith (1822-1823), and is located in Saint John's Episcopal Church Cemetery on Underhill Street in Yonkers. Eighteenth-century sandstones usually have a symbol carved at the top. While a few sandstones depict macabre symbols such as skulls and bones, the majority are inscribed with "soul effigies" in the form of a winged head. The inscriptions on these markers have held up very well, and intact sandstones are as legible now as they were over 200 years ago. Unfortunately, sandstones are susceptible to damage from rain and freezing temperatures. Water can seep between the layers of the sedimentary rock, where it freezes and expands, causing the layers to split and flake off

-**Slate tombstones** were produced exclusively in New England and occasionally imported into Westchester during the 18th century. Only two slate tombstones may be found in the municipalities that are covered in this volume. They are depicted on pages 24 and 56.

Marble tombstones came into fashion about the beginning of the 19th century. Many of the marble tombstones in Westchester County during the antebellum period usually feature symbols of mourning such as a weeping willow or a funerary urn. The tombstones of children usually feature depictions of lambs or doves, while those of teenagers and young adults may have carvings of flowers. Most of the marble tombstones in Westchester have not held up well against the elements, and their inscriptions have often faded. The marble tombstone at top right marks the graves of Henry and Ann Disbrow in the Disbrow Family Burial Ground, Mamaroneck.

Granite tombstones came into fashion during the late 19th century. Today, granite is the preferred choice for virtually all the tombstones that are cut in Westchester County.

Zinc monuments were made by the Monumental Bronze Company of Bridgeport, Connecticut, from 1875 to 1912. Although they were not commonly used, these hollow memorials have held up very well against the elements, and are generally in very good condition. The monument at top left contains a zinc base, and marks the graves of three children of Frank H. and Catharine Connolly: Emma (1877-1878), Frank H. (1873-1874), and F. Halcyon (1877).

Town of Eastchester

Left: Holy Mount Cemetery in 2008. The monument in the foreground is the tallest in the cemetery and marks the graves of members of the Forrest and Leary families.

Right: This 2008 photo shows the marker placed by the Daughters of the American Revolution at Saint Paul's Church Cemetery in Mount Vernon to mark the site of the reburials from the Winter Hill Burying Ground near Ward's house in Tuckahoe.

Bronxville Cemetery	2
Bronxville Reformed Church Burying Ground and Vault	5
Holy Mount Cemetery	6
Immaculate Conception Burying Ground	7
Ward's House Revolutionary War Burials	8
Winter Hill Burying Ground	8

Prior to 1892 the City of Mount Vernon was part of the Town of Eastchester. Thus, the early residents of the town would have interred their friends and family at Saint Paul's Church in present-day Mount Vernon. In fact, the eastern section of the cemetery at Saint Paul's was reserved as a burial place for Eastchester residents who were not of the Episcopal faith. Present-day Eastchester boasts relatively few cemeteries, and the majority of these were removed from their original locations. Interestingly, both of the active burial grounds were founded by religious congregations whose churchyards became inadequate. The Reformed Presbyterian Church of Manhattan founded the Bronxville Cemetery during the mid-19th century after burials were prohibited at their churchyard in New York City, while the pastor of the Roman Catholic Church of the Immaculate Conception established Holy Mount Cemetery during the late 19th century when the graveyard that adjoined his house of worship could not properly support the burial needs of his parishioners. Additionally, two long-lost 18th-century burial sites in Tuckahoe were uncovered during the early 20th century. A small colonial graveyard, the Winter Hill Burying Ground, and the burial place of the American soldiers who were killed during a Revolutionary War skirmish at Ward's house on the White Plains Post Road were rediscovered during two different construction projects in Tuckahoe.

Bronxville Cemetery
Eastchester (Bronxville)

Above: Looking northwest at the western half of Bronxville Cemetery in 2008.

Location: West side of Palumbo Place between Midland and Gramatan avenues. Note that a portion of the cemetery is located in the City of Mount Vernon.

Dates of Activity: 1852 – Present.

Other Names: Covenantor Cemetery, Reformed Presbyterian Cemetery, Scotch Presbyterian Cemetery, Shoemakers Yard.

Inscriptions: *WCHS* Book #8 (p.68-87).

Mailing Address: 18 Midland Avenue, Bronxville, NY 10708.

Notes: Although the land on which Bronxville Cemetery is situated was purchased for burial purposes in 1852, visitors to this graveyard will find several tombstones in the graveyard that date from the first half of the 19th century. In 1992 cemetery manager Dr. Richard B. Weir described the origins of the burial ground in an article for *The Villager*:

> "What a beautiful cemetery. How old is it?" To this I answer, "We are 140 years old, and can you guess where the cemetery was located before 1852?" Of course they don't even have an idea, but it is interesting to watch their faces when I tell them that it [was located] in New York City. The Reformed Presbyterian Church which founded Bronxville Cemetery was located on 11th Street in Manhattan. During the middle of the last century the Harlem Division of the New York Central Railroad was built [and the church's cemetery was] moved out to land along that line.[1]

The oldest tombstone in the cemetery marks the burial of "a child, little Eliza Acheson…who died April 13, 1805, at the age of one year, five months, and 18 days." Eliza was among the 38 persons whose remains were removed to Bronxville from the original cemetery in Manhattan, which had been located on "the south side of 41st Street between Ninth and Tenth Avenues," thirty blocks north of the church itself.[2] Richard Weir's son and successor in the management of the cemetery, Dr. David A. Weir, added the following information regarding the cemetery:

> The Bronxville Cemetery, however, has no connection with any Village church. It has always been owned by the Reformed Presbyterian Church of North America (Covenanter Synod).... The Church purchased 14.19 acres of land on August 22, 1851 from Cornelius Winter Bolton and other members of the Bolton family. The tract of land stretched down to the Bronx River and encompassed the future Alden Place site. After it had laid out the Cemetery, the Church sold the remaining acreage to F.W. Edmonds, who lived at the Crow's Nest.[3]

In 1899 a house was built next to the Midland Avenue entrance to the cemetery to serve as a caretaker's cottage. Since 1900 all of the cemetery caretakers have resided at this home. The cemetery had but one vehicle entrance until 1957, when the gate and entranceway on Palumbo Place were constructed.[4] Although the cemetery is "of Protestant heritage," the burial of persons of all faiths is permitted. As of 1974 the cemetery contained the remains of "three veterans of the Civil War, one of the Mexican War, about forty-five of the two World Wars and an Englishman of the Royal Army Service Corps."[5]

Left: The much-faded headstone of one-year-old Eliza Acheson, who died in 1805, is the oldest tombstone in Bronxville Cemetery and the Town of Eastchester. Like all of the tombstones which pre-date the 1852 founding of Bronxville Cemetery, Eliza's headstone was moved to this burial ground from its original location in the cemetery of the Reformed Presbyterian Church on 41st Street in Manhattan.

Right: The electricians who served aboard the battleship *USS Oklahoma* erected this monument at the grave of George H. Kennedy (1893-1917), who lost his life in battle practice shortly before America's entry into World War I.

Above: Two of the more elaborate monuments in Bronxville Cemetery in 2010. The taller monument at left marks the grave of Sarah Bell, who died in 1861 at the age of 47, while the one on the right marks the grave of her daughter, also named Sarah, who died in 1874 at the age of 25. Both of the monuments feature upside-down torches, which symbolize life snuffed out. The tombstone that is partially visible at far left marks the grave of Thomas Bell, husband of the elder Sarah and father of the younger Sarah, who died in 1869 at the age of 59.

4

Bronxville Reformed Church Burying Ground and Vault

Eastchester (Bronxville)

Location: 180 Pondfield Road (northwest corner of the intersection of Pondfield Road and Midland Avenue). The churchyard was located on the north side of the original church. When the present church was constructed, the remains from the churchyard were removed to a vault which is located in front of the pulpit.

Dates of Activity: 1850 – 1900.

Notes: The Reverend Cornelius Winter Bolton, son of Robert Bolton, author of *A History of the County of Westchester*, donated a piece of land at the settlement of present-day Bronxville, then called Underhill's Crossing, to "the Rev. Abel T. Stewart, minister of the Gospel" in 1849, "for the purpose of furnishing a site for a place of worship for a Dutch Reformed Society, the buildings and burying ground appertaining thereto, and for no other purpose whatsoever; and which church is to be erected within two years from the date hereof, and in default thereof this conveyance is to be void."[6] The Reformed Church congregation complied with the terms of the deed, dedicating their church on April 9, 1850. However, funds were needed to pay off the construction debt. A history of the church written in 1951 discussed how the creation of a burial ground solved this problem:

> ...on the gently sloping north side [of the church], a little burying ground was laid out where "each person who has contributed or shall contribute the sum of fifty dollars or more towards the erection of this church edifice be entitled to a lot for burial, and that such disposal of lots cease with the church debt." During the following decade or two, some sixty interments were made in the little church yard cemetery. For the greater part, the deceased were children of the workers in the factory and the stone quarry, who had died of cholera or some other epidemic which in the early days swept through the community.[7]

By 1924 the congregation had outgrown its original church building, and in order to make room for a larger edifice, a decision was made to remove the interments from the churchyard to a new vault. By this time "there were only two grave stone markers and a few small mounds" remaining in the churchyard "to indicate where these loved ones had been interred." In October of that year, these remains were "reverently placed in a vault built under the nave" of the new church, which is marked by a tablet in front of the pulpit.[8] The site of the original church is now occupied by a courtyard on the north side of the present edifice, while the location of the churchyard is now occupied by a building containing the church offices. Today, the congregation is not without an active place of interment, as a columbarium is located on the church grounds.

Right: This tablet lies in front of the pulpit and on top of the vault which contains the removals from the churchyard at the Bronxville Reformed Church. The top portion of the tablet reads:

"THAT HE MIGHT BE LORD OF
BOTH THE DEAD AND THE LIVING."

IN THE VAULT
BENEATH THIS STONE
LIE THE EARTHLY REMAINS
OF THOSE WHO WERE BURIED
IN THE CHURCHYARD · 1850 · 1900

Holy Mount Cemetery

Eastchester

Above: An aerial view of Holy Mount Cemetery about 1953. Photo courtesy Immaculate Conception Church.

Right: This veteran's marker denotes the grave of William H. Ebelt, who enlisted in Company M of the 8th New York Volunteer Infantry Regiment during the Spanish-American War. Although it was in service for six months, Ebelt's regiment never actually left the United States.

Location: At the end of Cemetery Lane, a street located on the east side of California Road about 300 feet east from its intersection with White Plains Road (Route 22).

Dates of Activity: 1882 – Present.

Mailing Address: c/o Immaculate Conception Church, 53 Winter Hill Road, Tuckahoe, NY, 10707.

Notes: Prior to the founding of Holy Mount Cemetery, the Roman Catholics of Eastchester buried their dead alongside the original Church of the Immaculate Conception in the neighborhood of Waverly. As this churchyard was insufficient to accommodate the burial needs of the parishioners, the decision was made to establish a larger cemetery for Roman Catholics of Eastchester and its surrounding area:

> In December of 1882, nearly ten acres of land were acquired for cemetery purposes, at a cost of $1,350, at the eastern extremity of the Sebastopol neighborhood (that is, the northern end of today's California Road) from John Lynch of Eastchester. There, a new cemetery was laid out of half of the tract and named Holy Mount. In 1895, the pastor, Father [John B.] Salter, was able to sell that portion which had not been laid out for burial purposes to Adrian Iselin for $5,000.... Today, more than one hundred years later, Holy Mount, which is financially self-sustaining, maintains a beauty and dignity seldom found in other Westchester cemeteries. It may be said, with all due respect, that buried there is the collective history of Immaculate Conception and modern Eastchester.[9]

The money received for the five acres sold to Mr. Iselin in 1895 "enabled Father Salter to reduce the Church's debt which he said was then 'crushing the parish.'" Father Salter noted this trend in a letter he wrote to Archbishop Michael Corrigan on May 18, 1895, at which time he requested permission to sell the five acres:

> There are ten acres of ground in the parochial cemetery five of which have not been laid out. Each adjoining parish has its own place of interment & since the opening of the White Plains cemetery the people of that place have been removing their dead from here. There are not twenty interments in a year & few of them in new ground. Consequently five acres of ground will suffice this neighborhood for generations to come.[10]

Nearly all of the burial space at Holy Mount has been sold at this time.

Immaculate Conception Church Burying Ground

Eastchester

Above Left and Above Right: These two headstones in Holy Mount Cemetery were presumably moved to that graveyard from the burying ground at the old Immaculate Conception Church. The tombstone at left marks the grave of 12-year-old Sarah Holohan, who died on December 27, 1866, while that on the right marks the grave of 5-year-old W.H. O'Gorman, who died in September 1875.

Location: Formerly at the site of the first Immaculate Conception Church (opposite Tuckahoe Avenue at its intersection with Main Street), which is presently occupied by the Eastchester Volunteer Ambulance Corps.

Dates of Activity: 1863 – 1882.

Removed: To Holy Mount Cemetery (Section M) c.1882.

Notes: The original Roman Catholic Church of the Immaculate Conception was built on Main Street in the Waverly neighborhood of Eastchester in 1856. "Like so many other nineteenth century country cemeteries, the Church's cemetery started out on the very grounds of the Church in Waverly Square where the first burial took place in 1863."[11] This churchyard was used until the parish established Holy Mount Cemetery on a 10-acre parcel in northern Eastchester in 1882. At some point thereafter, the tombstones and remains in the churchyard were removed to Holy Mount. The original Immaculate Conception church was demolished after a new house of worship was completed on Winter Hill Road in 1911.

Above: This photo depicts the original Immaculate Conception Church. It was taken sometime after the opening of Holy Mount Cemetery in 1882.

Winter Hill Burying Ground
Ward's House Revolutionary War Burials
Eastchester (Tuckahoe)

Location: Winter Hill Burying Ground was located on the west side of White Plains Post Road (Rt. 22) in the vicinity of its intersection with Winter Hill Road. The Revolutionary War burials at Ward's house were discovered between Midland Place and Midland Avenue.

Dates of Activity: Winter Hill Burying Ground, early 18th century; Ward's House Revolutionary War Burials, 1776.

Removed: The remains from Winter Hill Burying Ground were removed to Saint Paul's Church Cemetery (Section 5, Lot M, Grave 59) in 1908. The Ward's House Revolutionary War Burials were apparently reinterred on the east side of the Tuckahoe World War I monument in 1937.

Notes: The October 1908 edition of *Westchester County Magazine* reported the discovery of remains on Winter Hill:

> Near the corner of Main Street and the White Plains or New York Post Road, Tuckahoe, Westchester County, there is a knoll which, for many a year, has been known as "The Soldier's Burying Ground." Before the Civil War, some little headstones were still standing as markers for graves of the almost forgotten soldiers said to have fallen in the Revolution.
>
> In mid-September 1908, some workmen, excavating for a cellar, uncovered at this point the skeletons of about fifty men. If it can be fully established that these are the remains of American soldiers of the Revolution, the Daughters of the American Revolution of Mount Vernon, the nearest Chapter to the scene where the skeletons were unearthed, will re-inter the bones in the historic St. Paul's Church Cemetery. The place will be suitably marked.
>
> The question arises among local historians as to what soldiers these might have been. Near where the skeletons were found stood on the present site of the Gifford mansion, the famous Ward house, or tavern. In Revolutionary days it was the property of Judge Stephen Ward, a very prominent Whig. His house became such a rendezvous of the American soldiers that the British finally burned it in November, 1778. On October 24, 1776, while the American army was marching up the west side of the Bronx River to White Plains, and Howe's army up the east side to the same point, a party of Americans dashed across the Bronx, fell upon a detachment of Hessians, routed them, killed ten or more of their number and took some prisoners back with them. This skirmish was very near Ward's house.
>
> [On March 16, 1777,] the British, led by Captains Brandon and Campbell, wholly surprised the Americans who took refuge in the Ward house. The enemy battered down the barricades, entered the house, when a terrible hand to hand conflict followed. Captain Campbell himself was killed while fighting on the stairs. How many the British lost does not seem certain. Between forty and fifty Americans, and probably a few [Stockbridge] Indians, were slain, while twenty-seven were taken away prisoners. It is believed by students of local history that the dead in the two encounters we have described were buried where the skeletons have just been unearthed.[12]

According to John Dibble, "one of the American soldiers who took an active part" in the 1776 skirmish, there were but six Americans and eight British killed in this action. These soldiers were buried the next day by the returning patriots. According to the Reverend Robert Bolton, the burial site of those who fell in that action was located "in a beautiful locust grove west of [Ward's] house and directly in the rear of the barn on the opposite side of the post-road leading to White Plains."[13] Although some of the remains unearthed in 1908 may have been those of Revolutionary soldiers, it is much more likely that these bones were those of persons who were buried there before 1776. While discussing the rebuilt Ward house (which stands today at the southeast corner of Route 22 and Winslow Circle opposite Winter Hill Road), Bolton mentioned "the Winter Hill burying ground" which contained "some ancient memorials to the Hodens and Hunts. One of the headstones is inscribed 'S.1719,' another, 'Mary Hoden deceased March ye 10th, 1731.'"[14] Therefore, the headstones in the "Soldier's Burying Ground" mentioned in the above article most likely marked the burials of civilians rather than soldiers.

Beyond these observations, little else is definitively known about the Winter Hill Burying Ground. A newspaper article written at the time noted that "there are many who hold to the belief that the spot" where the remains were uncovered in 1908 "is the site of a family cemetery."[15] The 1908 find included "several skeletons with high cheek bones and evidences of Indian physique" as well as the bones of an infant.[16] Unfortunately, none of the contemporary accounts refer to the exact site of the burials, save for a 1908 newspaper article placing the graves "about one hundred feet" from Ward's house.[17] The remains which were found in 1908 were re-interred "in a big plain board coffin" at Saint Paul's Church Cemetery in Mount Vernon, not far from the burial place of the Hessian soldiers who died at that house of worship during the Revolution.[18] In 1910 a marble marker was placed at the re-interment site by the Daughters of the American Revolution. Historian Otto Hufeland gave his own account of the burial ground:

There were parts of 36 skeletons in [the 1908] "find" on the site of what is believed to have been a negro and pauper burying ground. Only six Americans were killed at the skirmish at Ward's house and these were buried close by on the other side of the W.P. Road. The daughters [sic] evidently gave some one who had bones a decent burial. When I told [the Reverend Doctor William S.] Coffey, the good old rector of Saint Paul's who performed the burial service, of the facts he smiled and said: "The Episcopal service may help them awaken if there is any chance after a hundred years."[19]

Right: This c.1927 photo depicts the marker placed by the Daughters of the American Revolution at Saint Paul's Church Cemetery to mark the site of the reburials from the Winter Hill Burying Ground near Ward's House.

The true site of the Ward's House Revolutionary War Burials was finally found in 1922, when the bodies of three Revolutionary soldiers, including one "little more than a boy," were discovered on Midland Place. A large ceremony, which included a wreath sent from General John Pershing, a message from President Warren Harding, and a procession of 250 children from the Hebrew Orphan Asylum, was held at the Tuckahoe Village Hall to commemorate these men.[20] The ceremony was described in *The New York Times*:

The townspeople of Tuckahoe filed through to lay their flowers on the coffin until it was buried beneath their blossoms, and only bits of the vivid red, white and blue flag shone through. They stood with bared heads for a little while, soldiers keeping guard at the head and foot, and then passed on.... Hundreds of children, many of them not more than six years old, walked in a half shy, half scared way beside this long, grim box.... They did not know what the Revolution was, why it had freed their country was something that they had not yet comprehended, [and] General Washington was a name only. But they placed their little wreaths beside the coffin, and the solemnity of the small rotunda will probably remain with them until they learn to connect it with that tribute of respect for men who fought their last fight in a great cause.[21]

The author's grandfather, who was a nine-year-old living in Tuckahoe at the time, remembered the event well and later recounted it to his sons. For several years, the bones were stored in a vault in village hall until they were interred next to the Tuckahoe World War I memorial, as Mayor Walter D. Crouch noted in 1937:

The bones of the Revolutionary Soldiers are buried at the easterly side of the war memorial, which was erected and dedicated in 1930. The vault box, casket and contents were interred by members of the Village organization. The interment was quietly, unobtrusively and reverently made. A flag of the United States was placed on the burial box. I offer the following suggestion: If there is a patriotic organization that desires to place a bronze Memorial Tablet on the eastern side of the War Memorial, I am sure permission would be given.[22]

Unfortunately, no tablet denoting the re-interment was ever placed on the monument. The burial of the bones became a campaign issue in the 1937 village election, as some of Mayor Crouch's opponents charged that the remains had been lost:

Le Roy Lockwood, civic worker, Republican and World War veteran, said he attended the 1930 [war memorial dedication] and heard no mention of the [burial]. "I understand the bones were put in an ashcan and were taken to the incinerator," said Mr. Lockwood. "It was just an accident. Men were clearing the basement for a police shooting gallery."[23]

Village Clerk John C. McDonnell responded to the allegations:

> John C. McDonnell, village clerk, said he took office in 1929 and "inherited" the bones, encased in an expensive casket, which were stored in the basement of the two-story brick Village Hall at Depot Square. "I made all the arrangements and had them interred beside [the] World War monument," he said. "I had the burial made shortly before the Armistice Day parade and celebration in 1930. I have been telling people this fact and I am surprised they don't believe me. It is true nothing particularly was said about the burial during the celebration, but there are many people who saw the burials take place."[24]

Mayor Crouch was re-elected by a margin of 2-to-1, so the charges did not make an impact on the Tuckahoe electorate. Optimistic readers may choose to believe Mayor Crouch's account that the bones lie close by the World War I monument, while pessimists may opt to agree with Mr. Lockwood's statement that the remains received an accidental, non-ceremonial cremation.[25]

Top Right: This monument was erected by the Village of Tuckahoe to commemorate the residents of the village who served their country and lost their lives during World War I. It stands at the intersection of Main Street and Winter Hill Road. The American soldiers who were killed in action during the skirmish at Ward's House during the Revolutionary War were supposedly re-interred between the monument and the flagpole in 1930.

Bottom Right: Lieutenant Samuel Crawford, Sr. of the Westchester County Militia was killed at a second skirmish at Ward's house in 1777. This cenotaph, which lists an incorrect year of death, is located in the Crawford family plot in Christ Church Cemetery in the City of Rye. It reads:

IN MEMORY OF
OUR GRANDFATHER
SAMUEL CRAWFORD SR.
WHO DIED IN DEFENSE OF
AMERICAN LIBERTY
AT TUCKAHOE, N.Y.
1776

"WHERE THE TREE FALLETH THERE IT SHALL BE"

Additionally, a monument was placed to the memory of Lieutenant Crawford at the intersection of White Plains Road (Rt. 22) and Winter Hill Road in Eastchester. It is not known if any of the men who were killed during this second skirmish were among those interred near Ward's house.

Town of Mamaroneck

Above: The Disbrow Family Burial Ground overlooks Rockland Avenue and is accessed by a stairway which leads upward through a terraced slope.

DeLancey Family Burial Ground	12	Mamaroneck Quaker Cemetery	30
Disbrow Family Burial Ground	15	Palmer-Barker Family Burial Ground	30
Florence-Powell Family Burial Ground	17	Nelson Family Burial Ground	33
Gedney Family Cemetery (Eleazer)	19	Palmer, Bloomer & Haight Burial Ground	35
Hadden Family Burial Ground	25	Richbell Cemetery	37
Heathcote Hill Revolutionary War Burials	28	Town of Mamaroneck Cemetery	40
Mamaroneck Methodist Church Cemetery	29	Budd Family Burial Ground	40

Unlike neighboring Rye and New Rochelle, the Town of Mamaroneck does not have a Colonial public burying ground. Instead, the residents of Mamaroneck during the 17th and 18th centuries preferred to establish their own family cemeteries on their own properties. The Richbell Cemetery, the town's oldest graveyard, is also the oldest family burial ground in Westchester County. The DeLancey Family Burial Ground was established by John Peter DeLancey, a grandson of Caleb Heathcote, the father-in-law of author James Fenimore Cooper, and a loyalist soldier during the Revolutionary War. Polycarpus Nelson established his own family cemetery in the early 18th century on his land near the Heathcote property. His interesting tombstone, which was the only grave marker in this cemetery, began a decades-long journey in the mid-19th century that ended 70 miles from the headstone's original location. The town government finally established a public cemetery in 1829 on a portion of the property formerly owned by patriot Colonel Gilbert Budd, who served his country with distinction during the Revolutionary War. In fact, the Budd Family Burial Ground became a part of this new municipal graveyard.

Many of the town's burial grounds fell into disrepair during much of the 20th century due to vandalism and neglect. The Hadden Family Burial Ground was destroyed during construction of the New England Thruway, while many tombstones in the Town of Mamaroneck Cemetery were vandalized. Recent efforts made by the municipality, as well as the Mamaroneck Historical Society, however, have resulted in improved maintenance of the town's cemeteries.

Please note that there are three cemeteries that are located in the portion of the Village of Mamaroneck that is located in the Town of Rye: the (Solomon) Gedney Family Burial Ground, the Guion Family Burial Ground, and the Griffen-Rogers Family Burial Ground.

DeLancey Family Burial Ground

Mamaroneck (Mamaroneck Village)

Right: Looking west along the remnants of the rear wall of the DeLancey Family Burial Ground in 2008. A piece of the headstone of Elizabeth Floyd DeLancey (1768-1820), wife of the cemetery's founder, John Peter DeLancey, can be seen at the bottom left hand corner of the photo.

Location: South side of Palmer Avenue between Delancey and Heathcote avenues.

Dates of Activity: 1806 – 1905.

Inscriptions: *WCHS* Book #8 (p.57).

Notes: Caleb Heathcote, one-time mayor of New York City, who was "known as the richest man in the colonies," purchased 1,000 acres of land in present-day Mamaroneck and Scarsdale from John Richbell's widow, Ann, in 1698.[1] Three years later, he received his royal patent to the "Manor of Scarsdale."[2] Colonel Heathcote built his manor house just east of Delancey Avenue between Cortlandt Avenue and the Boston Post Road on the hill which bears his name. His daughter and heiress, Anne, married James DeLancey, a future lieutenant governor of New York and one of the founders of King's College, now Columbia University.[3] The DeLancey family lost their Mamaroneck home to a fire just prior to the outbreak of the Revolutionary War. During the Revolution, the DeLanceys remained loyal to the British crown.

Although he served in the British Army during the Revolution and left for England at the close of that conflict, John Peter DeLancey, a grandson of Caleb Heathcote, returned to the United States in 1789. Three years later he rebuilt a family residence on the site that had been established by his grandfather.[4] On January 1, 1811, this home was the scene of the marriage of John Peter's daughter, Susan Augusta, to author James Fenimore Cooper.[5]

The "rights to burial" in the DeLancey's family vault at Trinity Church in New York City "had been canceled" as a result of the Revolutionary War, so John Peter decided to inter his deceased relatives in a plot on his own farm. This graveyard was reserved when Mr. DeLancey left his property to his sons in his will:

> …a small piece of land now enclosed and used as my family burying ground…upon trust to hold the same forever as and for a family burying ground to be used for the purposes of burial by each and every [one] of my children and their families and decendants and to and for no other purposes whatever.[6]

James Fenimore Cooper's daughter, also named Susan Augusta, described the DeLancey homestead as she remembered it in her youth, including the surroundings of the family's cemetery:

> The house stood on the brow of a low hill immediately above the highway to Boston, and facing a broad bay of the sound. The view was very pleasing when the tide was in, but dismal at low tide, when a waste of black mud covered half the bay…. [The] garden lay at the rear [of the house] at some little distance. Beyond the garden rose another low hill. On climbing it one came to the cider mill and the peach orchard [and] apple orchards, very extensive, with the finest kinds of fruit. Beyond all these

orchards there rose a beautiful woods, the remains of the ancient forest, and within its shade there was an open enclosure, the family burying-ground, surrounded by a low stone wall.[7]

Susan Cooper's description of the DeLancey property explains why the inscribed sides of the tombstones face to the south and away from nearby Palmer Avenue, a road that did not exist for most of the time when the burial ground was being actively used. The DeLancey family would have walked up Heathcote Hill from their home and accessed the burial ground on its south side. Today, traces of the cemetery's back wall can be found behind the north row of tombstones. The final interments in this cemetery were those of John Peter's son, William Heathcote DeLancey (1797-1865), the first Episcopal bishop of Western New York, his wife, Frances Munro (1797-1869), and their son, Edward Floyd DeLancey (1821-1905).[8] In 1907 the remains of these three individuals were reinterred at Saint Peter's Church in Geneva, New York. As late as 1954 Bishop DeLancey's open tomb greeted visitors to the graveyard.[9] Years of neglect have resulted in the disappearance of most of the stone wall which once surrounded the cemetery as well as damage to some of the tombstones. However, the burial ground is now maintained and kept free from overgrowth as the result of efforts made by the Mamaroneck Historical Society. Although its future is uncertain, the DeLancey home, which was moved from its original location in the early 20th century, still stands at the corner of Fenimore Road and the Boston Post Road.

Above Left: This heavily damaged box monument marks the graves of Thomas James DeLancey (1789-1822) and his wife, Mary Ellison (1798-1842). It can be seen at the bottom right of the photos on the following page.

Above Right and Bottom Right: The headstone of two-month-old Josephine Floyd DeLancey leans against that of her great-grandfather, cemetery founder John Peter DeLancey (top right). Mr. DeLancey's headstone (bottom right) reads simply:

> JOHN PETER DE LANCEY,
> Born in the city of New York
> 15th July, 1753,
> Died at Mamaroneck
> 31st January, 1828

Above: The top photo depicts the DeLancey Family Burial Ground from its south side on August 5, 1907, shortly before three of the interments were exhumed to be reburied in Geneva, New York. The photo at the center of the page was taken from a similar angle in 2008. The telephone wires mark the location of Palmer Avenue.

Left: The western portion of the DeLancey Family Burial Ground in 1954. The tombstone and footstone at left mark the grave of cemetery founder John Peter DeLancey. The three tombstones standing in this photo can be seen in the left half of the photo at the center of this page.

14

Disbrow Family Burial Ground
Mamaroneck (Mamaroneck Village)

Top: Looking east in the Disbrow Family Burial Ground in 2004. The tombstone of Edward Merritt can be seen at the bottom left corner of the photo in the portion of the cemetery that was reserved for the descendants of Gilbert Merritt. A photo of Edward Merritt's tombstone can be found on page vii. The tombstones of the Disbrow family can be seen in the distance.

Bottom: This rectangular piece of marble is located near the tombstone of David Disbrow and can be seen in the right center of the photo on the previous page. It reads: "I believe in the forgiveness of sins and the life everlasting. Amen."

Location: East side of Rockland Avenue between Munro and Cortlandt avenues.

Dates of Activity: c.1811 – 1877.

Inscriptions: *WCHS* Books #17 (p.75) and #81 (p.70).

Notes: In 1674 John Disbrow arrived in what is now Mamaroneck, where he purchased a parcel of land from John Richbell.[10] The family was not new to Westchester County, however, as John's father, Peter Disbrow, was "one of the first and principal proprietors of Rye, in 1660."[11] At its greatest extent, the Disbrow estate "consisted of 700 acres, including a valuable tract of wood-land, called the Hickory grove" located on the east side of present-day Weaver Street north of Palmer Avenue.[12] In 1677 the family built their home on the south side of the Boston Post Road opposite Rockland Avenue. This house was destroyed by fire in the late 19th century.[13]

Mary Disbrow made an arrangement with her neighbor James Mott which permitted her relatives to be buried in the Richbell Family Burial Ground, as the Disbrows did not have a family cemetery of their own until many years after their settlement in Westchester. Although Henry Disbrow buried his 16-year-old daughter, Mary, in the Richbell Cemetery following her death in 1807, he interred his second wife, Ann, in 1811 at the top of a small hill overlooking Rockland Avenue, which was then called West Street. It is possible, however, that the date of the cemetery's founding was earlier, as is evidenced by the number of fieldstones which can be found in this graveyard.[14] Mr. Disbrow formally set out the burial ground in his will, which was written on October 20, 1821:

> I do will and ordain that my Executors at the sale of my Real estate...do reserve unto my heirs forever the burial ground situate on the road leading from the turnpike to Henry Merritts Dec'd and adjoining the lands of John P. DeLancey Esqr., the reservation herein mentioned shall be thirty feet in front on the said road and thirty feet in the rear and twenty five feet deep on each side, said reservation is in no case to be sold or conveyed in way or manner to any person, but to remain as a burial ground unto my heirs forever.[15]

Presently, the Disbrow cemetery has a frontage of about 70 feet on Rockland Avenue. This discrepancy occurred when Henry Disbrow granted a plot on the west side of the reservation to his neighbor Gilbert Merritt.[16] Henry Disbrow's executors sold his landed estate in 1837, at which time the cemetery was described as such:

> ...a burying ground...which contains EIGHT PERCHES AND SEVEN TENTHS OF A PERCH OF LAND which is hereby reserved for a burial place the west part of said burial ground is now fenced to the desendents of Gilbert Merritt, decd. and the ground east of and between that and Delancys land to the desendents of the said Henry Disbrow, deceased forever.[17]

The fence which once separated the Merritt and Disbrow plots no longer exists. There is but one inscribed tombstone in the portion of this burial ground which belongs to the Merritt family:

IN MEMORY OF
EDWARD MERRITT.
who died Sept. 16th, 1831,
Aged 40 years & 6 months.

When the last trumpet shall bid thee rise
We'll haste to meet thee in the skies
Where smiles of love eternal glow
And parting tears will never flow

Edward Merritt, a resident of Manhattan, was the brother of Gilbert Merritt.[18] His obituary, which appeared in the New York *Evening Post*, "respectfully invited" his friends "and also the officers of the Revenue...to meet at his late residence, No. 231 Bleecker street, on Sunday morning next, at half past 7 o'clock A.M., from whence his remains will be conveyed to Mamaroneck, West Chester county, to be placed in the family burying ground."[19]

Only five inscribed stones, marking a total of six burials, can be found in the section belonging to the Disbrow family. The last person to be buried here, David Disbrow, died while serving as a 2nd lieutenant with the 1st New York Cavalry Regiment during the Civil War.

Right: The tombstone of David Disbrow reads: "DAVID R. DISBROW. BORN IN NEW YORK CITY JUNE 2, 1826. SERVED AS A COMMISSIONED OFFICER IN THE FEDERAL ARMY DURING THE WAR OF THE REBELLION. DIED IN WASHINGTON, D.C. JAN 1, 1877."

Florence-Powell Family Burial Ground
Mamaroneck (Mamaroneck Village)

Above: The Florence-Powell Family Burial Ground in 2007. The sandstones which mark the graves of Peter and Sarah Florence are visible at left.

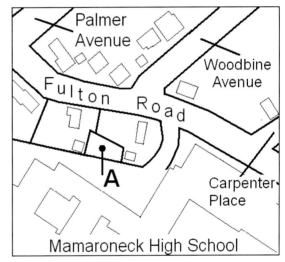

Location: The cemetery (A) can be accessed by the Fulton Road entranceway to the Mamaroneck High School. It is on the right side of the driveway about 200 feet from Fulton Road.

Dates of Activity: 1808 – 1883.

Inscriptions: *WCHS* Books #17 (p.74) and #81 (p.6).

Notes: The Florence family owned much of the land between present-day Rockland Avenue and the present Mamaroneck High School in the early 19th century. The first two persons interred in this small cemetery were Peter Florence (c.1751-1808) and his wife, Sarah (1752-1826), whose sandstones adjoin each other at the entrance to the burial ground. Although Sarah's stone is not adorned by any design, Peter's memorial is graced by an interesting border on its top and sides. In 1859 Peter and Sarah's son Benjamin transferred 11 1/2 acres of his property to Effie M. and Mary A. Florence with the exception of "the Old family Burying Ground" located on the west side of the property, "to be used as a Family Burying Ground forever by the Family of said Benjamin Florence and his relatives with a Right of Way to said Burying Ground forever to bury the dead."[20] The cemetery was used sparingly throughout the next quarter-century after this transaction was made. The final interment, that of William J. Florence, was made in 1883.

In 1940 Mamaroneck High School student Milton Prigoff noted that the burial ground was "not in marvelous condition due to vandalous [sic] students, who have destroyed a stone which had fallen and also due to debris scattered through the cemetery."[21] Today, only the stones of Peter and Sarah Florence remain intact within the Florence-Powell Family Burial Ground. The gravestone of their son William is lying on the ground in one piece, while a large stone containing the names of three members of the Powell family (William, his wife, Abigail, and their son Thomas) is scattered about in a number of pieces. The headstone of Benjamin Florence, another son of Peter and Sarah, disappeared well before 1940, and that of his wife, Elizabeth, has been split in two, with the top half lying on the ground next to the bottom. A number of pieces of other head and foot stones have been scattered throughout the little burial plot.

Above Left: The headstone of William J. Florence, the last person interred in the Florence-Powell Family Burial Ground, lies fallen on the ground next to its base.

Above Right: This damaged headstone marked the graves of the three members of the Powell family who are interred in the Florence-Powell Family Burial Ground: William Powell (1769-1856), his wife Abigail (1773-1856), and their son Thomas (1813-1838). The visible portion of this stone honors Abigail Powell, who was born on June 17, 1773. It mentions that she was the wife of William Powell.

Bottom Right: The headstone of Peter Florence reads:

P.F

In memory of
Peter Florence,
who died
Nov[r] 30th, 1808,
Aged 57 years 3
months & 10 days.

My glass is run, my days are spent,
My life is gone, it was but lent;
And as I am so must you be,
Therefore prepare, to follow me

Gedney Family Cemetery (Eleazar)
Mamaroneck (Mamaroneck Village)

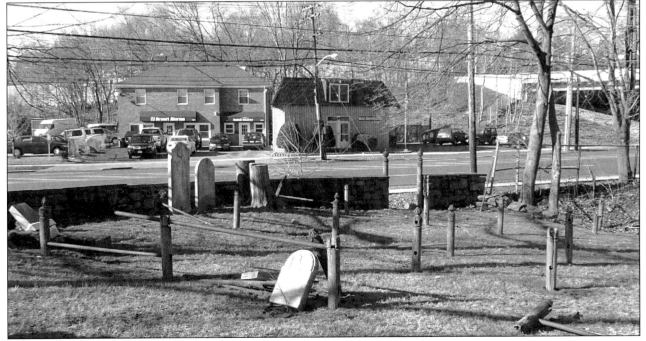

Top: The gate to the Gedney Family Cemetery in 2008.

Bottom: A number of wooden plot posts can still be found within the Gedney Family Cemetery. They are among the few remaining in Westchester County. The tombstone in the center foreground of the photo is depicted on page 23.

Location: East side of Mamaroneck Avenue about 300 feet north of its intersection with North Barry Avenue. The cemetery is located inside the northbound exit ramp from I-95.

Dates of Activity: 1722 – 1942.

Other Names: Harbor Heights Cemetery.

Inscriptions: *WCHS* Books #8 (p.89-97), #80 (p.28-33) and #81 (p.9-14).

Notes: Eleazer Gedney, the first member of his family to settle in Westchester County, moved to Mamaroneck from his native Salem, Massachusetts, in 1697. Eleazer's sons John, James and Eleazer founded this family cemetery when they buried their father atop a small knoll overlooking the Mamaroneck River following his death in 1722. Mr. Gedney's wife, Anna, was buried alongside her husband following her death.

Right: The tombstones of Anna (left) and Eleazar Gedney in the late 1950s. Eleazar's stone can no longer be found in the cemetery.

HERE
LIES ANNA
GEDNEY
HIS WIFE

1722
HERE LIES
ELEAZAR
GEDNEY DESEAS
OCTOBER 27
BORN IN BOSTON
GOVERNMENT

The first mention of the Gedney Family Cemetery in the land records of Westchester County dates from 1793, when Eleazer's grandson Absalom Gedney (c.1732-1816) sold his portion of the family estate to William Gray with the following stipulation:

> ...the said William Gray his heirs, and assigns shall not break the ground nor till the land containing the Graves of deceased persons already buried in the Burying ground in said farm for planting sowing or raising Grain in said Burying Ground.[22]

William Lawrence, who purchased the land surrounding the Gedney cemetery in the mid-19th century, decided to create his own burial lot adjacent to the northeast side of the Gedney Family Cemetery. The Lawrence plot was formally annexed to the Gedney burial ground on September 1, 1856.[23] The final boundaries of the Gedney cemetery were formally set out on March 10, 1868, as part of an agreement between the Lawrence family and Silvanus Gedney. In addition to determining that the cemetery would comprise a total of 60 rods of land as well as a right-of-way, the agreement also permitted the Lawrence family to have some unusual rights to the burial ground:

> Reserving nevertheless to the [Lawrence family] full right and authority forever hereafter to mow or pasture the [cemetery] also all the grass, herbage, fruit tree or trees now growing or hereafter to grow thereon, to take and carry away at his and their pleasure but not in any event to plough the aforesaid lot or any part thereof or to injure or molest any grave on said lot.[24]

In 1925 Mrs. Selleck E. Coles wrote a piece for the *New York Genealogical and Biographical Record* concerning the Gedney cemetery. The following is an abridged version of that article:

> The Gedney Burial Ground on Mamaroneck Avenue, Mamaroneck, N.Y., contains the oldest graves of this family in Westchester County. It is situated on the east side of the avenue, between it and the Mamaroneck River...and contains about half an acre. It is on a sandy knoll and the enclosure is of an irregular diamond shape, conforming to the contour of the knoll on which it is located. The stone wall surrounding it is in fair condition, but the ground is neglected. In the northeastern part a number of the Lawrence family are buried [and] there are about twenty stones and a number of unmarked graves in this part. Other names found on stones in the Gedney plot also belong to those who have married into the family. Before Mamaroneck Avenue was laid out (about 1872) there was an old lane or right of way leading from the old road through the land once Eleazer Gedney's to the graveyard, which lane was laid out on his land. Eleazar Gedney was the first of his name to settle in Westchester County, coming here

from Salem, Mass., in 1697. He is buried in the family burying ground having departed this life in 1722. Beside him lies his wife Ann[a], and nearby is his son John who was born in 1695, and who was the first proprietor of Gedney Farms in White Plains, he having bought the land in 1740 for his son Bartholomew. The estate with subsequent additions remained in the family until 1903, and a portion of it is still owned by his descendants of the sixth generation.[25]

Above: The tombstones of James Gedney (left) and his wife, Phebe Horton, are located near the graves of James's parents, Eleazer and Anna Gedney. Thomas Brown, a carver from New York City, carved the headstone of James Gedney.

In
Memory of
James Gedney
who Dep[td] this Life 27th
of Jan[ry] 1766
in the 64th Year of his Age.

Here lies
the body of
PHEBE,
wife of James Gedney
who departed this life
Aug[st] 10th 1799,
aged 94 years 6
months & 8 days.

Right: This tombstone stands at the grave of Mary Dixon (c.1758-1811).

Stop!
Reader Eer
the passeth this stone
nor regardless be told
that nears its Bass lies deposited
the remains of
MARY DIXON,
Wife of John Dixon;
a Woman whose reputation was spotless
and whose life was spent in the practice
of virtue, having by her unshaken fortitude
and native independence of Soul
commanded the esteem of all who knew
her. She departed this life August 12th
1811 aged 53 Years.

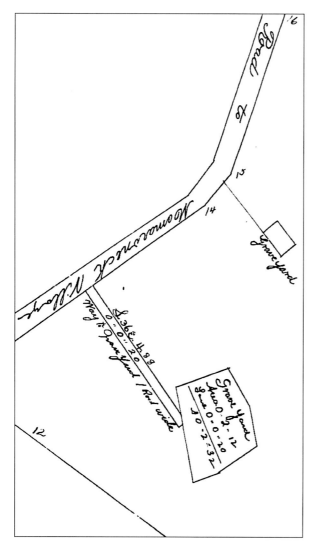

The Gedney Family Cemetery was still being used (albeit sparingly) when Mrs. Coles visited that graveyard. The final interment in the cemetery, that of Genevra Lawrence, was made in 1942. In the late 1920s the land on the east side of Mamaroneck Avenue that surrounded the Gedney cemetery was purchased by Westchester County for the proposed Pelham-Port Chester Parkway. When the right-of-way for that road was finally developed in the 1950s, the graveyard was surrounded by entrance and exit ramps for the northbound lanes of the New England Thruway. The Gedney cemetery is quite large compared to the other family burial grounds in Westchester County, and is also unique in that there are several smaller plots within its boundaries. Today, many of the weather-worn wooden posts which delineated the plots remain in place. Unfortunately, the cemetery was vandalized throughout the 20th century, as is evidenced by the number of damaged monuments and tombstones in the burial ground, which were long ago wrenched from their proper positions.

Top Left: Prior to the construction of Mamaroneck Avenue about 1870, the Gedney Family Cemetery was accessed via a right-of-way which led northwest from the cemetery gate to Winfield Avenue, a road that was eradicated by the construction of the New England Thruway in the early 1950s. The graveyard to the north of the Gedney cemetery is the Hadden Family Burial Ground, which was also destroyed during the construction of the Thruway (Westchester County Clerk Map #318).[26]

Top and Bottom Right: The tombstone of John Townsend (top right) contains an engraving of a crossbones and reads:

In Memory of
Iohn Townsend
who Died Jan[ry]. y[e] 7th, 1771
Aged 54 Years.

Interestingly, Mr. Townsend's footstone (bottom right) contains information regarding his place of birth:

I · Townsend
Born in Norwich
At Oysterbay L Iland
1716.

Above Left:

Here Lies
the Remains
of Hannah the Wife
of
Solomon Gedney
Who Dep^{td} this Life 5th
April 1788 Aged 37 Ye^{rs}

Above Right: The tombstone of five-year-old Paulina Gedney depicts an angel carrying the deceased child to heaven. The verse at the bottom reads: "She is not dead, the child of our affection—But has gone to realms above." The tombstone can be seen lying on a railing in the bottom center of the photo on page 19.

Bottom Left: Although it is now much faded and worn, the tombstone of Bartholomew Gedney, son of John Gedney and grandson of Eleazar and Anna Gedney, contains an epitaph with an ominous warning to its readers:

In Memory of
Barth^{w}. Gedney
who Dep^{td} this Life 27th
of Aug^{st}. 1775 in the 55th
Year of his Age.

Reader! Stand still & view this place
And ------ thyself
For soon thou must to this -----
Thy Awful Judge himself -----
Therefore be wise improve each hour
For now alone 'tis in thy power.

Above: The slate tombstone of John Gedney, eldest son of Eleazar and Anna Gedney, lies flat and broken on the ground in the Gedney Family Cemetery. It was carved by Thomas Brown. The item that appears to be a circle intertwined with the crossbones at the top of the tombstone is actually a snake with its tail in its mouth, which symbolizes eternity. The inscription on the tombstone is given at right.

Time how short

Eternity how Long

In Memory of
JOHN GEDNEY who
Dep[td] this Life Oct. 3rd
1766 Aged 71 Years
Death is y[e] Curse produc[d] by sin
through Christ Eternal Life
we win

Hadden Family Burial Ground
Mamaroneck (Mamaroneck Village)

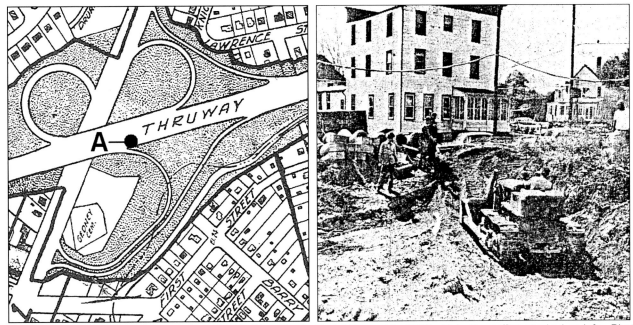

Top Right: The removal of graves from the Hadden Family Burial Ground in 1956. Note the coffins stacked at left. Photo courtesy Mamaroneck Village Historian Gloria P. Pritts.

Location: Prior to the construction of the New England Thruway, Barry Avenue continued straight until it reached Mamaroneck Avenue; the Hadden Family Burial Ground was located on the north side of this now-eradicated portion of Barry Avenue about 85 feet east of Mamaroneck Avenue. The site of the cemetery (A) is located beneath the Thruway near where the northbound exit ramp for Mamaroneck Avenue leaves the highway.

Dates of Activity: 1761 – 1856.

Other Names: Dingee Cemetery, Donaldson Cemetery.

Inscriptions: *WCHS* Book #80 (p.33-34).

Notes: This burial ground was founded by the Hadden family, whose surname is occasionally spelled Heady, Heddy and Hedden. The earliest known burial in this graveyard was that of Thomas Hadden (c.1676-1761), a Scarsdale farmer and the father of Lazarus Heady, a preacher who founded his own family cemetery in New Castle. Three decades after the burial of Thomas, the 1790 census listed Bartholomew Hadden as the head of a household in Mamaroneck consisting of three adult males, two females and three slaves.[1] On April 4, 1826, Lott and William Hadden reserved their family's burial ground when they sold a portion of their land on the west side of the Mamaroneck River to James Lawrence, Jr.:

> ...reserving to [Lott and William Hadden] and their heirs and assigns a passway six feet wide and one hundred and twenty three feet in length from the road...for the purpose of the going to and returning from the cemetery...the gate leading from the road in said passway and the fence arount [sic] the said Cemetery to be made and always hereafter to be kept in repair by the party of the first part, their heirs and assigns.[2]

The land surrounding this burial ground was owned by the Dingee family during the latter half of the 19th century. As a result, the Hadden graveyard is often known by the surname of that family. Originally, this cemetery was accessed by a right-of-way which led westward to Winfield Avenue. Following the construction of Mamaroneck Avenue and the northern extension of Barry Avenue, the burial ground was accessed by a right-of-way six feet wide and 20 feet long that led from the southeast corner of the graveyard to the latter street.[3] In 1905 members of the Underhill Society of America reported that they could not enter the burial ground as it "had been surrounded by a high board fence by the Harbor Heights Association, rendering it unapproachable."[4] In her 1925 article for the *New York Genealogical and Biographical Record* regarding the nearby Gedney Family Burial Ground, Mrs. Selleck E. Coles noted the condition of the Hadden Family Burial Ground, which was located about 300 feet north of the former graveyard:

The fence of this graveyard is entirely gone and only a few stones are still standing, others having fallen or having been broken or having disappeared entirely. There are about nine old weather-worn granite (native stone) markers with no inscriptions visible, which markers appear to be older than the [inscribed] stones which are of marble.[5]

The Hadden cemetery had the misfortune of being directly in the middle of the planned Pelham-Port Chester Parkway, and as a result it was taken by eminent domain by the State of New York for the construction of the New England Thruway on August 23, 1955.[6] The following article regarding the cemetery appeared in the Mamaroneck *Daily Times* on September 19, 1956:

An undertaking crew and New England Thruway engineers yesterday exhumed the graves of 13 persons in the Hadden Burial Grounds at Mamaroneck Avenue & North Barry Avenue, Mamaroneck, and when they were through they had the remains of 29 more persons than they'd bargained for. According to all available records, there should have been 13 members of the Hadden family of this area interred at the small plot across from Huber's Winfield Hotel. But, according to a thruway official, the undertaking crew counted the burials at the plot as having taken place from 1830 to 1885. However, the records are incomplete, and 8 of the 13 are unaccounted for except by name. The gravemarkers and tombstones have long been broken and taken from the cemetery.

According to records, also, the plot is now called the Dingee Burial Ground, which would seem at odds with the fact of the 13 Haddens. However, Frank Huber remembers that Mamaroneck real estate operator Stanley Hare had relatives buried there.... Mr. [J.M.] Spader recalled that his grandmother, Ophelia Maria Hadden, was buried at the cemetery, and that Job Hadden, owner of the grist mill at the site now occupied by the Westchester Joint Water Works, was also buried there, but he could recall no dates. Then Mr. Spader recalled the grounds had originally been owned by the Hadden family, and that a man named John Dingee, who once ran a summer hotel in Harbor Heights, had taken the grounds over. According to Mr. Spader, Mr. Dingee was the man who surveyed Mamaroneck Avenue from White Plains to Mamaroneck Harbor.... [7]

Although this article provided no clue as to where the remains were reinterred, a 1961 article in *The Standard Star* mentioned that "an old cemetery which was moved from Mamaroneck to make way for the New York Thruway" had been relocated to Greenwood Union Cemetery in the City of Rye. The Hadden Family Burial Ground is the only burial ground that fits this description.[8]

Above: The remains from the Hadden Family Burial Ground were probably moved to the unmarked plots in the easternmost portion of Greenwood Union Cemetery in the City of Rye.

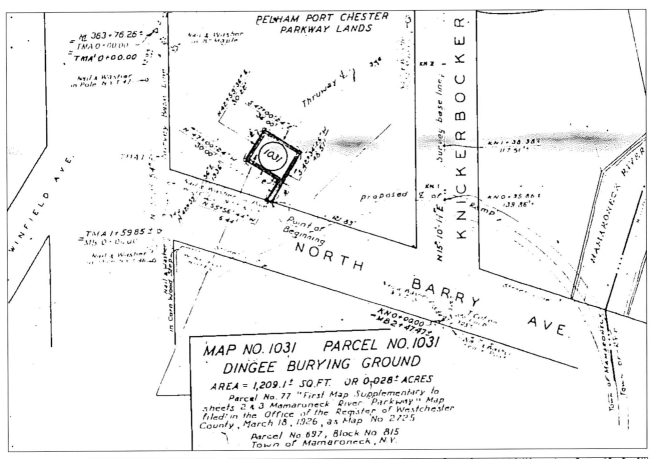

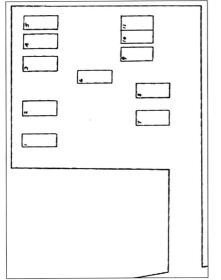

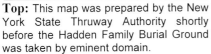

Top: This map was prepared by the New York State Thruway Authority shortly before the Hadden Family Burial Ground was taken by eminent domain.

Bottom Left: This map of the Hadden Family Burial Ground was drawn by the WPA in the 1930s. Each rectangle represents a marked grave.

Bottom Right: This 1930 map shows the location of the Hadden Family Burial Ground (just above the upside-down "AVE." and to the left of the large "M") in relation to the Gedney Family Cemetery.

27

Heathcote Hill Revolutionary War Burials

Mamaroneck (Mamaroneck Village)

Right: This 2005 photo was taken looking east at the stretch of Munro Avenue where the Heathcote Hill Revolutionary War burials were discovered.

Location: Underneath Munro Avenue between Heathcote and Delancey avenues.

Dates of Activity: 1776.

Notes: A prelude to the Battle of White Plains, the skirmish at Heathcote Hill occurred on October 22, 1776, when a contingent of 750 American soldiers under the command of Colonel John Haslet surprised a "regiment of loyalists...commanded by the renegade Colonel Robert Rogers" at Mamaroneck during a night attack.[9] In a letter to his father, Lieutenant Colonel Tench Tilgham reported that "Colonel Haslet killed and wounded a considerable number carried back to White Plains 36 prisoners and included among the trophies, a 'pair of colors', 60 stands of arms and a variety of plunder among, the latter of which were a good many blankets."[10] Tilgham reported that the Americans "counted 25 killed in one orchard."[11] On the following day, those who were wounded in this skirmish were "removed in ox-carts to New Rochelle Church [Trinity Episcopal] where nearly all of them died."[12] Nelson Schofield, a man who witnessed the removal of the wounded, remembered that "the cries of the wounded were dreadful: 'Oh, how cold I am! Oh, give me some water! Oh, what pain I'm in!'"[13] Mr. Schofield also told of the burial of those soldiers who were killed in this action:

> The killed were buried on Heathcote's heights, but covered so slightly that the dogs scratched off the dirt and attacked the dead bodies so that the neighbours turned out and covered them again – throwing stones upon the holes made by the dogs.[14]

Although no effort was made to properly mark this burial site, its location was apparently passed down in local lore. Edward Floyd De Lancey described the burial site as it appeared in 1886:

> All of both sides were buried just over the top of the ridge directly north of the Heathcote Hill house, in the angle formed by the present farm lane and the east fence of the field next to the ridge. There graves lie together friend and foe but all Americans. The late Stephen Hall, a boy of 17 or 18 at the time, said they were buried the morning after the fight and that he saw nine laid in one large grave.... My father told me when he was a boy their green graves were distinctly visible.[15]

This burial site was unearthed as a result of the development of Heathcote Hill into a residential neighborhood early in the 20th century:

> The exact location of the fight is confirmed in a very interesting manner. Edward F. DeLancey, a descendant of the builder of the house and at one time owner of the property, told Charles M. Baxter [that] a neighbor named Isaac Hall, then an old man, had described the event to him. Mr. Hall, who was a boy at the time of the battle, lived upon a hill across the harbor and had seen the conflict between the American troops and the Loyalists. Afterwards, he had come over to the place of conflict and has seen the twenty-seven men who had been killed buried immediately over the brow of the hill where Munro Avenue is now located. When the Heathcote Company [was] putting in the water and gas mains in that street, they came to the sand bank where evidence of the buried soldiers could be seen and where some bones were found and reinterred. Men working on the roads found a number of coins and silver faced buttons with the figure of a crown and numbers, 3 and 60.[16]

Charles M. Baxter, the overseer of this work, reported that "his worker's spades had turned up some black loam earth mixed with bone fragments [but] there was, unfortunately, nothing left of anyone or anything that had been buried there."[17]

Mamaroneck Methodist Church Cemetery

Mamaroneck (Mamaroneck Village)

Right: The tombstone of William Taylor (1771-1834) and his wife, Eleanor Cornell (1775-1828) once stood in the Mamaroneck Methodist Church Cemetery and now lies cracked on the ground in Greenwood Union Cemetery. It contains a passage written by John Wesley:

> Lo! The prisoners are released
> Lighten'd of their fleshly load,
> Where the weary are at rest
> They are gather'd unto God
> Lo! The pain of life is past,
> All their warfare now is o'er,
> Death and hell behind are cast;
> Grief and suffering are no more.

Location: Formerly at the northeast corner of the intersection of Prospect and Mount Pleasant avenues.

Dates of Activity: 1830 – 1861.

Removed: To Greenwood Union Cemetery (a plot in the Beechmont Acre section about 40 yards south of the maintenance building) in 1900.

Notes: Although the first Methodist services in Mamaroneck were conducted by Francis Asbury before the Revolutionary War, "the real beginning of a permanent Methodist Episcopal organization" in the town occurred when a society of this denomination formed on April 8, 1813, at the home of Hester Sands. Built in 1814, the society's first church was located on High Street, now called Prospect Avenue. When this meeting house burned on February 12, 1845, it was replaced by a new structure on the same site in October of that year.[18] The congregation did not remain in this new house of worship for long, as they decided to build their third and final church on the Boston Post Road in 1859.[19]

By 1830 the congregation had begun to use the ground which adjoined the west side of their original church as a place of interment. This cemetery had a frontage of 68 feet on Prospect Avenue and 164 feet on Mount Pleasant Avenue.[20] Mamaroneck High School student Alberta R. Tropp gave a brief history of this burial plot, along with a list of inscriptions, in her 1942 seminar paper entitled "Methodist Episcopal Church in Mamaroneck":

> In the days when the Methodist Episcopal Church was situated on [Prospect Avenue], the land on the [west] side of the edifice was a burial ground. Later, in order to sell the land on High Street, the Board of Trustees raised enough money to reinter the bodies in the Greenwood Union Cemetery of Rye. On March 14, 1900, a plot of ground, 25' by 28' was purchased in the cemetery in Rye for $196.00. To this property, the remains were removed. Mr. Louis Kolter, who was contracted for the job, reported the work completed on May 7, 1900.[21]

A total of 22 marked graves were removed to Greenwood Union Cemetery where the tombstones were placed flat on the ground; hence, their inscriptions have mostly faded. Following the transfer of remains, the trustees of the Mamaroneck Methodist Episcopal Church sold the site of the burial ground on October 7, 1904.[22] In 1905 a building was constructed on the cemetery site to house a kindergarten. Today, the lot is occupied by the Mamaroneck Seventh Day Adventist Church.

Mamaroneck Quaker Cemetery
Palmer-Barker Family Burial Ground
Mamaroneck (Larchmont)

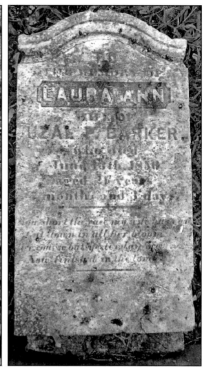

Left: Looking north in the Mamaroneck Quaker Cemetery in 2005.

Right: The tombstone of Laura Ann Barker lies face-up on the ground in the Palmer-Barker Family Burial Ground.

Location: North side of Boston Post Road about 125 yards west of Larchmont Avenue.

Dates of Activity: Quaker Cemetery c.1735 – 1905; Palmer-Barker Family Burial Ground, c.1752 – 1899.

Other Names: Howell Cemetery.

Inscriptions: *WCHS* Book #11 (p.8-9).

TO
THE MEMORY OF
LAURA ANN
WIFE OF
UZAL P. BARKER.
who died
June 13th (18th), 1850
aged 21 years
7 months and 3 days.

How short the race my wife has run
Cut down in all her bloom,
Her course but yesterday begun
Now finished in the tomb

Notes: The first European family to permanently settle in what is now Larchmont, the Palmers arrived in Mamaroneck in the mid-1690s from the town of Westchester in present-day Bronx County.[23] Samuel Palmer (c.1647-1716) purchased most of the land that now comprises the village from John Richbell and Native American Sachem Anhook. Having already held several offices in the Town of Westchester, Samuel was an ideal choice for supervisor of the Town of Mamaroneck, and was elected to this position at the inaugural town meeting on April 2, 1697.[24] Samuel and his wife, Mary Drake, held meetings of the Society of Friends in their home beginning in 1704, as is indicated by the following petition to the Westchester County Court of General Sessions: "…the meetings of the Decenters Pordestants [sic] called Quakers shall be held at John Ferris in Westchester and Samuel Palmer in Memoroneck accordingly."[25] In 1735 Samuel Palmer's son, Solomon, built a meeting house on his property located on the north side of the Boston Post Road. It is assumed that the Friends began to use the space next to this edifice as a burial place shortly thereafter. The Palmers did not remain in southern Mamaroneck for very long, and many members of the family relocated to North Salem about the year 1751, where they became associated with the Peach Pond Meeting.[26] On March 23, 1752, a deed to the Friends from Solomon Palmer established the boundaries for the Palmer-Barker and Quaker cemeteries:

Beginning at the northeast corner of the Meeting House and running from thence Eastwardly 40 ½ rods to a stake with some stones about it; thence running southwardly 30 ½ rods and about two feet to a stake with stones about it standing near the fence on the North side of the Boston Post Road including the land within the said fence lines and the Meeting House to have and to hold...the premises for the use of a burying ground...reserving only unto the said Solomon Palmer and his heirs the privilege of burying in the said ground whensoever he or they shall desire it.[27]

By 1768 many of the Mamaroneck Friends had relocated to the north part of the town. As a result, the meeting house was "relocated to the [southeast] corner of Weaver Street and Griffen Avenue" in that same year, though the congregation continued to use their burial ground in Larchmont until 1905.[28] In keeping with the burial customs of the Society of Friends, the early graves in this cemetery are marked by fieldstones, while the later interments are marked by small headstones which give the deceased's name, date of birth, and date of death.

As was mentioned in the deed for the Quaker Cemetery, the Palmer family was permitted to use a portion of the meeting house lot for their own burial ground. The Palmers used a portion of the lot located next to the Boston Post Road for their cemetery, which eventually became known as the Palmer-Barker Family Burial Ground. The connection between these families is explained by the marriage of Mary Palmer to Daniel Barker.[29] The vault in the cemetery was constructed by James Donaldson, a Mamaroneck landowner who had married into the Barker family.[30] The final interment in the graveyard, that of Samuel Barker's wife, Elisabeth A. Bruce, was made in 1899.

Above: The Palmer-Barker Family Burial Ground in 2005.

In 1931 a small portion from each of these cemeteries was acquired by Westchester County for the widening of the Boston Post Road. The graves of two persons were disturbed during this project, which required the excavation of about nine feet of land from each of the cemeteries.[31] Sadly, little attention was paid to the upkeep of these burial grounds during much of the 20th century, when the cemeteries became a favorite target of vandals. In 1974 the Mamaroneck *Daily Times* published a three-part series concerning the state of the cemeteries, which highlighted their shameful condition:

> Orange, blue and silver paint has been sprayed throughout the area, fully covering some graves. Many of the stones have been broken, separated from the bases and scattered – evidence of visitors armed with hammers and chisels. A large mausoleum in the Barker area, constructed of three layers of cement, slate and brick and encased in metal, is most severely damaged. Large sections of the roof and side have been torn off by vandals and the elements. The original door is gone and its replacement shows signs of ruin. A skull and crossbones and the words "savage skulls" have been sprayed on the side in multicolor paint.... The weather has also taken its toll in the form of fallen trees and overgrown brush. But the elements did not deposit a rusty bicycle, the cracked bottles and paper bags.[32]

The condition of the cemetery has improved since this series was published, as the grounds are kept free from debris and overgrowth. Nevertheless, the vandalism of years past is still evident.

Above: The tombstone of Isaac Secor (1790-1879) in the Mamaroneck Quaker Cemetery is inscribed in a format that is usually referred to as the "Quaker Method." The deceased's date of death is listed first and includes the number rather than the name of the month of the death. At the time, the Quakers preferred not to use the pagan names of months. Additionally, the age of the deceased in years, months and days is listed.

Right: The headstone of Margaret Cornell (1757-1847) is surrounded by beer bottles and trash in this 1974 photo. Fortunately, the cemetery is now kept clean by the Village of Larchmont.

Left: Although it has been cleaned, traces of paint are still visible on the headstone of Clara Roulstone.

SACRED
to the memory of
M^RS CLARA
wife of
Geo. S.F. Roulstone
and daughter of
Samuel & Mary Barker
who died March 10, 1838
aged 27 Years and 1 day

Our hearts assure us thou are at rest
In sweet repose upon thy Saviours breast,
And when thy pulse of life did almost cease to beat
Thy faltering words were,

Death shall not destroy my comfort
Christ shall lead me through the gloom

Nelson Family Burial Ground
Mamaroneck (Mamaroneck Village)

Location: Formerly located north of the site of the Polycarpus Nelson house (west side of Fenimore Road between Boston Post Road and Cortlandt Avenue).

Dates of Activity: c.1738.

Removed: Although the cemetery no longer exists, the tombstone of Polycarpus Nelson is now located in Rhinebeck Cemetery in Dutchess County, New York (Section A, Lots 448 and 449).

Notes: John Nelson, an English immigrant, arrived in Mamaroneck from Flatbush, Long Island, sometime before 1683 and purchased from John Richbell a parcel of land, which encompassed much of the land presently bounded by the Boston Post Road, Fenimore Road, Maple Avenue and the Sheldrake River.[33] Mr. Nelson transferred a piece of his land to his son, Polycarpus, in 1707, the latter having been named after a "benevolent French physician named Polycarpus" who "aided and sheltered" John Nelson when his ship was wrecked off the coast of France en route to New York from the County of Norfolk. The elder Nelson "promised through gratitude to name his first son after [the doctor] when he reached America and found a wife."[34] Polycarpus Nelson served his town as constable and overseer of highways, and was a landowner in Dutchess County as well.[35] He was one of the signers of "the famous declaration by the chief citizens" of Westchester "in support of William and Mary, and in opposition to the House of Stuart."[36]

Polycarpus was interred in a family burial plot on his estate following his death in 1738. The Reverend Robert Bolton gave a description of this burial ground as it appeared in 1848:

> Several members of the Nelson family are interred north of [the Nelson homestead]. Upon the only tombstone remaining, are chiseled two open hands pointing to a heart, with the following inscription:
>
> PALYCARPES
> NELSON
> WAS   BORN
> IVLY · 21 · ABOT · 4 ·
> A · CLOCK · IN · THE · MO
> RNING · IN · THE · YEAR ·
> 1688 · I · FINNIST · MY · CORS
> AND · QVIT · THE · LAND · IN ·
> WITNES · HERE · OF · MY · HART · MY ·
> HAND · DESESED · DESEMBER · 19
> 1738 [37]

The Reverend Bolton erroneously stated that the name of one of Polycarpus' sons, Mahar-shalal-hash-baz, is "supposed to have been derived from his maternal ancestor Akabashka, one of the [Native American] witnesses to the sale of [the future town of Harrison to] John Harrison in 1695."[38] In fact, the devout Polycarpus took that name from the Book of Isaiah in the Old Testament.[39] Maher's son, James, sold the Nelson homestead of 34 acres to Isaac Gedney, Jr., on June 19th, 1784, without making any reservation for the burial ground.[40]

Over the next 150 years, the tombstone of Polycarpus Nelson went on a strange odyssey before reaching its final home in Dutchess County. Sometime between 1848 and 1895, the tombstone was removed from the family burial ground and taken to Sleepy Hollow Cemetery.[41] However, the latter burial ground does not have any record of remains being transferred to its property. The marker did not remain in Sleepy Hollow for long. In 1895 "Van Wyck & Collins of Poughkeepsie erected a Nelson monument at Sleepy Hollow" and the tombstone of Polycarpus, "being in the way, was brought to [the company's] marble yard at Poughkeepsie" for storage. [42] Some 20 years later, Robert James Nelson, Sr., found the tombstone in the marble yard and took it to the Nelson plot in Rhinebeck Cemetery:

> In about 1915 Ralph Prowell and I made a boat trip up the Hudson River in one of the steamers and got off at the landing at Poughkeepsie, New York. As we ascended the inclined road up from the steamer we became aware of a stonemason shop off to our left. The name turned out to be Van Weike [sic] and that fitted in with some information given by letter to James H. Nelson by an off branch old lady Dougherty. So I went over to the building. The third stone in the second tier to the left turned out to be the long hunted stone! When we arrived back home in New York City I told dad about it and he arranged with Uncle Theo to get it to the cemetery. It was late in 1922 before this was finally accomplished.[43]

Above: The tombstone of Polycarpus Nelson in Rhinebeck Cemetery in 2008. The clasped hands on the tombstone indicate that it was carved by a member of the Stanclift family of Connecticut carvers.

Palmer, Bloomer & Haight Burial Ground

Mamaroneck

E 40' x 18'

C 49'6" x 49'6"

D 40' x 96'

B 49'6" x 16'5"

A 49'6" x 49'6"

Cooper Lane

Above: Looking northwest in the Palmer, Bloomer and Haight Family Burial Ground in 2007. The fieldstones in the foreground are located in the portion of the cemetery that was reserved by the Bloomer family, while the tombstones in the background are located in the section of the burial ground that was reserved by the Palmer family.

Location: North side of Cooper Lane between Weaver Street and Mardon Road.

Dates of Activity: c.1802 – 1917.

Other Names: Palmer Cemetery.

Inscriptions: *WCHS* Books #81 (p.22-24) and p.47-66).

Notes: Usually referred to as the Palmer Cemetery, this graveyard was set aside for burial purposes by four different families during the 18th and 19th centuries. Josiah Haight (1747-1812), a carpenter, appears to be the founder of the east half of the cemetery. Although the oldest tombstone dates from 1812, the large number of fieldstones indicates that the burial ground was probably founded at an earlier date.[44] The earliest record of the cemetery dates from April 13, 1802, when Josiah Haight and his wife, Anne Bloomer, reserved a burial ground about 75 links square (marked "A" on the map at top right) when they sold 22 acres of their land to Arnold and John Bloomer.[45] During their ownership of the land, the Bloomer family added an additional parcel (B) to expand the small graveyard[46] In 1813 the land on the east side of the cemetery was acquired by the Mott family. By the time they sold their land in 1841, the Motts had nearly doubled the size of the cemetery by adding a parcel on the north side of the burial ground (C). This final addition brought the boundaries of the graveyard to seven rods on the east and west sides and three rods on the north and south sides.[47] Together, the parcels that were reserved by the Haight, Bloomer and Mott families became known as the Bloomer & Haight Burial Ground, a graveyard that was used by neighboring families throughout the 19th and early 20th centuries.

Meanwhile, the Palmer family, who owned the land on the west side of the Bloomer & Haight Burial Ground, created their own family cemetery adjacent to that graveyard. The first interment in the Palmer portion of the cemetery occurred in 1812 when John Palmer (1792-1872), whose wife Mary (1787-1867) was a daughter of Josiah and Anne Haight, interred his father, Elihu (b.1759), a few yards west of the Bloomer & Haight Burial Ground.[48] Elihu Palmer was a great-grandson of Samuel Palmer, who in turn was the first of his family to settle in Mamaroneck. Samuel's son was the founder of the Palmer-Barker Family Burial Ground in Larchmont.[49] On January 18, 1868, John Palmer deeded the parcel (D) in which he had interred his father as well as some other relatives to his sons Benjamin F., William D, and John W. Palmer "for the use and purpose of a Burying ground for them and their heirs forever."[50] John W. Palmer deeded a small parcel (E) adjacent to the northern end of his family's plot to his siblings for the burial of their heirs on February 27, 1874.[51] Unfortunately, a feud had developed between John W. Palmer and Harriet M. Palmer resulting in John's refusal to grant Harriet permission to cross the southern portion of the family cemetery so that she could inter her daughter, Eliza, in the northwest portion of the burial ground.[52] Ultimately, the case reached the New York State Court of Appeals, which ruled in Harriet's favor.[53]

In 1941 Mamaroneck High School student Robert Flagg described the condition of the burial ground, which was largely forgotten at the time:

> Since the graveyard has been abandoned for twenty-four years, it is now overgrown with sumac trees, blackberry bushes, honeysuckle vines, and other shrubs, making access to some sections impossible. Some of the stones are buried, broken, or almost illegible, and many have fallen down, due to the loamy soil and to vandals.... Members of the Bloomer, Coles, Davis, Griffin, Haight, Hutton, Ireland, Irvine, Lockwood, Longley, Palmer, Robinson, Schofield, Scholefield, and Secor families are buried here. Some years ago, members of the Higby and Bedell families were removed from this graveyard.[54]

The remains and tombstones of four members of the Robinson family who had been interred in this cemetery were removed to the Robinson Family Burial Ground in New Rochelle about the year 1894.[55] Restoration work conducted by the Town of Mamaroneck in 1952 found 76 marked graves in this cemetery. Additionally, there are at least 26 fieldstones in this cemetery, which mark the earliest interments in the burial ground.[56]

Above: Looking east in the northern portion of the cemetery in 2008. Note the remains of a plot enclosure.

Right: The eastern portion of the cemetery in the 1980s. The fieldstones which mark the graves of the Bloomer and Haight families can be seen in the right foreground. A larger fence has since been constructed to separate the cemetery from the neighboring houses.

Richbell Cemetery
Mamaroneck (Mamaroneck Village)

Above: Looking southeast at Richbell Cemetery in 2005. The monument erected on the occasion of the 300th anniversary of Richbell's purchase is partly shielded by the trees at left.

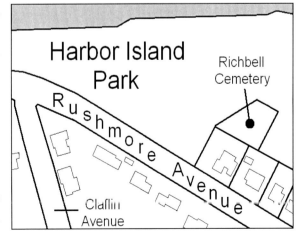

Location: Near the southeast corner of Harbor Island Park about 600 feet west of the intersection of Rushmore and Claflin avenues and 150 feet north of Rushmore Avenue.

Dates of Activity: c.1682 – 1827.

Other Names: John Richbell Burial Ground, Mott Cemetery, Richbell-Williams Cemetery.

Inscriptions: *WCHS* Book #17 (p.34-35).

Notes: "The oldest burial place of civilized man in the town of Mamaroneck" and the oldest surviving family cemetery in Westchester County, the small burying ground in Harbor Island Park was used by the family of John Richbell, who purchased what is now the Town of Mamaroneck from the Siwanoy Indians in 1661.[57] A merchant and native of Hampshire, England, Mr. Richbell had originally settled 13 years earlier in Charlestown, Massachusetts. However, his business lost a great deal of money as a result of the Navigation Act of King Charles I.[58] "In defiance of the English navigation laws," Richbell sought out a trading base in the Dutch colony of New

Netherland, resulting in his move to the shores of Long Island Sound.[59] Mr. Richbell divided his purchase into several tracts of land. The present neighborhood of Orienta was given to his daughter, Mary, and it was on her land that John Richbell was buried following his death on July 26, 1684.[60] Mary's husband, Captain James Mott (1651-1707), officially set out the family cemetery in the early 1700s in a statement that was recorded by the Mamaroneck Town Clerk:

> I James mott do give and grant to margeret disbrow and her three Sons hennery john and beniamin all belonging to momoronack to them and their famylies for ever the Liberty of burying their dead whether father or mother husband or wife brother or sister son or daughter in a certain peace of Land Lying near the Salt medow where mr John richbell and his wifes mother and my wife mary mott was buried in my home Lott or Feild adioning to my house writen by william palmer Clerk of momoroneck by order of Capt Jeames mott.[61]

The cemetery was used by the descendants of John Richbell and his wife, Ann, as well as their neighbors throughout the 18th and early 19th centuries. In 1848 the Reverend Robert Bolton stated that the burial ground on "Seaman's Point or Neck" contained "several memorials to the Bain, Disbrow, and Vanderbilt families."[62] The aforementioned geographical feature took its name from Giles Seaman (1748-1827), the "venerable old Quaker" who was the great-great-nephew of Captain James Mott.[63] Giles was the last relative of John Richbell to inhabit the Mott family farm, and his burial in Richbell Cemetery was the final interment made in that graveyard.[64] In his will, Giles reserved the cemetery from any posthumous sale of his land: "The Burying ground where my wife Lydia Lyes shall not be sold but kept fenced in big enough to inclose her and some other parts of my family with myself If I end my days in a reasonable distance."[65] Writing about the cemetery for Scharf's *History of Westchester County, New York*, in 1886, Edward Floyd De Lancey described the cemetery and mentioned his hope that the burial place of Mamaroneck's founder would one day be appropriately marked:

> The spot is on the property of Mr. Thomas L. Rushmore on the little knoll between the Harbour and Delancey Avenue, marked by a few trees and a few half buried tombstones of a comparatively later date. How many of the Disbrows are buried there nought remains to tell.... It is the oldest burial place of civilized man in the town, and it is hoped that some proper historic monument may yet mark this spot so sacred in the memory of the earliest settler of Mamaroneck and his family and friends.[66]

Evelyn Briggs Baldwin, a recorder of the tombstone inscriptions in many of southern Westchester's old cemeteries, visited the burial ground in the early 20th century and found the tombstones of Agnes Bain (c.1755-1792) and Mary Disbrow (1791-1807), as well as three rough stones marking the graves of a C.H. who died in 1728, a J.B. who died at the age of 84 in 1765, and an A.B. who died in 1793 at the age of 69.[67] Unfortunately, the cemetery remained in a state of neglect through much of the 20th century. Mamaroneck historian William Fulcher recounted his visit to the burial ground in 1936:

> After plowing through the brush and blackberry bushes, [I] found what appeared to be the remains of half a dozen tombstones and one stone which was a few inches below the surface of the ground, lying flat in a good state of preservation with the date 1807 and the name Disbrow on it.... Another stone bears the name of Hains [sic], 1796 and part of a stone has just been uncovered which has a heart and vines carved on it with the date March 15, 1728. No name can be found to identify this stone. It is the oldest dated stone in any of the cemeteries in the town of Mamaroneck.[68]

Above: Two tombstones in Richbell Cemetery in the late 1950s.

Four years later, Mamaroneck High School student Milton Prigoff detailed the condition of the cemetery:

> This is perhaps the most tragic of all [Mamaroneck's] graveyards, for the soil, being of an absorbent nature, has swallowed up all the stones. About eight to ten years ago, in building a house nearby, bricks and other debris were thrown on the lot. Until Mr. William G. Fulcher, local historian,

unearthed four or five tombstones, there was nothing to show that it was a cemetery at all. The lot is badly overgrown with clinging vines and blackberry bushes. It is no individual's fault that this graveyard is in such bad condition but it reflects badly on the town that it has done nothing to preserve this historical spot.[69]

Above: Looking south in Richbell Cemetery in 2005. A 21st-century Mamaroneck family makes its home next to the final resting place of the town's 17th- and 18th-century residents.

In 1954 a reporter for the *Mount Vernon Daily Argus* noted that the burial ground had been "forgotten and neglected by all but children who love the story of the Indians and the brave adventure tales of the early days."[70] The appropriate recognition of Richbell Cemetery finally came when "a granite monument, with a bronze tablet affixed to it describing [Richbell's] acquisition, was erected in 1961 to commemorate the 300th anniversary of Richbell's Purchase."[71] Many of the sunken fieldstones were raised at that time as well. The cemetery has since become a part of Harbor Island Park, and is now kept free from overgrowth and pollution.

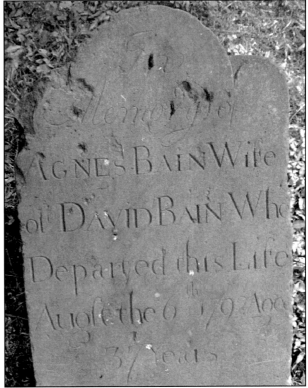

Right: The headstone of Agnes Bain is the only remaining inscribed tombstone in Richbell Cemetery. It reads:

In
Memory of
AGNES BAIN Wife
of DAVID BAIN Who
Departed this Life
August the 6th 1792 Aged
37 Years

Town of Mamaroneck Cemetery
Budd Family Burial Ground
Mamaroneck (Mamaroneck Village)

Above: The Budd Family Burial Ground in the Town of Mamaroneck Cemetery in 2007.

Location: The Town of Mamaroneck Cemetery is located on the west side of Mount Pleasant Avenue between Mamaroneck and Stanley avenues. The Budd Family Burial Ground is in the southwest corner of the Town cemetery.

Dates of Activity: Budd Family Burial Ground, 1754 – 1813; Town of Mamaroneck Cemetery, 1829 – 1957.

Other Names: Cemetery behind Kindergarten, Old Town of Mamaroneck Cemetery.

Inscriptions: *WCHS* Books #11 (p.71-77) and #81 (p.19-21).

Notes: The cemetery on Mount Pleasant Avenue originated as the burial ground of a branch of the Budd family in 1754, when Jane Barker (c.1712-1754) was interred on a rise overlooking the Sheldrake River. One year later, Mary Budd (1710-1798) buried her husband, Underhill (1708-1755), in this burial ground. Underhill Budd was the proprietor of the Mamaroneck portion of Budd's Neck, a 1,250-acre purchase made by his grandfather, John Budd, in 1661.[72] Underhill's son Gilbert (1744-1813) "served with great distinction in the continental army during the Revolution" as the Lieutenant Colonel of the 2nd Westchester County Militia Regiment. In peacetime Gilbert served four terms as clerk and two terms as supervisor of the Town of Mamaroneck.[73] Colonel Budd was apparently the namesake of his uncle, Dr. Gilbert Budd (1718-1805), a former surgeon in the British Royal Navy whose burial in this cemetery was very simple in accordance to his will:

> …my burial I request and hereby positively order to be as private as possible and particularly
> dispence with that ridiculous custom of inviting people to attend the burial, that each person who has the
> trouble of carrying the corpse to the place of interment be allowed one dollar each and further that the

ceremony of the clergy be dispensed with upon this principle that we ought not to leave to bungling journeymen after death what our duty demanded from us while living. [74]

The central monument of the Budd plot is a box monument which lists the names of six members of the Budd family who are interred beneath it. The much-faded inscription at the top of this memorial reads:

UNDERHILL BUDD
Died May 1755

SARAH
Wife of Underhill Budd
Died Aug. 17, 1798. Aged 88.

MARY BUDD
Died 1756. Aged 10.

Col. GILBERT BUDD
Died Sept. 7, 1813. Aged 69.

SARAH
Wife of Andrew Lyon

Dr. GILBERT BUDD,
who died Oct. 14th, 1805,
aged 87 years.

Whoe'er thou art, with silent footsteps tread
The hollow mould where he reclines his head;
Let not thoughtless mirth one dear deny,
But pensive, pause, where truth and honour lie.
His the gay wit that fond attention drew,
Oft heard delighted by the friendly few;
The heart, that melted at another's grief;
The hand, in secret, that bestowed relief.
Perhaps e'en now, from yonder realm of day,
To his lov'd relatives he sends a ray;
Pleased to behold affections like his own,
With filial duty raised this votive stone.

Sarah Lyon was the daughter of Underhill Budd.[75] Following his death in 1813, Colonel Gilbert Budd was the last person with his surname interred in this graveyard. However, a few members of the Barker family were interred in the Budd Family Burial Ground during the first half of the 19th century. In 1817 Dr. Guy C. Bayley purchased Colonel Budd's estate, at which time the following reservation was made for the Budd Family Burial Ground:

...reserving to the representatives, heirs and family of Gilbert Budd, deceased the burial ground belonging to them and a convenient way to and from the same with horses, wagons, carts and carriages forever at their free will and pleasure.[76]

Although the Budd cemetery's usefulness as a private graveyard had largely ended with the death of Gilbert Budd, its rededication as a public burial ground occurred less than 20 years after the Colonel's demise. The following resolution was made at Mamaroneck's annual town meeting on April 7, 1829:

Resolved that Walter Marshall, John Morrill, and James R. Hadden be a Committee to Call on Guy C Bay[ley] to get from him a good Deed for half Acre of Land for a Town Berring Ground and if they obtain said Deed they are then to be the Committee to fence Said Ground With a good Stone fence....[77]

No progress was made on this matter over a year following this action. As a result, another resolution regarding a town cemetery was passed at the annual meeting held on April 6, 1830:

Resolved that Peter Ferris, James H. Guion & Monmouth Lyon be the Committee to Call on henry Munro and get from him $100 Dollars which was raised last year to fence a Town Berring Ground and to Call on Guy C Bayley and get the Deed for Said Ground then to fence the Ground....[78]

Interestingly, the deed which transferred the half-acre of land to Mamaroneck Town Supervisor Henry Munro from Guy C. Bayley "for the use of the inhabitants of the Town of Mamaroneck to be used by them as a public burying ground forever" was dated November 1829, a date which conflicts with the resolution made at the 1830 town meeting. Additionally, the deed excepted "a piece of ground in the South corner" of the parcel "known as the Burying Ground belonging to the Estate of Gilbert Budd, deceased."[79] After this transaction was completed, the annual town meetings appointed a committee of three persons "to take Charge of the Publick Burying Ground."[80] By the 1870s, this task was assigned to only one person. The last burial, that of Edward Riley, was made in 1957.

Despite its historic significance, the Town of Mamaroneck Cemetery was much neglected throughout the 20th century. The cemetery does not boast a picturesque location, as it is hemmed in on the west and south sides by apartment buildings. Although many of its damaged tombstones are in poor condition, the status of the cemetery has improved due to efforts made by the Town and Village of Mamaroneck, as well as the Mamaroneck Historical Society.

Top: Looking east from the Budd Family Burial Ground in the Town of Mamaroneck Cemetery in 2007.

Bottom: Looking west in the Town of Mamaroneck Cemetery in 2007. Note the construction of the building in the rear of the cemetery. The box monument in the Budd Family Burial Ground is located directly behind the cross at the center of the photo.

42

City of Mount Vernon

New York Infant Asylum Cemetery   44   Wartburg Cemetery   58
Saint Paul's Church Cemetery   45

Above: An aerial view of Saint Paul's Church and cemetery about 1930.

Right: This tombstone in Saint Paul's Church Cemetery marks the body of a militia officer whose date of birth was not known: "Here Lays the Body of Cap Will Pinkney Deceas[d] 11th day of March 1755 Aged about 75 Years." According to the Reverend Robert Bolton, "there is a tradition in the Pinkney family that one of its early members presented the land to the church, embracing the present green, church-yard and adjoining property, for which they enjoy the privilege of free interment."[1]

Four cemeteries were located within the present boundaries of the City of Mount Vernon. The remains from two of these burial grounds, the New York Infant Asylum Cemetery and the Wartburg Cemetery, were removed in 1902 and 1934, respectively. The burial ground of the Farrington family is discussed in the Appendix. The city's only surviving cemetery is part of the only national park in Westchester County. The churchyard at Saint Paul's Church National Historic Site was used as an active burial ground for four centuries, and contains an interesting mix of fieldstones, sandstones, marble tombstones, granite monuments and vaults. Among the prominent citizens of southern Westchester who are interred at Saint Paul's is the Reverend William S. Coffey, who served as rector of the church from 1852 to 1909 and encouraged his flock to visit the burial ground:

> With but few exceptions, [the] old friends of the Church repose in its quiet grave yard. As then from time to time, you go thither to pass some profitable hour, in reading the varied inscriptions on its tomb stones, seek out the mounds, which cover the resting places of these faithful ones, and in expressions audible to the quick ear of your own grateful instincts, if not to them, offer the tribute of reverence and regard, which is their due. Shall you not be greatly benefited by such an employment?[2]

New York Infant Asylum Cemetery

Mount Vernon

Right: The empty space that stretches from the bottom of this photo to the tall tree at right is the unmarked plot which contains the remains that were removed from the New York Infant Asylum Cemetery to Kensico Cemetery in 1902.

Location: Although the precise location of the cemetery is unknown, the New York Infant Asylum was located on the east side of Columbus Avenue (Route 22) between California Road and the border of Mount Vernon and Eastchester.

Dates of Activity: 1878 – 1902.

Removed: To an unmarked plot in Kensico Cemetery (Section 24) in 1902.

Notes: The New York Infant Asylum, which was established in 1865 "primarily to provide care for foundlings and abandoned chil-

dren," opened a "general hospital and asylum" in Mount Vernon in 1878.[3] In 1893 the asylum was "said to be the most complete institution of its kind in the world," and by 1896 there were "over 500 babies" being cared for at the Mount Vernon campus.[4] The management of the asylum established a cemetery about "100 feet square" on the campus.[5] Unfortunately, little information is available regarding this cemetery, which served as the final resting place for "most of the children and many of the women" who died at the asylum.[6] In 1897 the *New York Times* reported on a complaint regarding the method of burials in the cemetery:

> Robert Catterson, a monument dealer, of [Mount Vernon], has filed complaint with the Board of Health, in which he charges improper methods of burial on the part of those employed by the New York Infant Asylum in interring the bodies of the children dying in that institution. It is the custom, he says, for six and eight bodies to be placed in a single grave. The caskets are placed one on top of another. He also asserts that the graves are not covered except with oilcloth until they are filled as high as intended with caskets. He claims that in some cases the top casket is not more than two feet below the surface, despite the law requiring six feet.[7]

A committee that investigated Mr. Catterson's complaint cleared the asylum of all charges.[8] The asylum closed its Mount Vernon branch in 1902. The following article appeared in the *New York Times* on October 19, 1902:

> Nine petrified bodies have just been found in the cemetery attached to the New York Infant Asylum here. The asylum was closed recently, and the land was sold to a syndicate that proposes to develop the property. Three hundred bodies are to be transferred to the Kensico Cemetery. To-day the workmen exhumed nine bodies that had become petrified. The bodies have the appearance of white marble. The soil there is sandy.[9]

There were "over 300 bodies" interred in this cemetery.[10] The Mount Vernon *Daily Argus* reported that in purchasing a plot in Kensico Cemetery, the trustees of the asylum chose "as desirable a spot as though they were the children of the trustees themselves." The Daily Argus went on to note that "while in some institutions it is the custom to consider any place good enough for the burial of people who have died at such places, the trustees of this asylum have been more thoughtful and have purchased this expensive land."[11] Nevertheless, there is no marker of any kind at the asylum's plot in Kensico Cemetery.

Saint Paul's Church Cemetery
Mount Vernon

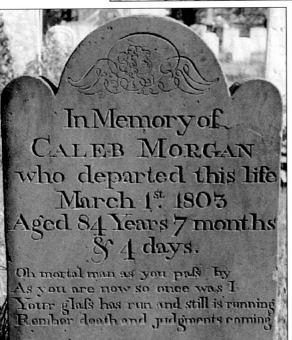

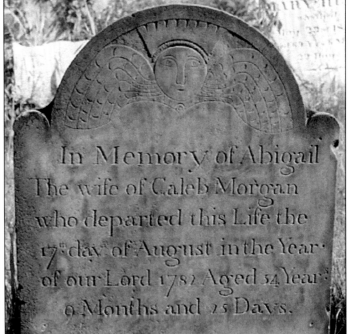

Top: Saint Paul's Church and Cemetery in 1886.

Bottom: The headstone of Caleb Morgan (left) was carved by Thomas Brown. Mr. Brown originally carved skulls and bones on his tombstones, but switched to cherubic angels such as this one after the Revolutionary War. Mr. Morgan is buried between his two wives, Abigail Drake (1727-1782) and Isabella Guion Johnson (1717-1800). Abigail's tombstone (right) features a fairly elaborate winged soul effigy, and was probably carved long after her death.

Location: South side of South Columbus Avenue between South Fulton Avenue and South 3rd Street.

Dates of Activity: c.1693 – Present.

Other Names: Eastchester Cemetery, Eastchester Churchyard.

Inscriptions: *WCHS* Book #13 and #14.

Mailing Address: Saint Paul's Church National Historic Site, 897 South Columbus Avenue, Mount Vernon, NY 10550.

Notes: The history of Saint Paul's Church can be traced back to May 9, 1693, when the inhabitants of Eastchester resolved to build a meeting house on the south side of the village green. By 1696 a meeting house roughly 28 feet square had been completed about 200 feet east of the present church.[12] Although the precise date of the founding of the church cemetery is unknown, by 1704 burials were being made on the south side of the original meeting house. Today, a number of crudely inscribed gravestones marking the earliest burials in the cemetery can be found in the northwest portion of the churchyard. Unlike burials made by future church members in the properly laid-out plots located in the central and southern portions of the cemetery, interments made by colonial parishioners were made with no clear distinction for family or class, save for that of slave and free, as the former were interred in a piece of land about 250 feet behind the graves of their owners.

Maintenance of the cemetery at Saint Paul's was an affair of both church and state. For example, the Eastchester town records note that at a meeting held on April 1, 1755, it was resolved, "That Richard Stevens be appointed grave-digger for the town, for the year ensuing, and to dig a grown person's grave for six shillings and three shillings for children."[13] Eleven years later, Marcus Christian was "appointed sexton for the town" and was directed to "take care of the Green, to see that hogs don't dig, and to dig graves, and to find a good bier."[14] It is known that two burials were made underneath both the old and new churches, as the Reverend Doctor Thomas Standard, minister of the church from 1726 to 1760 and donor of the congregation's bell, was buried "by the side of his wife, beneath the chancel of the old church on the green…. In 1818, their bodies were removed by order of the Vestry and interred under the communion table" of the present church.[15] At the time of this exhumation, the remains of the Standards "were found in a good state of preservation, but crumbled to pieces on exposure to the atmosphere. Tradition says, that Mr. Standard gave certain lands to the church on condition that the remains of himself and wife should be removed whenever the new edifice should be built."[16]

Above: The marker placed at the site of the sand pit where the Hessians who died at Saint Paul's were buried, c.1927 (left) and 2007 (right).

As the town of Eastchester grew, so did the need for a new, larger meeting house. In 1761 the Reverend John Milner noted that "the people of Eastchester have laid the foundation of a new church of stone, seventy-one feet by eighty-eight, in the room of a small decayed wooden building erected in the infancy of the settlement."[17] The construction of this new church was very costly to its members, who were not able to raise funds for the completion of the roof until 1767. However, these monetary concerns would not be nearly as pressing for the congregation as the Revolutionary War would eventually become.[18] Following the Battle of Pell's Point in 1776, the church was used as a hospital by the British army's Hessian allies, and those soldiers who died there were buried in a sand pit about 250 feet south of the church. This site was partially uncovered "when a grave was being dug" in the early 20th century, at which time "brass buttons and buckles that had lain there for centuries were found in the earth."[19] Although "estimates of the number of soldiers buried in the pit sometimes reached 100...the actual number seems to have been much smaller."[20]

With the completion of the new church, the focal point of the cemetery moved easterly and away from the site of the original meeting house. It should also be noted that the environment surrounding the cemetery's southern side at this time was quite different from today's situation. Before the Hutchinson River was straightened into a canal during the late 19th century, the marshlands which presently border the river at Pelham Bay Park once continued northerly into Westchester, hence the need for the declaration of a right of way through the cemetery to the owners of the "salt meadow" in 1792.[21] Only by understanding these geographical differences can one realize why the inhabitants of Eastchester would have seen this ground as such an ideal place to bury their friends and family.

The ratification of the United States Constitution in 1788 marked the beginning of a separation of the affairs of church and state, an idea which would be reflected in the management of the cemetery at Saint Paul's. At the 1792 Eastchester town meeting, it was resolved "that the burial ground shall, and of right, ought to belong to the Church."[22] As a result, the sexton of the cemetery was appointed by the church trustees rather than the town government. (A year earlier, sexton Marcus Christian had been dismissed from his post after admitting to selling liquor in the church's bell tower.) The Minutes of the Vestry for March 1793 record that "a committee of three were appointed to enclose the Church ground, with a board fence on the whole front, or north side, and with a post or rail fence, or board fence on the other sides."[23] In 1809, this fence, "very much decayed, gave place to the present one of stone, toward which the town of East Chester voted $100, the rest of the amount required, being raised by subscription." It is this stone wall which, repaired and improved over the next two centuries, presently marks the north side of the cemetery.

Above: The Drake (left) and Morgan family vaults are located just west of Saint Paul's Church In 1829 the body of George Washington Adams, eldest son of President John Quincy Adams, washed up on the shore of City Island six weeks after he fell (or jumped) off a steamer in Long Island Sound. His remains were taken to Saint Paul's and temporarily interred in the Drake family vault. As a token of gratitude for the church's assistance, First Lady Louisa Adams donated a chalice to the congregation.

The Reverend William S. Coffey, rector of Saint Paul's from 1850 to 1909, gave an interesting description of the cemetery, particularly in regard to its numerous vaults, for Scharf's *History of Westchester County New York* in 1886:

ST. PAUL'S CHURCH-YARD contains about three and a half acres of land, and, it is estimated, holds in sacred trust over six thousand bodies. This burying-place was started in the very infancy of the town. The oldest inscriptions legible are those of "M.V.D." who deceased "FEB. 15, 1704," and of "R.S.," the date of whose death was Dec. 14th, of the same year. The monument to William Crawford, which rests horizontally upon brick walls, seems to have been the most conspicuous in the yard before the Revolution. The following family names of the town are read frequently upon the tomb-stones: Pinkney, Drake, Fowler, Shute, Hunt, Ward, Valentine, Pell, Sherwood, Underhill, Morgan, Briggs, Searing, Purdy, Reid, Barker, Bertine, Odell. There are vaults in this cemetery belonging to the Pell, Hill, Grigg, Prime, Sands, Morgan, Valentine, Masterton, Kain, H.R. Morgan, Drake, Seaman, Coutant, Oakley, Beekman, Farrington, Schieffelin, Dooley, Skidmore, Fowler and Street families. The Comfort Sands vault bears the date of 1790, but its erection here was at a much later period, the remains in it being transferred with the slab from Brooklyn [sic] to this church-yard.... The Fowler vault contains the remains of Capt. Jonathan Fowler, of the French [and Indian] War, and of his son, Capt Theodosius Fowler, of Revolutionary fame. In the "Prevost Plot" are buried Major George W. Prevost, of the British army, and the Rev. Augustine P. Prevost, who was at his death Rector of St. John's Church, Canandaigua. In this yard are also the remains of Philip Pell, Judge-Advocate of the American army, and those of his brother, Major Samuel Pell. A spot is pointed out in this cemetery where the sand for the mortar used in erecting the church was obtained. It has the added interest of being the burial-place of a large number of soldiers who died at the time of the Revolution, of the prevailing disease (bloody flux), in the church, then used as a hospital.[24]

The stone inscribed "R.S." marks the grave of Richard Shute (c.1632-1704), a founder of the town of Eastchester who served the municipality as town clerk for 30 years. Although Mr. Shute's inscription is quite primitive in comparison to the memorials of the present day, the fact that his tombstone contained a carving denoted his status within the small community of Eastchester.

Above: Looking south near the southwest corner of Saint Paul's Episcopal Church Cemetery in 2008. The space in the foreground was used by the congregation of Saint Paul's as a plot for the burial of their slaves.

Left: This headstone, which can be seen in front of the tree in the photo on the previous page, marks the burial of a slave named Thomas:

In
Memory of
THOMAS,
a Servant of Philip
and Deborah Rhineland
who departed this life
September 2nd, 1813
Aged 21 Years.

Well done thy good and faithfull
Servant; enter thou into the
joy of the LORD.

Right: The bottom portion of Samuel Nelson's headstone reads: "For thirty years attached to the family of John Grigg." During his escape from slavery in 1837, Mr. Nelson "knocked on the door" of Mr. Grigg, who lived across from the church. Mr. Nelson worked as a gravedigger in the cemetery where he was laid to rest, and "was paid with items such as suspenders, fish hooks, candy, and a bottle of beer."

Below: Looking southeast at Saint Paul's Church and cemetery, c.1910. Note the row of vaults at right.

The portion of the cemetery located east of the church was used as a public burial ground for nearly a century. At the 1849 annual town meeting, the municipal officers of Eastchester resolved to appropriate "the Towns lot of ground back of the shed and adjoining the burial ground attached to the Church as Town burial ground" and to "raise by tax the sum of one hundred and fifty dollars to fence the Town burial ground."[25] This claim was apparently questioned by Saint Paul's, for in 1850 the town officers resolved "that the Town claims the Inalienable right to the Burial ground around the Protestant Episcopal Church, and they will use all Lawful means to preserve, sustain and perpetuate the same." The town also determined to "defend [against] any suit" that sought to prevent "full free use of [the] ground as a Town Cemetery."[26] In 1851 the following resolution regarding the municipal burial ground was passed at the annual town meeting:

> That the surface of the ground be made smooth and it be divided into lots of twenty six feet or such number of feet as will make four divisions running parallel...and it shall be the duty of the town to employ some person or surveyor to measure such pieces or plots of ground...and when so arranged it shall be the duty of the Trustees [of the town] to give notice that the ground is ready for interments, [and] that families may select out such pieces of ground for their Family Interments as may be reasonable and proper.... [27]

In 1854 the Eastchester town officers resolved the following:

> [The town burying ground] shall forever herafter be free for the use of the Inhabitants, their families & relatives of this Town as a burial place subject only to a reasonable charge for opening graves... the fees for digging, filling and sodding Graves be as follows: in open seasons $2.00 in Frost seasons $2.50.[28]

Mount Vernon, which became a separate city in 1892, used this same parcel as its own municipal cemetery until the 1940s.[29] As such, the persons interred in this space were not necessarily congregants of Saint Paul's. The 1910 *Fairchild Cemetery Manual* noted that interment in this section was "free to the poor of the City of Mt. Vernon" who could present an "affidavit of citizenship" and a burial permit from the commissioner of charities.[30]

A number of gravestones are located alongside the church at the foot of the belfry. These gravestones represented persons who had originally been interred in the Underhill Family Burial Ground in the Bronx.[31] Saint Paul's ceased to operate as an active church in the 1970s and was opened to the public as a unit of the National Park Service in 1984. Today, burials can still be made by families who already own plots in the cemetery.

Above and Right: The veterans' marker in the foreground of the photo at right honors the military service of Captain Frederick Whittaker (1838-1889), an English immigrant who served in the Union cavalry during the Civil War. In 1876 Whittaker wrote *A Complete Life of Gen. George A. Custer*, a work which, though it contained many inaccuracies, helped contribute to the "Custer Legend." Captain Whittaker lived in Mount Vernon and was interred at Saint Paul's following his death from a self-inflicted gunshot wound. The sculpture of the baby (above) marks the grave of Captain Whittaker's eight-day-old great-granddaughter, Jacqueline Barneto, who died on December 11, 1919.

50

Top: This fieldstone has been placed inside a granite enclosure. Its inscription, which is given on the back of the granite enclosure, reads:

HEARE LYETH
THE BODY OF CAPTAIN
JOSEPH + DRAKE
DESECED + MARCH
THE + 16 + DAY + 1731
IN THE + 70 + YEAR
OF + HIS + AGE

Bottom Left: Peter Briggs, Jr. had this marble memorial placed at the grave of his wife, Eustatia (1832-1870). Note the wedding ring on the hand at left.

Bottom Right: The headstone of Revolutionary War veteran Charles Turnbull proudly notes his country of birth as well as the fact that he fought to liberate his adopted nation from it. The inscription is given at right.

In
Memory of
Charles Turnbull
(*A Native of Kingston on Thames*
Old England.)
who departed this life the 19th
Dec[r]. 1795 Aged
42 years 3 months & 14 days.
Major in the American Army.
My flesh shall slumber in the ground
Till the last Trumpet joyful sound;
Then burst the Grave with sweet surprise
And in my Saviours Image rise.

51

R S · D
DECEM
BER
14 1704

Above and Right: The tombstone of Richard Shute in the early 20th century (top left) and 2003 (top right) shortly before it was placed inside the museum at St. Paul's. The tombstone indicates that Mr. Shute died on December 14, 1704. A blank fieldstone has been placed at the gravesite (bottom right). Mr. Shute was interred within sight of his home lot, which was located on the west side of South 3rd Avenue between South Columbus Avenue and East 7th Street.[32] Note the absence of a plot enclosure in the photo at bottom right. Most of the posts and railings which enclosed family plots have been removed from cemeteries throughout Westchester to provide for easier landscaping access.

Top and Bottom Left: Marked "M V D FEB 14 1704," this fieldstone, which is located just south of the location of the original Saint Paul's Church, is the oldest dated grave marker in the cemetery at Saint Paul's as well as in all of Westchester County. The photo at the top of the page depicts the stone about 1910, while that at bottom left shows a similar view in 2008. Note the location of the two tombstones, which have been switched. Although the exact identity of "M.V." is unknown, it is believed that he or she was a member of the Valentine family.

Bottom Right: This fieldstone reads: "W B D IVLY 28 1741." It marks the grave of William Baker, who died on July 28, 1741. Mr. Baker "owned one of Eastchester's earliest taverns, located on the Boston Post Road."[33]

Above: These two crudely carved markers are among the oldest headstones in the churchyard at St. Paul's that contain legible inscriptions with full words. The tombstone at top left marks the grave of Cate Drake, while that at right stands at the grave of Rachel Gee.

17 * 49

Hear · Lieth · YE

Body · of · Cate

Drake · Wife

of · Ioseph ·

Drake

HER

LIETH · THE

BoDY · OF GE

RECHEl · E

DE · MA · YE

20 1752

Center Left: The headstone which marks the grave of Elizabeth Clements, who died on August 15, 1762, at the age of 30, is one of the earliest sandstones at St. Paul's. It is believed that the inscription on the stone was carved by a local blacksmith who ran out of room on the third line, which runs upward on the right side of the tombstone. Although the inscription was carved by a local, the stone and soul effigy were cut by John Zuricher, one of the most prolific carvers of colonial New York.

Here·Lyes·y^e

Bodyof·Elezebeth y^e 15

Clements·AUGUST

HO DPArted·ThS·LiFe

In y^e yeAr·1762 AGed

30 yer

Bottom Left: This headstone marks the grave of Jeremiah Fowler, who died on November 14, 1724.

IF D NOUE

MBERTHEFOURT

EEN DAY 1724

54

Above and Right: The graves of three Revolutionary War veterans in the churchyard at Saint Paul's. The headstones above mark the graves of Philip Pell (right) and his son, Samuel T. Pell. Samuel's expensive tombstone was carved by Thomas Brown. Legend has it that while the Marquis de Lafayette was traveling from New York to Boston in 1825, he stopped at Saint Paul's to pay his respects at Philip's grave.[34] The tombstone at bottom right marks the grave of Stephen Ward, whose house in Eastchester was the site of a skirmish during the war. Ward served at different times as a state assemblyman, state senator, county judge, Eastchester town supervisor, presidential elector and United States congressman.

In Memory of
Maj. SAMUEL T. PELL
who died the 29th
of December AD. 1786,
in the 32d Year of
his age.

Thus after returning Victorious
From the Field of Mars he
cheerfully obeys the summons
to Eternity from whence
there is no return.

In
Memory of
PHILIP PELL
Esq. who Deptd. this Life
on the 23rd of May 1788
56 Year of his Age.

He was patient under his suff-
erings and obedient to the
call of Heaven.

In
Memory of
STEPHEN WARD, ESQ.
who died 8th Dec'r. 1797
Aged 67 Years 9 Months
& 17 Days.

Sons of America!

Mourn for your country, she has lost a friend,
Who did her rights and liberties defend;
May rising patriots keep those rights secure
And hand them down to latest ages pure.
Mourn too, ye friends and relatives who knew
His worth, his kindness, and his love to you;
But duty bids us all resign, and say,
Thy will be done, who gave and took away.

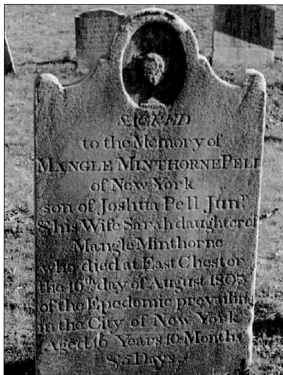

Top Left: This faded veteran's marker is located at the grave of Doctor Charles Sabin Taft. On April 14, 1865, Doctor Taft followed Doctor Charles Augustus Leale (who is interred at Oakland Cemetery in Yonkers) into the President's box at Ford's Theatre to assist the fatally wounded Abraham Lincoln.

Top Right: This much-damaged headstone is the only slate tombstone in the cemetery at Saint Paul's. It was probably imported from Massachusetts or Rhode Island.

Bottom Left: This marble tombstone marks the grave of Mangle Minthorne Pell, a young man who fell victim to yellow fever.

Bottom Right: This sandstone marks the grave of Dr. Thomas Wright's wife, Eliza (1761-1796). At the annual Eastchester town meeting on April 7, 1767, "it was agreed Doctor Wright should not be molested in his Buring yard on ye Green."[35] The reason behind this resolution is unknown.

Bottom Left:

SACRED
to the Memory of
MANGLE MINTHORNE
PELL
of New York
son of Joshua Pell Jun[r]
& his Wife Sarah daughter of
Mangle Minthorne
who died at East Chester
the 16th day of August 1805
of the Epedemic prevailing
in the City of New York
Aged 16 Years 10 Months
& 5 Days.

Top Right:

Ellener Daughter To
Benjamin & Mary
Drake Aged 4
years & 7 mo
june ye 10th 1729

Bottom Right:

Remember to Die

In Memory of Eliza[beth]
Wife of Doc[tr] Thomas
Wright
who Died March 20th 1796
Aged 34 Years 7 Mo.

Mortals be wise improve ye day
While vital spirits animate ye clay

Wartburg Cemetery
Mount Vernon

Above: Looking west in the Wartburg Cemetery. Photo courtesy Wartburg Care Community.

Location: As is indicated in the 1933 map at bottom right, the cemetery was formerly located near the intersection of Stuyvesant Plaza and Audubon Avenue. The gray rectangle on the modern map at top right indicates the approximate site of the cemetery (A) between Audubon Avenue (B) and the Cross County Parkway.

Dates of Activity: 1900 – 1918.

Removed: To Beechwoods Cemetery (Section 9) in New Rochelle in 1934.

Notes: The Wartburg Adult Care Community was founded in 1865 when the Reverend Doctor William A. Passavant, a Lutheran minister, established the Lutheran Deaconess Institution of the State of New York. The original purpose of the institution was to serve as "an orphans' home for children who had lost their fathers in the Civil War."[36] The institution had acquired two farms totaling 125 acres in the Town of Eastchester. This land included much of the present-day Mount Vernon High School campus. The property was called the Wartburg, as someone, perhaps the Reverend Passavant himself, remarked that it was "something like the site of the Wartburg where Luther translated the New Testament."[37] By 1872 a total of 57 orphans were residing at the Wartburg. In 1892 the Wartburg became part of Mount Vernon following the incorporation of that city.

In 1899 the Marie Louise Heins Memorial Home was opened at the Wartburg, an event which marked the beginning of the institution's program of caring for the elderly. During the following year, the Wartburg established a small cemetery on its property. Unlike the burial ground of the nearby New York Orphan Asylum, which was solely intended as a burial place for orphans, the graveyard at the Wartburg was also a place of interment for staff members and elderly persons as well. The first interment in the cemetery was that of Auguste Peters, who died on April 21, 1900. Over the next 18 years a total of 20 adults and 12 children were laid to rest in the 60' x 44' burial ground, which was located in a wooded area on the western portion of the institution's property.

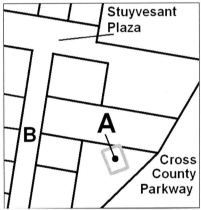

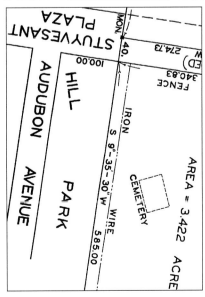

Above: Looking west at the Wartburg Cemetery. Photo courtesy Wartburg Care Community.

Right: A plan of the Wartburg Cemetery, 1931. Courtesy Wartburg Care Community.

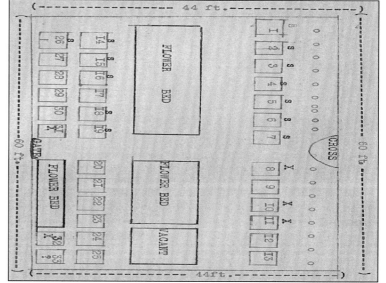

The Wartburg was a bilingual institution during the early years of its existence, and as such the burial ground was also known by the German word for cemetery, *friedhof* (literally, "peace yard"). Many of the grave markers in the cemetery were inscribed in German:

Ernestine Louise	Charlotte Fuessguss
Sommer	Geb. 26 Aug. 1886
Geb. 26 Apr. 1830	Gest. 19 Maerz 1907
i Neusalz A.O.	Auf Wiedershen.
6 Juli 1900 Wartburg	
	[Born 26 August 1886
[Born 26 April 1830	Died 19 March 1907
in Neusalz-an-der-Oder]	Until we see again.]

The cemetery was used briefly, as the Wartburg purchased a plot in Beechwoods Cemetery in New Rochelle after the end of World War I. In 1934 the remains from the Wartburg Cemetery were removed to Beechwoods to make way for the Cross County Parkway. Although much of the land that originally comprised the Wartburg has been sold, the institution continues to be a leader in the area of adult care.

Bottom Right: The monument in the Wartburg plot at Beechwoods Cemetery, 2011.

City of New Rochelle

Above: Thomas Paine's burial site and house, May 15, 1910. The sign on the tree at the left reads, "On the site of this tree was the grave of Thomas Paine." Today, a plaque marks the burial site.

Allaire Family Burial Ground	60	Huguenot Burying Ground	87
Beechwoods Cemetery	64	Lispenard Family Burial Ground	101
Carpenter Cemetery	67	Leonard Lispenard Tomb	101
Christ Methodist Church Cemetery	70	New Rochelle Presbyterian Church Cemetery	102
Seacord Family Burial Ground	70	Old Catholic Cemetery	103
Coutant Cemetery	74	Saint Joseph's Cemetery	103
Robinson Family Burial Ground	74	Pugsley Family Burial Ground	108
Davids Island Cemetery	77	Saint John's Methodist Church Cemetery	110
DeVeau Family Burial Ground	78	Shute Family Burial Ground	112
Flandreau Family Burial Ground	79	Thomas Paine Burial Plot	114
Harrison Family Tomb	83	Trinity Episcopal Church Cemetery	117
Holy Sepulchre Cemetery	84	Trinity Episcopal Church African Cemetery	120

The City of New Rochelle has been the home to more than 20 burial places ranging from small family plots to Westchester's oldest Catholic cemetery, and from a 17th-century community burial ground to the grave of one of America's founding fathers. New Rochelle is also home to the Carpenter Cemetery, a burial ground founded for the African Americans of southeast Westchester by a white Quaker abolitionist and his wife. Unfortunately, nearly one third of the city's burial places have been destroyed or removed from their original locations due to urban renewal, highway construction, and commercial and residential development. The most bizarre case of destruction of a burial place in Westchester County occurred in 1819 when William Cobbett, a British journalist, stole the remains of Thomas Paine from their original resting place on his New Rochelle farm. Additionally, other graveyards such as the Carpenter Cemetery and the Flandreau Family Burial Ground have suffered greatly from neglect over the past century.

Fortunately, New Rochelle's cemeteries are among the best documented of any municipality in Westchester County. In 1941 the Daughters of the American Revolution produced *New Rochelle Tombstone Inscriptions: A Record of All Inscriptions in the Old Cemeteries*. This invaluable resource contains maps and tombstone inscriptions from every burial ground in New Rochelle except for Beechwoods and Holy Sepulchre cemeteries. It is indispensable for anyone who is looking for a gravesite in that city.

Allaire Family Burial Ground
New Rochelle

Above: Taken on December 3, 1911, this photo depicts the monument which was located near the northeast corner of the Allaire Family Burial Ground. The monument does not mark the interments of members of the Allaire family, but was erected by Alexander B. Allaire to "transmit to posterity the origin of the Allaire family in the United States."

Location: Formerly where I-95 passes behind the Odell Place Apartments (see map on page 89).

Removed: to Trinity Episcopal Church Cemetery in September 1956.

Dates of Activity: c.1823 – 1943.

Inscriptions: *WCHS* Book #18 (p.54-61).

Notes: Alexander Allaire, a native of the French city of La Rochelle, was among the Huguenot refugees who fled to North America following the revocation of the Edict of Nantes in 1685.[1] He originally went to the West Indies, and from there he traveled to New York City and then to New Rochelle, where he obtained a "home lot" in the early 1690s. In 1693 he was "licensed to keep a tavern."[2] One of the members of the French Church who refused to conform to the Church of England in 1709, he preferred instead to lead "the Calvinists in the continuation of their church organization."[3] He remained a popular citizen of New Rochelle, however, and was elected to two terms as town clerk.[4]

Peter Alexander Allaire, a grandson of Alexander Allaire, deeded a piece of land adjacent to the Huguenot Burying Ground to his four sons and their descendants for use as a cemetery on October 8, 1823.[5] The exact date of the founding of this burial ground has not been ascertained, as the Daughters of the American Revolution noted in their description of the cemetery in 1941:

The Allaire Cemetery is located immediately to the south west of the Old Huguenot Burying Ground. It is a small plot, surrounded by a good iron fence with a small gate leading from a lane which runs beside it and the Old Huguenot Cemetery from the corner of Division Street and Union Avenue….

The earliest date of death appearing on a stone in the cemetery is 1782. This appears on a stone erected to the memory of Capt. Alexander Allaire who died in 1782, aged 80 years. There is no way of telling whether stones represent actual burials, whether they have been erected in memory of the persons named or whether they are removals from some other cemetery….

The New Rochelle Trust Co., 542 Main Street, New Rochelle, N.Y., has partial charge of this cemetery. They hold two trust funds, to be used for the care of two plots in the cemetery. These plots are Isaac Allaire's Plot and Taulman Allaire's Plot. If there is any money left, after caring for the above named plots it is used in the general upkeep of the cemetery. As a matter of fact, the cemetery is well kept.[6]

Above: Looking south at the northwest corner of the Allaire Family Burying Ground in 1954. The small plaque on the gate read "ALLAIRE CEMETERY."

Right: A group of men from Trinity Episcopal Church cleaning up the Allaire Family Burial Ground in 1950.

Among those interred in Taulman Allaire's plot was his son, William (1854-1884), a civil engineer whose monument notes that he assisted Henry H. Gorrange with the transfer of Cleopatra's Needle from the *Dessoug* to its position in Central Park in 1880. The cemetery was still used by the Allaire family throughout the early 20th century. The final burial, that of Robert A. Allaire, was made in 1943. The coffers of the two aforementioned trust funds had dwindled by the late 1940s, and as a result the burial ground began to feel the effects of vandalism and overgrowth. In 1950 a contingent of men from Trinity Episcopal Church conducted a cleanup of the lot and repaired many of its tombstones.[7] However, the cemetery's days were numbered because of the construction of the New England Thruway, and its interments were removed in 1956 to their current resting place, a plot in the rear of Trinity Church Cemetery.[8] More than two decades later, the remains of a member of the Allaire family, Eloise Allaire Close, were buried in the Allaire plot alongside those of her ancestors.

Above: Looking north inside the Allaire Family Burial Ground in 1954. The gate at the end of the path is the same as that depicted in the foreground of the photo on the previous page.

Left: Formerly located near the northeast corner of the Allaire Family Burial Ground, these headstones were among the oldest tombstones in the cemetery. The two headstones in the top photo read:

IN
MEMORY OF
CAPT. ALEX. ALLAIRE.
DIED 1782.
AGED 80 YEARS.

IN
memory
of
MARIA (a native of the
Island of S^t. Thomas in
the West Indies) Wife of
Alexander Allaire
who died January the 6th
1805
Aged 93 Years & 6 Days.

This stone is erected as a tribute
Of respect to an affectionate and tender
Mother by her dutiful Children.

Captain Allaire's headstone was the oldest dated tombstone in the Allaire Family Burial Ground. As the tombstone predates the purchase of the cemetery land by more than 40 years, it is unknown if it actually marked a burial that was removed from another graveyard, or if it was a cenotaph. The two headstones in the bottom photo mark the graves of Peter Alexander Allaire, who "died 9th March 1839 in the 90th year of his age," and his wife, Frances, who died on February 5, 1807, at the age of 53 years, 8 months and 23 days.

Top Left: Taken from the New Rochelle *Standard Star*, this photo shows the re-interment ceremony that was held in Trinity Episcopal Church Cemetery over the boxes containing remains from the Allaire Family Burial Ground.

Top Right: Shaded by the branches of a small tree, the grave of two-month-old Peter Erickson Allaire, who died on January 8, 1849, was among those removed from the Allaire Family Burial Ground to Trinity Episcopal Church Cemetery.

Bottom: The tombstones and remains from the Allaire Family Burial Ground have been placed in a special plot on the north side of Trinity Episcopal Church Cemetery. The circular plot in the background contains the tombstones that were formerly located in the Guion family plots in the Old Huguenot Burying Ground.

Beechwoods Cemetery
New Rochelle

Right: One of the first portions of Beechwoods Cemetery that was developed following the cemetery's founding in 1854 is a hill located near the center of the burial ground. This hill contains a number of vaults and monuments that were constructed by the leading citizens of mid-19th-century New Rochelle. Today, their graves overlook the growing skyline of the community where they lived and worked.

Location: At the western end of Beechwood Avenue.

Dates of Activity: 1854 – Present.

Inscriptions: *WCHS* Book #19 (Part II).

Mailing Address: 179 Beechwood Avenue, New Rochelle, NY, 10801.

Notes: The following excerpt written by the Reverend Charles E. Lindsley for Scharf's *History of Westchester County, New York*, summarizes the founding of New Rochelle's largest burial place, Beechwoods Cemetery:

> For many years the town of New Rochelle had felt the need of some better place for the burial of the dead, the growing population having no other facilities for this purpose than the private or denominational burying-grounds afforded. On the 30th of January, 1854, the Beechwoods Cemetery was incorporated upon land owned by the late Dr. Albert Smith, of New Rochelle. It was chiefly Dr. Smith's energy and liberality that this new burial-place was opened to the public, he having contributed largely both of time and money to this object. The position is convenient and well-adapted to the purpose designed, and it is now the principal place of interment, both for the town and the vicinity.[9]

Dr. Smith transferred 31 acres of his estate to the Beechwoods Cemetery Association on April 16, 1855.[10] At the time of its founding, Beechwoods Cemetery was surrounded on three sides by farmland. In fact, Beechwood Avenue was laid out over Dr. Smith's estate so that the cemetery could be accessed across from Main Street.[11] Unfortunately, it appears that this street became a favorite haunt of vagabonds from the nearby railroad during the late 19th century:

> The tramps were especially troublesome in Beechwood Avenue, where they annoyed women and children on their way to Beechwoods Cemetery. The favorite haunt of the tramps is near a spring north of Beechwood Avenue.... This spring is famous far and wide among the members of the tramp guild. One man who was sent to jail not long ago for vagrancy told Police Captain Timmins that he had left his ordinary route to visit New Rochelle because of stories he had heard in California about this spring.[12]

The grave of Dr. Albert Smith is situated atop a hill in the north central portion of the cemetery. This hill is also the location of most of the vaults and tombs in the burial ground. Interestingly, the earliest date on any of these vaults is the one belonging to the family of Elbert Roosevelt–1843, 11 years before Beechwoods was founded. This discrepancy results from the fact that the remains of the Roosevelts were removed to Beechwoods from a crypt located beneath the Church of Christ the Redeemer in Pelham Manor. Along with presidents Theodore and Franklin Delano Roosevelt, Elbert was a descendant of Claes Martensze Rosenvelt, an early settler of New Amsterdam.[13]

Perhaps the most interesting story concerning a burial at Beechwoods relates to that of the Sickles family. George Garrett Sickles, father of Civil War General Daniel E. Sickles, was interred in a vault at Beechwoods following his death in 1887:

The body was placed in a tomb which Mr. Sickles had had specially built for himself and the members of his household. It is constructed of solid granite and is 12 feet in depth. The top of the tomb projects about 18 inches above ground. The body of Mr. Sickles was placed upon the lowest tier and surmounted by a solid granite slab which was hermetically sealed to the sides of the tomb. The same plan will be followed in the case of each additional body placed in the tomb.[14]

In the summer of 1905, General Sickles had the remains of his dog, Bo-Bo, buried in the plot of his father and late stepmother, Mary S. Sickles. The *New York Times* reported that "the body of Bo-Bo was brought from New York in a suit case and taken to the cemetery, where John Ross, the Superintendent, acting under instructions of Gen. Sickles, placed it in a pine box and buried it."[15] Although Mrs. Sickles' stepson objected to the burial, it appears that Bo-Bo was not removed, as the cemetery's "charter contain[ed] no clause preventing the burial of animals in the cemetery."[16] Today, the interment of animals in a regular cemetery is prohibited by New York law.

Left: The Sickles family plot in Beechwoods Cemetery.

Right: Beechwoods Cemetery is the final resting place of two soldiers who won the Medal of Honor during the Indian Wars. Sergeant William B. Lewis (top right) was awarded the medal for bravery during a skirmish with the Northern Cheyenne at Bluff Station, Wyoming, on January 20-22, 1879. Lieutenant Robert Temple Emmet (bottom right), who is buried in his family's large plot near the southwest corner of the cemetery, covered a retreating force of soldiers at Las Animas Canyon, New Mexico, on September 18, 1879, in the face of 200 Apache warriors. A graduate of West Point, Emmet first held off the attacking force with five of his comrades and then faced the Apaches by himself so that his fellow soldiers could recover their horses. Emmet's unit, the 9th Cavalry, was comprised of white officers and black enlisted men. Note the extra "T" in his surname on the veteran's stone.

Left: This tombstone reads:

TO THE BELOVED MEMORY OF
NORMAN WILSON CROSBY
ELDEST SON OF
HORACE AND JENNIE E. CROSBY,
WHO DIED IN THE SERVICE OF HIS COUNTRY
SEPT. 3, 1898, AGED 24

NOT THE
"SURVIVAL OF THE FITTEST,"
BUT THE
SACRIFICE OF THE BEST
PROMOTES THE CIVILIZATION OF MAN
AND REDOUNDS TO THE GLORY OF GOD.

TO THE DEAR MEMORY OF
HORACE FRANKLIN CROSBY
SECOND SON
DIED JAN. 8, 1902, AGED 21

Both of the Crosby brothers served in the 71st New York Volunteer Infantry Regiment during the Spanish-American War. Norman was a graduate of Cornell University, while Horace graduated from New York University. Norman contracted typhoid fever while in Cuba and died shortly after returning to the United States.[17]

Horace Crosby, who also served in the Spanish-American War and was employed as an office clerk with American Locomotive Works, was a victim of the 1902 Park Avenue Tunnel Collision in Manhattan. The last car on the Danbury-New York train, which was only opened to passengers in New Rochelle, was struck by another train that missed a signal in the steam-filled tunnel. Seventeen New Rochelle residents, including Horace, were killed. The *New Rochelle Pioneer* reported that "the young man's death has caused much sorrow and the grief of Mr. Crosby and his daughters was among the most pitiful of the heart-breaking scenes at the railroad depot."[18] The event was one of the most tragic in New Rochelle's history, as was reflected by the *Pioneer*'s headline: "ENTIRE CITY FILLED WITH UNPARALLELED REMORSE."

Above and Right: Several mid-19th century marble tombstones in Beechwoods Cemetery feature hands pointing upward to heaven. The tombstone of "Dannie" and "Harrie" at bottom left depicts a hand pointing to the adjacent grave with the words, "THERE LIES MOTHER." The photo at right depicts the tombstone of Augusta Boulle, who died in 1877 at the age of 11.

66

Carpenter Cemetery
New Rochelle

Right: The three white markers in the photo at top right indicate the boundaries of a small family plot, and are among the few remaining grave markers in the Carpenter Cemetery. The post on the left, which is depicted in the photo at bottom right, is marked with a "B." This may be the plot which contains the graves of T. Cornelius Bonnett (died October 22, 1901) and his wife, Eliza (died June 13, 1899, aged 75 years), whose headstones were the only inscribed tombstones recorded by the Daughters of the American Revolution in 1940.

Location: North side of Stratton Road between the driveway for the Saint Nersess Armenian Seminary and the Iona Preparatory School athletic fields (about four-tenths of a mile east of Wilmot Road).

Dates of Activity: 1838 – 1905.

Notes: Joseph Carpenter was an "old Quaker gentlemen" who owned a farm which during the mid-19th century stretched westward from Weaver Street to the present site of the Saint Nersess Armenian Seminary. Mr. Carpenter served as the executor of the will of Joseph Thomas Turpin, a former slave who owned a parcel on Pelham Road that had once been used by Trinity Church as a cemetery for African Americans.[19] Perhaps through his connection with Mr. Turpin, Joseph Carpenter realized the need for a proper burial place for the black citizens of New Rochelle and its surrounding area. To solve this problem, he donated an acre of his land for use as a cemetery for African Americans in this 1838 deed transferring the land to several municipalities in southern Westchester County:

WITNESSETH: That Joseph CARPENTER and his wife, MARGARET of the town of New Rochelle, County of Westchester and State of New York, being desirous of having a place of general Cemetery or burying ground, to be used for to inter any person that may die in either or any of the towns of New Rochelle, Mamaroneck, Scarsdale or Eastchester, all towns in the County of Westchester aforesaid, and such other persons as may die in other towns adjoining the aforenamed towns and such as may die elsewhere who have had relations intered in the piece of ground intended hereby to be granted to the said Towns....

AND WHEREAS: as aforesaid, the said Joseph Carpenter and his wife, Margaret, are desirous of granting the privilege of a general cemetery or burial ground to the four towns herein before particularly named, and a conditional privilege for the interment from other places do hereby grant to the towns, New Rochelle, Mamaroneck, Scarsdale and Eastchester the privilege of using the said piece of land particularly described for a general cemetery or burial ground forever under such restrictions regulations and on such conditions as is herein pointed out--namely that Timothy Bonnett, David, Harry and Jacob Landrine, of the said town of New Rochelle, Abraham Bonnett Jun. of the said town of Mamaroneck, and Henry

Thompson, of the town of Yonkers Westchester County, or their successors or a majority of them or a majority of their successors shall be superintendents of the said piece of ground, for interments as to them shall seem advisable they shall at all times when requested so to do point out such place as they deem advisable for the interment of any person who dies in any of the before mentioned four towns to which this grant is made.

And they shall also, if it appears proper, permit the interment of persons of said towns who shall have relations buried in said ground, or others who shall die near adjoining said four towns. The said Timothy Bonnett, David Harry, Jacob Landrine, Abraham Bonnett, Jun. and Henry Thompson, or their successors shall put up or procure to put up for the said four towns (if the towns give them the necessary assistance, or by other means if they choose) a good and substantial fence on the line designated adjoining other lands of Joseph Carpenter and maintain the same in good condition, [as well as] all other fences appertaining to said piece of land forever.

No charge shall at any time be made by the said superintendents or either of them or any of them or either or any of their successors for the privilege of interment. That there may always continue to be a body of superintendents of said ground, I empower those that remain of the five named Superintendents after any vacancy may happen to fill such a vacancy or vacancies, as the case may be, by one or more of their number giving the other superintendents three days notice of the time and place of meeting to fill any vacancy or vacancies that may exist in their body, and such vacancy shall be filled by a majority met for that purpose, and all vacancies that may happen shall be so filled in all time to come. And the board of superintendents that may be elected or partly elected shall have the same power and be under the same restrictions as the present five named are, and for the more full and quiet enjoyment of the said described piece of ground for a cemetery or burial ground, to those to whom it is granted.

We do stipulate for ourselves our heirs and assigns, that we will not erect any building or buildings plant any tree or trees thereon nor brake the soil thereof, nor suffer it to be done by others, except as is herein granted for the purpose of burial.

And that the ground may be kept in a suitable order for interments we grant the privilege to the superintendents forever to remove from said grounds any stones not erected as monuments, trees, brush, briars or noxious weeds.[20]

Aaron M. Powell, a prominent Quaker and member of the Anti-Slavery Society, commented on Mr. Carpenter's commitment to providing a suitable burial place for the black citizens of southeast Westchester:

There was much prejudice against colored people in this region, so much, that at that time in New Rochelle colored people were denied burial in any of its cemeteries or burial places. To meet this difficulty Joseph Carpenter set apart a portion of one of the fields of his [New Rochelle] farm as a burial plot for the colored people. By his direction his own body was interred therein. I visited him a short time previous to his death, when he acquainted me with this arrangement for the disposition of his body, as a last testimony against the then prevailing – and, alas, still prevalent – unchristian color prejudice. In accordance with his wish I also attended his funeral, and to those assembled bore my testimony to his memory and great personal worth. It was an occasion long to be remembered. His body, clothed in his wonted plain Friendly costume, was placed for burial, as he had also directed, in a plain, unstained pine coffin. At the conclusion of the services the coffin was carried out upon the lawn, in the shade of the trees he loved so well, and then those in attendance, colored and white, gathered about it to take a last look at the face of him whom they loved and reverenced. Then it was borne by colored men, who had requested the privilege, to its final resting place, among those of the proscribed colored people whom he had befriended. At a later period the body of Margaret Carpenter, the wife, a woman of sterling worth, sharing fully the deep feeling of her husband concerning the great injustice from which the colored people, both bond and free, were sufferers, was also interred in this unique, and now historic, burial plot.[21]

In 1889 George T. Davis noted that the number of burials in the cemetery "average[d] about 10 per year."[22] Among those interred in the Carpenter Cemetery was Mrs. Carrie Gifelt (b.1848), whose funeral procession on April 21, 1896, attracted a considerable amount of interest:

[Mrs. Gilfert] was a devout Christian lady, and a member of the Ladies Aid Society of the [A.M.E.] church…. Six members of the Ladies Aid Society, attired in long mourning gowns of black and white, officiated as pall-bearers, and escorted her remains to the Church and thence to the Upper New Rochelle Colored Cemetery…. This is the first occasion in New Rochelle of an adult's funeral attended by female pall-bearers, and was quite a novelty to the spectators who witnessed the funeral en-route to the cemetery.[23]

The farm which bordered the east side of this cemetery remained in the hands of the Carpenter family until 1906, when Phila Jane Carpenter sold the parcel to Francis A. Stratton.[24] This transaction caused some concern among the friends and relatives of those who were interred there, as was noted by the *New York Times*:

> President F.A. Stratton of the Westchester Lighting Company, who recently paid $65,000 for a farm on the Wilmot Road in Upper New Rochelle, finds that he is also the possessor of a negro cemetery with 400 graves in it…. The last burial there was that of a white woman who had a negro husband. She was buried a week ago. The negroes of New Rochelle are very much concerned because they have heard that Mr. Stratton intends to build a mansion on the place, which will mean that the cemetery will be wiped out and the gravestones raised. The negroes have no control over the graveyard because the man who deeded the property to them named a board of trustees, and the last member of the original board of trustees died twenty years ago. Mr. Stratton is in Maine on his vacation, and a gang of men is clearing the land for building purposes.[25]

These fears were unsubstantiated as the deed for Mr. Stratton's property noted that his purchase did not include the graveyard. Nevertheless, this transaction marked the end of the Carpenter Cemetery's existence as an active burial ground.[26] In 1939 Morgan Seacord noted that the "earliest known stone" in the Carpenter Cemetery "is that of James Tudor, 1839. The names of others suggest retainers of early white families of New Rochelle, among whom are Landrine, Bonnet, Pugsley, and Bailey."[27] Unfortunately, the condition of the cemetery deteriorated in the first half of the 20th century, a fact that was noted by the DAR in their 1940 survey of burial grounds in New Rochelle:

> The cemetery is in a most neglected state at the present time. There are many stones, set up in rows, most of them plain field stones without marks. A number of small stones have initials on them. The only stone with an inscription at present standing is a double stone to T. Cornelius [d.1901] and Eliza Bonnett [d.1899].[28]

Sadly, the neglect mentioned above has continued to the present, as the cemetery is full of the "trees, brush, briars [and] noxious weeds" that Joseph Carpenter had empowered the superintendents of the burial ground to remove.[29] There is no sign or marker to denote the cemetery's existence, and to the unknowing observer it appears to be nothing more than an overgrown patch of land.

Above: Looking east along Stratton Road in 2005. The sign next to the driveway for Saint Nersess Armenian Seminary is near the southwest corner of the Carpenter Cemetery, which in turn is located in the woods on the left side of the street.

Christ Methodist Church Cemetery
Seacord Family Burial Ground

New Rochelle

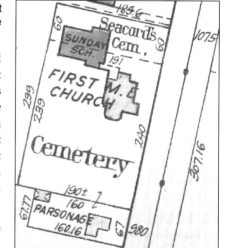

Above: This c.1890 photo depicts the second building used by the First Methodist Church. This church stood from 1838 to July 11, 1897, when it destroyed by fire. The northeast corner of the cemetery is visible at left.[30]

Location: Christ Methodist Church Cemetery adjoins the south side of the old First Methodist Church building (1228 North Avenue, west side of the road about 150 yards north of Disbrow Lane). The 1929 map at right depicts the church as well as the site of the Seacord Family Burial Ground, which was located on the northwest portion of the church's lawn. In 2004 the headstones and remains from the Seacord Family Burial Ground were removed to a plot in the Christ Methodist Church Cemetery just north of the church's former parsonage. Christ Methodist Church Cemetery also contains the removals from Saint John's Methodist Church Cemetery. These removals are located in a plot next to removals from the Seacord Family Burial Ground.

Dates of Activity: Christ Methodist Church Cemetery, 1794 – mid-20th century; Seacord Family Burial Ground, 1794 – 1896.

Removed: The interments and headstones in the Seacord Family Burial Ground were removed to the Christ Methodist Church Cemetery in 2004.

Other Names: First Methodist Church Cemetery (official name prior to 1966).

Inscriptions: Christ Methodist Church Cemetery: *WCHS* Books #8 (p.104-133), #18 (p.86-129), and #19 (Part I, p.41-75). Seacord Family Burial Ground: *WCHS* Books #8 (p.102-103) and #19 (Part I, p.76).

Notes: Methodism arrived in New Rochelle in 1771 when "two missionaries working out of the John Street Methodist Church in New York City" visited the home of Frederick DeVeau and assisted his ailing wife with her conversion to this faith.[31] A Methodist society was formed shortly thereafter, and its meetings were held at the homes of Mr. DeVeau and Peter Bonnett, the first being a loyalist and the latter a patriot. Following the end of the Revolutionary War, the DeVeau estate was confiscated by New York State and awarded to Thomas Paine. Services were occasionally held at the Bonnett home until 1787, when Israel and Jane Seacord donated a half-acre plot to the trustees of the congregation.[32] Three years after acquiring this land, the society was incorporated as the Methodist Episcopal Church of Upper New Rochelle.

According to the 1940 DAR survey, the "first interments which have been found in [this] cemetery are for the year 1794. Deeds to the plots in the cemetery were sold to church members soon after the organization of the church."[33] The churchyard was apparently an integrated one from its earliest days, as there are "numerous references to the burial of blacks in the family plots of the people with whom they had long been associated, both as slaves and freedmen."[34] In 1889 George T. Davis provided the following information regarding the cemetery:

> Within its limits lie buried many of the settlers of that part of the town. It contains two vaults (one, that of John Bonnett, and the other, that of Stephen Renoud, which was just a mound with a small stone at the entrance. This mound has long since been leveled) and several monuments.... The interments average about five per year.[35]

At one point the church had plotted the land in the northwest corner of its property for use as a cemetery. However, no burials were made in this area, and a Sunday school was constructed on that site instead.[36] In 1940 the DAR noted the state of the cemetery at that time:

> Deeds to plots in the cemetery were sold to church members soon after the organization of the church. Thus the cemetery developed. At present (for the past four years) there is about one interment per year. No more plots are being sold. Burials are allowed only when there is room [in] a plot and when the deed is held by some member of the family. The church does not keep up the cemetery. There are a few plots owned by people who pay for care. However, the grass seems to be kept cut in the front part of the cemetery.[37]

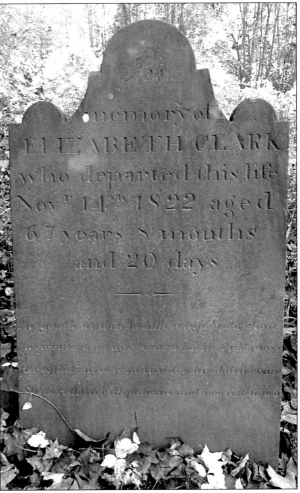

Above: The epitaph on the tombstone of Elizabeth Clark (1755-1822) reads:

> In youth and in health religion she chose
> In sickness and age 'twas a balm for her woes
> Her afflictions were many as years did increase
> She bore them with patience and now rests in peace.

The tombstone of Elizabeth's father, Moses, is depicted on page iv.

In 1962 Christ United Methodist Church was formed when the First Methodist Church merged with Saint John's Methodist Church. Three years later, the remains from Saint John's were reinterred in Christ Church's cemetery.[38] The newly-named congregation moved into its present building, located about 300 feet south of the cemetery. In 1966 the old church was then sold to an Orthodox Jewish congregation, Young Israel of New Rochelle.[39]

In describing the Israel Seacord house, a dwelling which still stands at the northeast corner of the junction of North Avenue and Quaker Ridge Road, New Rochelle historian Morgan Seacord gave the following background of that family, who were once the owners of much of the land in the vicinity of that intersection:

> James Seacord owned this property as early as the year 1755, and, upon his death in 1773, it passed to his son, Israel Seacord, who probably built the present home after 1773 and, with his family, occupied it during the Revolutionary War.... Israel Seacord was a Tory sympathizer, and, during the time General Howe's army was encamped in New Rochelle, British officers were visitors at his home... It remained in the ownership of his family until 1903.[40]

71

Above: Looking west at the Seacord Family Burial Ground during the mid-1950s. Note the obelisk behind the gate. The names of most of the persons interred in this burial ground are listed on this obelisk. Photo courtesy George Pouder.

Right: The obelisk visible in the photo above has since been removed to Christ Methodist Church Cemetery. The south face of this monument gives the name of Abraham Seacord (1785-1870) and contains a depiction of Masonic symbols.

The 1940 DAR study gave the following information concerning the Seacord Family Burial Ground, which was located on the lawn in front of the First Methodist Church:

> After selling this property to the church, [Israel Seacord] laid out a small plot to be used as his own family burying ground. This plot, located to the north of the church itself and east of the new parish school, is still the private plot of the heirs of Israel Seacord and is cared for by them. The church corporation neither owns nor controls it.[41]

In 2003 a descendant of the Seacords, Patricia Reed Perry, was contacted about the cemetery and decided to have the remains of her ancestors exhumed and re-interred in the burial ground belonging to the Christ Methodist Church:

> By the fall of 2003, tractors had been brought in and exhumation was under way. For weeks, experts worked, digging up trees and rubble in their search for whatever was left in the graves. It wasn't much—just a couple of shoe soles and a handful of bones. When the process was completed in the spring, Mrs. Perry held a small rededication ceremony.[42]

Mrs. Perry still has title to the parcel on which the cemetery was located. Young Israel of New Rochelle moved to a new building in 2008, and the fate of the old Methodist church building is undecided.

Above: Looking north in Christ Methodist Church Cemetery in 2009. The Bonnett family vault is located in the foreground.

Above: Christ Methodist Church Cemetery contains the removals from Saint John's Methodist Church Cemetery and the Seacord Family Durial Ground. This photo depicts the plots where these removals were reinterred. The flat stones mark the removals from Saint John's, while the obelisk marks the removals from the Seacord burial ground.

Right: This sandstone near the southeast corner of Christ Methodist Church Cemetery marks the grave of John Schureman, who died at the age of 62 on March 15, 1813. The epitaph at the bottom of his tombstone is given at right.

He was! But words are wanting
to say what.
Ask what a man should be: and
he was that.

Coutant Cemetery
Robinson Family Burial Ground
New Rochelle

Location: The Coutant Cemetery is located at the southeast corner of the intersection of Eastchester Road and Webster Avenue. The Robinson Family Burial Ground adjoins the east side of the Coutant Cemetery.

Dates of Activity: Coutant Cemetery, 1776 – Present; Robinson Family Burial Ground, 1894 – Present.

Inscriptions: Coutant Cemetery: *WCHS* Book #18 (p.62-85) and #19 (Part I, p.87-99); Robinson Cemetery: *WCHS* Book #18 (p.85).

Notes: One of the Huguenot refugees who fled France following the revocation of the Edict of Nantes, Jean Coutant (1658-1710) and his wife, Sarah Guion, moved to New Rochelle from New York City sometime between the fall of 1701 and January of 1703.[43] Prior to the outbreak of the Revolutionary War, members of the Coutant family, including Jean's sons, Jean Jr. (1695-1749) and Isaac (1697-1747), were interred in the Huguenot Burying Ground.[44]   The story of the founding of the Coutant Family Cemetery was recounted by Morgan Seacord in *Historical Landmarks of New Rochelle*:

> This is the family cemetery of Isaac Coutant [Jr.] and his descendants, and dates from 1776. It is owned and controlled by a family cemetery corporation. Isaac Coutant, Jr. [1723-1802], the founder, was the owner of the farm on which the cemetery is located when it was begun in 1776, and, with him, lived his aged mother, [Catherine Bonnefoy] the widow of Isaac Coutant, Sr. (who had died in 1747). On the 18th day of October, 1776, the aged Mrs. Coutant died and, due to the rapid approach of the British Army after the battle of Pell's Point, and the interference of military regulations, burial was not to be made in the public cemetery of the town, so Mrs. Coutant was buried here in a secluded part of the farm, this becoming the first interment in this cemetery. The Coutants' daughter, the wife of John Hudson, was the next burial, which occurred in 1778. Memorial stones for both of these were put up in the cemetery late in the nineteenth century, long after the cemetery had been permanently established.[45]

Above: The tombstone of Catherine Coutant notes that she "was buried Oct. 1776 while this ridge was held by the British," thus making her "the first interment in [the Coutant] Cemetery." The headstone of Mrs. Coutant's son Isaac, who chose the site of the cemetery, can be seen in the background.

Top: Looking northeast at the Coutant Cemetery and chapel during the early 20th century. Photo courtesy New Rochelle Public Library Local History Collection.

Bottom: The Coutant Cemetery in the early 20th century. Note the chapel entrance at right.

Isaac Coutant III, the son of the cemetery's founder, died in 1822 and left his property to his brothers John and Isaiah. On March 9, 1839, the octogenarian Coutant brothers transferred the cemetery to a four-person trustee group "on behalf of the Coutant Family to be used by them as a Family burying ground and for no other purpose whatever."[46] At this time the burial ground had a depth of 120 feet, a frontage of 60 feet on Eastchester Road, and contained about 35 tombstones.[47] On October 20, 1854, the Coutant Family Cemetery Association was incorporated to take charge of the burial ground, which by that time had grown to encompass half an acre of land.[48] From 1876 to 1889, the Coutant Family Cemetery Association added additional acreage to the burial ground.[49] At one point, a "little wooden chapel" was erected on the south side of the cemetery "but vandals broke the windows and caused so much damage that it was finally torn down" sometime prior to 1940.[50]. According to the 1910 *Fairchild Cemetery Manual*, the chapel could be used "for funeral services in stormy weather" for a fee of $5.[51] The Coutant Cemetery Association has retained ownership of the burial ground to this day, and as a result their family cemetery is one of the best kept of its kind in Westchester. Eligible persons may still be interred in this graveyard, with "burial [being] limited to direct descendants of the Isaac Coutant family and their wives or husbands."[52]

Adjoining the Coutant Cemetery on that burial place's east side, the Robinson Family Cemetery was founded by Israel P. Robinson when he "buried his wife Elizabeth Palmer there in 1894."[53] Interestingly, Mr. Robinson did not actually purchase the land on which the cemetery is located until July 11, 1895, and there is no record of his having sought permission of the Westchester County Board of Supervisors to dedicate the lot for burial purposes.[54] The DAR survey described the cemetery in 1940:

> It is enclosed with a stone wall and iron fence in front, and fence on the other sides. On the iron gate which opens on Eastchester Road, are the initials I.P.R. These stand for Israel P. Robinson, the founder of the cemetery.... About this time [1894] the bodies of four Robinsons and the stones marking their graves were moved from the old Palmer burying ground on Weaver Street, Larchmont. They are the four identical old marble stones which are laid flat in a row, bordering the fence dividing the Robinson and Coutant cemeteries. The oldest stone is that of Gilbert Robinson who died March 3, 1821. The most recent interment is that of James Robinson, who died June 1, 1939.[55]

The Robinson family continues to use this small cemetery, and the most recent burial here was made in 2007. Among those who are interred here is John J. Crowther (1923-1944), a Lieutenant in the US Army Air Forces who was killed in action during World War II.

Above: Looking south in the Robinson Family Burial Ground in 2008. The Coutant Cemetery is visible on the other side of the chain-link fence.

76

Davids Island Cemetery

New Rochelle

Above: Many of the markers in this row of tombstones in the Cypress Hills National Cemetery in Brooklyn identify the graves of soldiers whose remains were originally interred in the Davids Island Cemetery. The tombstone at left marks the grave of William Gibbs, a member of the 154th New York Volunteer Infantry Regiment who died at DeCamp General Hospital on Davids Island on April 19, 1863.

Location: Formerly on the northern portion of Davids Island. Following its removal in 1887, the cemetery was replaced by a brick barrack (marked "55" in the map at right), which in turn was removed during the demolition of the Davids Island buildings in 2006-08.

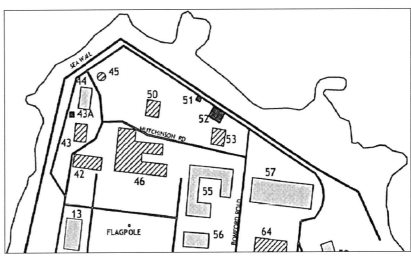

Dates of Activity: 1862 – 1887.

Removed: To Cypress Hill National Cemetery (Section 2) in Brooklyn in 1887.

Notes: The following passage explaining the origin of the United States Army presence at Davids Island appeared in Morgan Seacord's *Historical Landmarks of New Rochelle*:

> The island was rented by the United States Government in April, 1862, and was used for hospital purposes. Wooden structures were immediately erected which housed thousands of wounded prisoners from the battlefields of the Civil War. At the close of the war, Congress authorized its purchase for military purposes and it was conveyed to the United States in May, 1867. But it was not until April, 1868, that jurisdiction was ceded by the State of New York and then with the proviso that it should not be used for general hospital purposes.
>
> A number of soldiers who died at the hospital were interred in a plot located on the northern end of the island. The remains of "around 60" soldiers who were buried in the cemetery at Davids Island were exhumed and removed to Cypress Hills National Cemetery in 1887.[56]

77

DeVeau Family Burial Ground
New Rochelle

Location: This cemetery was destroyed in the late 19th century. The following points comprised the corners of the rectangular-shaped DeVeau farm: northwest corner, Saint John's Episcopal Church on Wilmot Road; northeast corner, a point on Van Etten Boulevard about 500 feet east of its intersection with Carol Lane; southwest corner, a point about 250 feet west of the intersection of Lovell Road and Mildred Parkway; southeast corner, a point in Ward Acres about 900 feet east of the southern intersection of Robert Drive and Saldo Circle.

Dates of Activity: c.1774 – c.1810.

Notes: This burial ground was created for members of the DeVeau family, who also used several different spellings of their surname, chief among them being Devaux, Devoue, and Devoe.[57] Abel DeVeau, Sr. (1688-1774), the son of Huguenot refugee Frederick De Veaux and a native of Morrisania in the Bronx, arrived in New Rochelle around 1718 after his father had purchased 200 acres of land there that same year.[58] His son, Abel Jr. (1719-1775), outlived his father by only one year and founded a small family cemetery for his relatives and descendants in his will:

> My Body is to be buried in a Christian like and decent manner, in the burying ground that I have reserved for a burying place for my family, or any of the Devoues, of my relations, and the free liberty of a road from the highway to said burying place, being 30 feet north and south, and 28 feet east and west.[59]

Among those who may have been interred in this cemetery is Jeremiah Schureman, who married Magdalen DeVeau, a sister of Abel DeVeau, Jr. Mr. Schureman was a "well-to-do farmer" in northern New Rochelle who met his death while British forces were encamped in New Rochelle in 1776:

> [Tory raiders] visited the premesis of Mr. Schureman, as they wanted his cattle to furnish [the British] troops with fresh beef. They took advantage of a dark, stormy night and drove his cattle out of their pens, which lay near the house, but the unusual and hurried steps of the cattle were heard by Schureman, who hastily arose from his bed and opened the upper half-door, and saw at least one of the thieves whom he knew, when he said: "I know you, boys; I'll report you to-morrow." At the same moment one of the scoundrels fired his musket at him and shot him down at his door, where he died a few moments after.[60]

The 104-acre parcel on which the burial ground was located was sold by Abel's sons Daniel and Abel III to Samuel Tedwell in 1787. Later, this parcel was occupied by Frederick Schureman, a son of Jeremiah and Magdalen DeVeau Schureman.[61] The following stipulation regarding the DeVeau Family Burial Ground is taken from an 1853 deed:

> <u>Excepting and reserving</u> such right to bury in a certain Burying ground on the above described farm...provided that said burying ground shall not take in more than two Rods square of land and shall be used for no other purpose than burying and by no other persons than to those whom the right is given.[62]

Sadly, it appears that the cemetery was forgotten by the family after they sold off their land in northern New Rochelle. In 1885 Thomas F. De Voe published *Genealogy of the De Veaux Family* in which he described a visit to this long-forgotten graveyard:

> With a descendant of the family, Mr. Darius A. Seacor, in the month of August, 1878, the author visited the above old burying-ground, where we found many of the old flat and rough head and foot stones removed, some of which had been placed on the stone wall adjoining on one side and others thrown against the wall on the other side of the angle, and but few were found remaining on the ground in sight, or perhaps had been covered by the plough of the owner adjoining this plot, who has wrongly taken possession of this reserved and sacred spot. It was supposed that there had been buried in this plot above 50 persons, beginning with [Abel DeVeau, Sr.]...and all of the descendants of [Abel Jr.'s] brothers, sisters, &c., up to and after the Revolution, who had resided in the neighborhood and other parts of the State. The site is a beautiful one, which lies some 300 or 400 paces from St. John's Church, near Cooper's Corners. Here on the highest elevation in the eastern angle of a heavy stone wall, partly shaded by friendly limbs of a large old apple-tree, will yet be found this old burial-place of the de Veaux family, almost obliterated.[63]

The length of time during which the DeVeau family used this plot is unknown. However, Abel, Jr.'s son, Daniel (1750-1804) and his wife, Mary, were buried in the Christ Methodist Church Cemetery.[64] It is presumed that the cemetery was destroyed when the old DeVeau farm was subdivided around the turn of the 20th century.

Flandreau Family Burying Ground
New Rochelle

Above: The Flandreau Family Burial Ground in 2004. The tombstone of Benjamin Flandreau (1718-1800) is visible leaning against a tree at the center of the photo.

Right: The tombstone of Benjamin Flandreau (1810-1844) in 1940. The verse on Benjamin's tombstone reads: "Affliction sore long time I bore / Physicians were in vain / Till God alone did hear my moan / And eas'd me of my pain."

Location: The cemetery is located on the west side of Chester Place about 150 feet south of Moran Place (adjoining the Mamaroneck/New Rochelle border to the north and #44 Chester Place to the south and west).

Dates of Activity: 1800 – 1892.

Inscriptions: *WCHS* Books #18 (p.147-153) and #81 (p.71-72).

Notes: Benjamin Flandreau, "the son of Jacques Flandreau, the Huguenot exile," was buried by his family in a plot on their farm following his death on February 19, 1800.[65] Mr. Flandreau's property stretched from the Boston Post Road to Long Island Sound (including the land that has since been developed into Premium Point), and his home was located on the north side of the Old Boston Post Road just west of its intersection with Route 1 and Cherry Avenue.[66] The burial ground where Benjamin had been interred was reserved by the Flandreau family when they sold their property to Christopher Hubbs on February 16, 1814:

> ...excepting and reserving a burying ground adjoining Pelton and Bonnetts land and CONTAINING on each side twenty eight yards and at each end thirteen yards to be used by [the Flandreaus] and their heirs and assigns as a burying place with a priviledge or right of way to pass and repass to and from the same on foot and on horse back, and with carriages at all times of the year forever with the right to take as much stone as will be necessary to fence in the said burying ground provided the same be taken before the first day of September next.[67]

In 1851 a significant portion of the old Flandreau property was purchased by Samuel T. Cowdrey, who named his estate "Hazelhurst." Mr. Cowdrey "wanted the [cemetery] as a part of his estate" and offered "to buy the plot and move, at his own expense, all of the bodies to a burial ground selected by the Flandreau heirs."[68] This offer was not accepted, as the "little graveyard was still being used and carefully cared for." [69] To separate the cemetery from his property, Mr. Cowdrey "had a hedge planted around the plot and it was also enclosed by a stone wall."[70] The last burial in this cemetery, that of Isabelle Flandreau, was made in 1892. Three years before, George T. Davis had written the following:

> This cemetery is situated on Main Street at the Mamaroneck line east of the residence of Mr. S.F. Cowdrey and can not be seen from the street. No persons except the Flandreau family are buried here. The interments average about one per year. Only one monument is erected here and that was erected to the memory of a young man who was killed during the [Civil] war.[71]

Above: This c.1923 photo depicts the damaged Harsen monument in the Flandreau Family Burial Ground prior to being removed to Beechwoods Cemetery.

Left: The Elisha Harsen monument in Beechwoods Cemetery in 2011. Now badly faded, the inscription on the monument reads:

[North side]
IN
MEMORY OF
ELISHA HARSEN,
Aged 23 yrs. & 4 mos.
1st Asst. Engineer in the
United States Navy on board
the Monitor Tecumseh who
perished in Mobile Bay on
Aug. 5th, 1864, when their
vessel was sunk by a rebel torpedo. This monument is erected by his parents, whose consolation is that their son died in
the service of his country.

[East side]
DULCE ET DECORUM EST PRO
PATRIA MORI

[West side]
He died doing what
he could to suppress the
wicked rebellion of the
slave states. While leading
the fleet which ran past
the forts of Mobile Bay, the
Tecumseh was struck by the
fatal torpedo which launched into eternity as brave a
crew as ever manned a vessel. They offered themselves
a sacrifice to their country,
met the fate they had some
reason to expect, and by

[South side]
bravely confronting
it, averted it from others. None but heroes would have consented to lead
through the terrible dangers
of that battle day; as heroes
they did their duty; while
at their posts they perished
and were buried in the
dark waters with more than a heroes salute; their
country will never cease to
cherish the fame they so gallantly won.

Little had changed in the condition of the cemetery by 1940, when the Daughters of the American Revolution noted the following:

> The cemetery – or what is left of it...is apparently abandoned, with no one left who is interested in its care.... [Few] of the stones are legible, and even fewer still are in their original positions. Scattered pieces of markers were found in all parts of the plot. An attempt was made to fit them together. It was sometimes possible to do this. However, it was impossible to locate the positions of the graves. [72]

Above: Damaged tombstones in the Flandreau Family Burial Ground in 1931.

Right: This photo of the Flandreau Family Burial Ground appeared in the *New York Times* in 1981. Note the shopping cart dumped near the tombstone next to the arrow.

Hazelhurst was sold and subdivided into a residential neighborhood following the death of Samuel Cowdrey in the late 1890s. Although this subdivision did not destroy the cemetery, it apparently caused some damage as the stone wall which surrounded the burial ground was removed. In the early 1920s, reporter Florence S. Bennett "found the little cemetery in a deplorable condition," with the "shaft of the monument" mentioned by Mr. Davis having "been forced off the base, and an effort had apparently been made to destroy it."[73] Shortly thereafter, this monument, which had been erected by the parents of Elisha Harsen, a naval officer killed in the Battle of Mobile Bay, was removed to Beechwoods Cemetery along with the stone of Theodore Flandreau, another Civil War veteran.[74] In 1931 *The Standard Star* reported that the tombstones in the graveyard were not visible "to one riding by...so overgrown with weeds, tall grass and trees has this cemetery become." More visible were the mounds of piled-up dirt, left, probably, from the construction of recently built houses" as well as "cans and stones strewn about—hardly by way of decoration."[75]

Left and Right: The tombstones of Benjamin Flandreau (left) and Joseph Mullinex (right). The backside of Mr. Mullinex's tombstone is visible next to that of Mr. Flandreau in the photo at left. The markings located near the bottom left of Mr. Flandreau's tombstone may represent the price of the marker.

In
Memory of
BENJAMIN FLANDRAU,
who departed this life
Feb[ry] 19th 1800
Aged 81 Years 5 month
and 15 days

Exult my soul with days that flow
From GOD'S Almighty hand
Whilst here my mouldering body lies
To rise at his command.

IN
Memory of
Ioseph Mullinex
Hoo Departed This
Life october the 28th day
1807 Aged 83 years
1 month 13 days

Above: This 2004 photo depicts some of the few remaining tombstones in the Flandreau Family Burial Ground. The tall sandstone belongs to Benjamin Flandreau (1718-1800), while the headstone at its base belongs to his son, Benjamin (1762-1807). The marble stone at the top right belongs to James A. Seacord. The tombstone of Benjamin Flandreau was apparently the first grave marker placed in the Flandreau Family Burial Ground.

The cemetery was in such poor condition that the DAR incorrectly claimed that "this old burial ground [had] only recently been destroyed" when they published a compendium of early New Rochelle wills in 1951.[76] In 1978 the Flandreau cemetery again made news when *The Standard Star* reported on the sad state of the burial ground:

If Benjamin Flandreau, Sara Esther and Joseph Mullins desire eternal peace, they'll have to wait until children stop playing on the swing set about three feet from their graves. The Flandreau, Esther and Mullins names are about the only ones still visible on the gravestones that lie broken and uprooted in [the] tiny Flandreau cemetery…. "The cemetery has become a dumping ground and a place to take your dog," complained Mrs. Elinor Katz…. "I would like to see people get together and restore it." But first they would have to remove the old shopping cart, trash and heaps of branches and other backyard refuse that have been dumped on the plot sandwiched between two houses…. Another neighbor has gone so far as to install a swingset among the remaining stones, most of which have worn away so that they are no longer readable.[77]

Recent efforts have resulted in the elimination of much of the overgrowth in the cemetery.

Right: The tombstone of James Seacord can be seen leaning against a tree in the top right corner of the photo at the top of this page. It reads: "IN memory of JAMES A. son of Leonard & Maria Seacord who died Oct. 13, 1842 aged 5 Years and 5 Mos."

Harrison Family Tomb

New Rochelle

Right: The Harrison Family Tomb in 2007. The entrance to the tomb is blocked by a large boulder.

Location: Located within Five Islands Park on the south side of Round Island (between Oakwood Island and Harrison Island).

Dates of Activity: 1878 – 1892.

Other Names: Graveyard Island, Harrison Cemetery.

Notes: Many visitors to Five Islands Park have wondered

about the interesting in-ground structure on Round Island. Few, however, would venture to guess that it was constructed as "a fine vault for 12 bodies."[78] David Harrison (c.1792-1878), "a prominent and wealthy Brooklyn lawyer," arrived in New Rochelle in 1827 and over time purchased all of the land which presently comprises Five Islands Park, as well as a significant amount of property on the mainland.[79] Mr. Harrison built a large summer home on Harrison's Island.[80] The *New York Times* reported on an interesting clause in his will:

> [Harrison's] eccentricity manifested itself in the shape of a clause providing a home for two destitute white female orphan children on [Harrison] Island…. The orphans were to be retained in the home until they had reached the age of womanhood, or until either of them married, when they were to be replaced by two other dependent white female orphans, who were to be maintained at the establishment subject to the same rules. Thus Mr. Harrison thought of perpetuating his home for the benefit of a limited number of young female orphans of successive generations.[81]

This plan was not enacted as the Harrison family successfully contested the will. However, another wish set down in this will was fulfilled. During his ownership of this land, Mr. Harrison built a vault on Round Island. In his will, he ordered that "Round Island be kept and used as a family burial ground for myself and family and relations who desire to be buried there, and I hereby order and direct my body to be buried there."[82] However, only he and his son, David Harrison, Jr. (d. 1892) were actually entombed there.[83] Mr. Harrison sold off most of his mainland property throughout the mid-1800s. The executors of his estate reserved Round Island when they sold the remainder of his land to Adrian Iselin, Jr., in 1892.[84]

During the early 20th century, Harrison's Island was leased by the New Rochelle Yacht Club, which established itself in the old Harrison house. In 1904 vandals broke into the vault and "smashed portions" of the elder David Harrison's casket "and scattered [its] contents about the tomb," although they did not take "the heavy silver handles and plates on the caskets."[85] Round Island was later "occupied by squatters" throughout much of the early- and mid-20th century, during which time the caskets were stolen.[86] Both Harrison's and Graveyard islands are now part of Five Islands Park.

Right: Looking inside the empty Harrison Family Tomb.

Holy Sepulchre Cemetery

New Rochelle

Top Right: This c.1912 photo depicts the grave of Father Thomas P. McLoughlin (1859-1912), which is located at the Kings Highway entrance to Holy Sepulchre Cemetery.

Location: North side of Kings Highway between Highland and Ancon avenues.

Dates of Activity: 1887 – Present.

Mailing Address: 15 Shea Place, New Rochelle, NY, 10801.

Notes: One of the primary places of interment for Roman Catholics living along the Sound Shore, Holy Sepulchre Cemetery was established as a result of an increase in that denomination's numbers in New Rochelle during the late 19th century. At that time, very few lots remained available for sale in the two small Catholic cemeteries near Drake Avenue. To remedy this problem, Saint Matthew's Parish purchased an 18-acre parcel from Alexander B. Hudson on February 27, 1886, for $7,308.[87] This land was dedicated as a cemetery by the Westchester County Board of Supervisors on January 4, 1887, and the first interment, that of Mary E. F. Siegel, was made in 1888.[88] The creation of this burial ground was largely the result of the work of Father Thomas McLoughlin (1826-1902), the founder of the Church of the Blessed Sacrament, who served as the pastor of that parish from 1853 until his death. The cemetery's development was fostered by McLoughlin's nephew, Father Thomas P. McLoughlin (1859-1912), who "following the example of his uncle...devoted a great deal of time to the work of laying out roads and otherwise beautifying Holy Sepulchre Cemetery, and encouraged his people to honor their dead by holding memorial services in the cemetery on Decoration Day."[89]

Bottom Right: The grave of Tom McNamara features the depiction of a golf club. McNamara was "one of the first great American-born" golfers.[90] A salesman in the Wanamaker Department Store's golf department, McNamara's suggestion of a national golf association provided the impetus for his boss, Rodman Wanamaker, to hold a meeting which led to the formation of the Professional Golfers' Association, better known as the PGA.

Up until at least 1940, a superintendent's home existed on the west side of the main entrance off Kings Highway just east of the maintenance building. This house has since been removed to provide for additional burying space.[91] In 1889, not long after the opening of this burial place, George T. Davis, founder of the George T. Davis Funeral Home, observed the ideal location of the Holy Sepulchre Cemetery, which included scenery that has since been obscured by development: "It is situated on the brow of a hill from which [the] Long Island Sound and part of Mt. Vernon can be seen. For cemetery purposes it is the finest in New Rochelle."[92]

Several notable persons from New Rochelle are buried in this cemetery. Civil War veteran Richard Beddows was awarded the Medal of Honor for saving his unit's flag during the Battle of Spotsylvania. Golfer Tom McNamara provided the idea which led to the formation of the Professional Golfers' Association, better known as the PGA. Perhaps the most notable persons interred at Holy Sepulchre are Eddie Foy and his family. The Foy family resided in New Rochelle and toured the nation for many years in the early 1900s as Eddie Foy and the Seven Little Foys, a popular vaudeville act. Eddie and six of his seven children are interred in a plot near the Kings Highway entrance to the cemetery.

Among the most moving sites in any burial place in Westchester are the two childrens' sections in Holy Sepulchre. The first section is located along the eastern edge of the cemetery and holds the graves of a number of children who fell victim to the influenza epidemic of 1918. These graves are marked by a variety of simple memorials, many of which appear to be homemade. The second childrens' section is located along the fence which marks the boundary between Holy Sepulchre and Beechwoods Cemetery, and contains graves from the late 1920s and early 1930s. Many of the burials in the second section are of the children of Italian immigrants, and are adorned with statues of angels.

Top Right: This memorial marks the grave of Corporal Edward J. Farrell Jr., who was killed in action near Chateau Thierry, France, during World War I. Corporal Farrell resided in Mount Vernon and served in Company C, 101st Battalion, Signal Corps.[93] The epitaph reads:

THE LAST CLAUSE OF HIS WILL READS
"TO THE OLD U.S.A. I GIVE MY LIFE
WILLINGLY, BECAUSE SHE IS THE
GRANDEST, GREATEST AND FREEST
COUNTRY IN THE WORLD. AND I HOPE
TO GOD THAT THE DAY WILL COME
WHEN SHE WILL BE INDEED
'AMERICA FOR AMERICANS' OF
UNDIVIDED ALLEGIANCE."

Bottom Right: This monument stands at the graves of Eddie and Madeline Foy, Madeline's sister, Clara, and six of the "Seven Little Foys." Bryan Foy, the seventh child, is buried in Calvary Cemetery in Los Angeles.

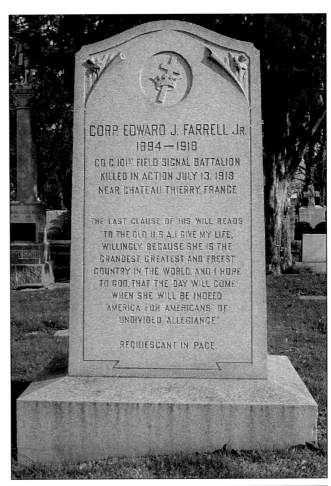

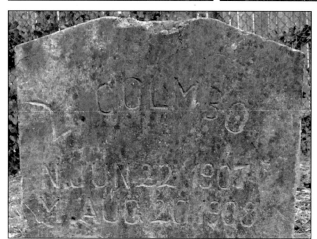

Top: The first children's section in Holy Sepulchre Cemetery, 2008.

Center Left: This monument in the children's section is inscribed in Italian and marks the grave of two infants who died in 1916 and 1917.

Center: Although the inscription on this tombstone has long since faded, two small statues of angels remain in place to stand watch over the grave which it marks.

Center Right: This face lies on the ground in the children's section.

Bottom Left: This marker reads:

L. COLMBO
N.JUN 22 1907
M.AUG 20 1908

The "N" stands for "nato," the Italian word for born, while the "M" stands for "morto," the Italian word for died.

Huguenot Burying Ground
New Rochelle

Top: The headstone of Susanne Landrine was once surrounded by fieldstones in the Huguenot Burying Ground; the back cover of this volume depicts this tombstone as it now appears in Trinity Episcopal Church Cemetery. The fieldstone on the right reads "S C T 1728" and was the oldest dated grave marker in the Huguenot Burying Ground. Today, it lies almost entirely covered by grass just a few feet south of Susanne Landrine's headstone.

Bottom: The Louis Guion plot in the Huguenot Burying Ground. The gate, which stands today in Trinity Episcopal Church Cemetery, reads: "The Descendants of Louis Guion A Native of France."

Above: Looking northwest from the southeast corner of the Huguenot Burying Ground (top) and north from the southwest corner of the cemetery (bottom) in 1955.

Location: The Huguenot Burying Ground and the Allaire Family Burial Ground were located at the southwest corner of the intersection of Union Avenue and Division Street. The map shows the location of the two cemeteries (marked in gray), which is now occupied by the New England Thruway (A), compared to the present landscape (marked in black). The Huguenot Burying Ground (B and C) was located on the west side of Division Street. The southern portion (C) of the Huguenot Burying Ground was removed to Trinity Episcopal Church Cemetery (D) in 1927 to make way for the proposed Pelham-Port Chester Parkway. The northern section (B) of the Huguenot Burial Ground, as well as the Allaire Family Burial Ground (D), were removed to Trinity in 1956 prior to the construction of the New England Thruway.

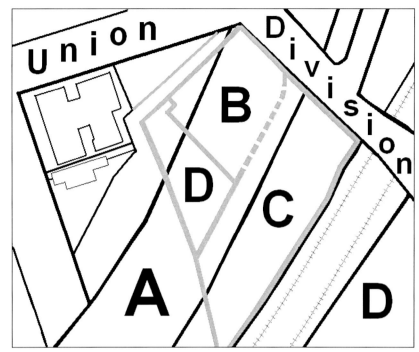

Dates of Activity: c.1690 – 1950.

Removed: To the north side of Trinity Episcopal Church Cemetery in September 1956.

Inscriptions: *WCHS* Books #8 (p.27-40) and #18 (p.9-22).

Right: The headstone of Pierre Parcot (c.1664-1730) as it appeared in 2007. Mr. Parcot was a native of Marennes, Saintonge, France. His tombstone can be seen in its original location in the top photo on page 94.[94]

Notes: Having fled from the religious persecution they encountered in their native France, a group of Huguenots settled in Westchester County in 1689 when they purchased present-day New Rochelle from John Pell.[95] Sometime between 1690 and 1693, Louis Bongrand gave "unto the inhabitants of New Rochelle...a church Yard to bury theirs dead conteyning forty paces square."[96] Most of the early burials in this cemetery were made in "well defined parallel rows" and marked by "small sunken uninscribed stones."[97] Later, the Huguenots marked their tombstones with the initials and year of death of the deceased. For example, "the stone of Pierre Parcot, one of the early Huguenot settlers," read simply "P P A 66 M 1730," which indicates that Mr. Parcot died in 1730 at the age of 66.[98] Several other stones from later dates were inscribed entirely in French or in English with very interesting spelling. The oldest identifiable tombstone in the cemetery, which can no longer be found today, read: "Here lies the body of James Flandreau Aged 69 Years Died, Feb. 19, 1726."[99]

The Huguenot Burying Ground contained several family plots. Two plots belonged to the Guion family, while the Allaire, Archer, Henderson and Parcot families each had one. Although the number of burials made in the Huguenot Burying Ground declined upon the establishment of nearby Trinity Church Cemetery, interments were continually made in the former graveyard throughout the 19th century, with a few stones even dating from the early 20th century. Nevertheless, it appears that little attention was paid to the maintenance of the cemetery following the Civil War, with the following observation being made on the state of this burial ground in 1890:

> In the old churchyard where the early Huguenots found their last resting place, very many graves are unmarked. Many markers have been destroyed or broken, as the grounds are no more than commons.[100]

Above: Looking northwest at the Huguenot Burying Ground from the Division Street bridge over the railroad, December 3, 1911.

The state of the cemetery had changed little by the 1920s, at which time there was "no doubt [that] some of the most interesting stones [had] disappeared."[101] Among the memorials that had deteriorated were those within the small plot containing the graves of Alexander Bampfield Henderson, a one-time surgeon with the British army in India who purchased Hunter's Island in the Bronx in 1797, and his adopted son, an "East Indian lad" named William.[102] In his will, William left trusts for the construction of New Rochelle's Presbyterian Church and first town hall.[103] An appropriation had been made at a New Rochelle town meeting on March 27, 1855, "for a fence to be put up around the Henderson plot, 'the cost to be paid by trustees of [the] town house out of the moneys in their hands.'"[104] Eighty-three years later, the fence had become "rusted and broken down," while Alexander Henderson's tombstone was "so worn and weather-beaten that the inscription [was] no longer decipherable."[105] The condition of these artifacts was symbolic of the "shameful spectacle of ruin and public indifference and neglect" that the cemetery had become.[106] In 1927 the southern half of the burial ground was purchased by Westchester County for the proposed Pelham-Port Chester Parkway, which required the relocation of the interments that had made in this area:

> ...after the sale Trinity Church had this section examined. All standing stones with the bodies were removed to Trinity Cemetery and reburied along the line of the railroad tracks at the back of the cemetery. All stones, many of them with no marks and long since fallen and buried under the sod, were dug up and placed, 49 of them near the Church House in Trinity Cemetery and the rest in the [remainder of] the Old Huguenot Burying Ground.[107]

The proposed parkway was not constructed, and the parcel between the burial ground and the railroad remained empty for the rest of the Huguenot Burial Ground's existence. Shortly thereafter, additional efforts were made to improve the condition of the cemetery:

During the observance of the 250th Anniversary of the Settlement of New Rochelle in June 1938, the fence around the Henderson plot was painted and the debris around the Henderson grave removed by the Corporation of Trinity Church. The Huguenot burying ground was explored by the rector and wardens of Trinity Church, many old grave markers [were] recovered, and efforts [were] made to restore the graveyard to a reasonably creditable condition.[108]

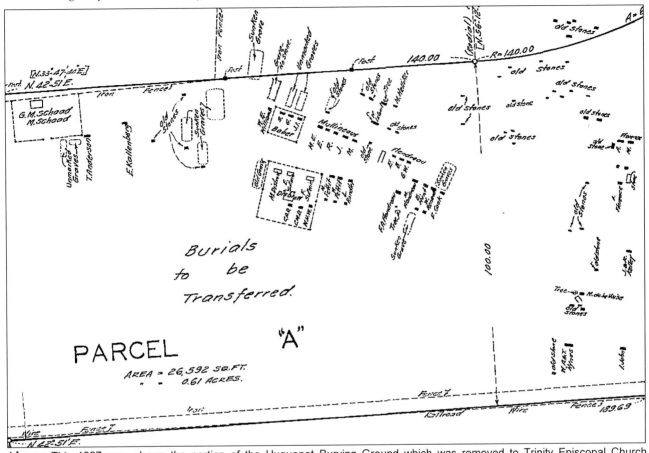

Above: This 1927 map shows the portion of the Huguenot Burying Ground which was removed to Trinity Episcopal Church Cemetery to make way for the proposed Pelham-Port Chester Parkway. Westchester County Clerk Map, Vol. 66, p.39.

The last two interments in the Huguenot Burying Ground, those of Louis L. Lawton and his wife, Henrietta, were made in 1925 and 1950, respectively.[109] Unfortunately, the renewed interest in the preservation of the cemetery would be short-lived, as the Huguenot Burying Ground would suffer its worst and final insult in the mid-1950s as a result of suburban progress. In order to construct the New England Thruway, the cemetery was taken by eminent domain on September 7, 1955.[110] The New York State Thruway Authority attempted to search for relatives of the deceased through ads in the Macy newspaper chain as well as letters. However, "very little response was received" through this outreach, and only "one person of the 1st generation" of descendants was actually located. A survey of the graveyard conducted during this time found 100 tombstones as well as 172 fieldstones.[111] Approval to remove the remains from the old cemetery to the Trinity church was granted by Judge Hugh S. Coyle on July 18, 1956, and the week-long transfer of graves and tombstones was completed on August 31st of that same year.[112] Sadly, it appears that the removal of the remains and headstones was not done with extreme care. The following passage is an abridged version of "Saint Bartholomew's Day 1956," a piece written by New Rochelle historian Morgan Seacord in response to the destruction of the cemetery:

AUGUST 24th, 1956 will long be remembered by those who are descended from the Huguenot settlers of New Rochelle. It was on that day that the foreign legion of the New York State Thruway struck its first blow for the destruction of the cemetery of the Huguenot exiles, of those who had settled and founded the city after fleeing from massacre [in France]; and their successors for two hundred and sixty years had been buried there, fondly hoping for peace in Christian burial in a foreign land. The day opened auspiciously with an attack on the Allaire family cemetery adjoining. The contractors first proceeded to demolish all tombstones and monuments in both cemeteries, breaking them off at the base, or breaking them at the ground level with sledge hammers, then transferring the wreckage to the Trinity Episcopal Church. The bulldozer then moved in with its gentle ministrations, tearing up the ground to the depth of five and six feet, and so operated under the shallow excuse of cutting off "the top soil" of the graves, but quickly tearing up the graves and dragging out scattered bones and corpses from the later graves. The bones and corpses were gathered up indiscriminately and put into small wooden boxes without lids, and these relics of the past removed for reinterment behind the Trinity Episcopal Church.

Representatives of the Allaire, Guion and Parcot families, the Huguenot and Historical Association, and the Westchester County Historical Society were present to witness this mutilation of their forefathers and relations. By Monday [the bulldozers] moved into the Allaire burial plot in the Huguenot cemetery, and later in the day into the Elias Guion plot.... [Police] were on hand all the while during this orgy of destruction to drive out the descendants and relations of those being rooted out of their last resting places, and threatened them with arrest if they persisted in being present to observe the sacrilege being carried on there....

As the work progressed, the plot of the Henderson graves was torn up. Here lay buried the young man who was probably the first benefactor of the early nineteenth century village, by donating the funds for building its first Town Hall, a building it doubtless would never have had for many long years to come if left to its own efforts to raise money for that purpose.... The work was soon extended to tearing up the second Guion plot where more corpses were rooted out of the ground and the bodies dumped out of their coffins, and one was cut up with an axe for boxing. Another, that of John Warren Lawton, an outstanding lawyer of the last century, a graduate of Harvard, and a leading local Democrat, had his legs cut off for the like purpose. The Parcot family plot was the last, after the balance of the old cemetery to the south, including the Archer family plot, was ripped up. This south section contained many very ancient tombstones of the field stone material, of which no account was had or taken, and they narrowly escaped going into the junk heap.[113]

Above: The Elias Guion plot on December 3, 1911. The triangle-shaped marker at the far right is the tombstone of Susanne Landrine, and the railing behind it enclosed the Louis Guion plot.

Far Left: This notice calling for bids to "Exhume and Reinter Human Remains" from the Huguenot Burying Ground and the Allaire Family Burial Ground appeared in the *New York Times*. Floyd F. Sorrentino submitted a low bid of $75,544.[114]

Left: The graves of Elizabeth (1773-1855) and Elias (1772-1855) Guion in 1955. These tombstones are visible at the far left of the Guion plot in the 1911 photo above. Mrs. Guion outlived her husband by less than two months.

In
Memory
of
ALEXANDER BAMPFIELD HENDERSON, ESQ.
a Native
of CHARLESTOWN in
South Carolina
but late of the Town of
PELHAM and
County of West Chester
who departed this Life
26th December, 1804,
Aged 47 years.

In
Memory
Of
WILLIAM HENDERSON
who departed this life
Jan. 19th, 1812
In the 25th Year of his
Age.

Top Row: The tombstone in the foreground of the photo at top left was located near the northwest corner of the Archer family plot. The elaborate fence surrounded the small Henderson family plot, which contained the tombstones of William (left) and Alexander Bampfield Henderson. The inscriptions of these monuments are given above. Today, the tombstone of Alexander Bampfield Henderson (top right) now lies flat on the ground in Trinity Episcopal Church Cemetery. The tombstone of William Henderson lies nearby and is illegible.

Center Left: The grave of John Warren Lawton (d.1911) was located at the southeast corner of the Louis Guion plot.

Bottom Left: "In memory of JOHN GUION of Rye who departed this life the 21st of July 1792 aged 69 years." Although he was interred in New Rochelle, Mr. Guion's children and their descendants founded their own burial ground on their property in Mamaroneck. This tombstone was carved by Solomon Brewer of Greenburgh.

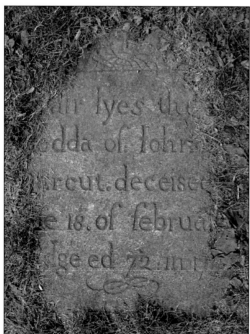

Above: The tombstone of John Parcot now lies flat on the ground in Trinity Episcopal Church Cemetery; it reads: "heair lyes the bodda of John parcut. Deceised the 18. of February adge ed 72: in 1772."

Top: The Parcot family plot, December 3, 1911. Left to right in the back row are the tombstones of John Parcot, Jr. (1740-1782), John Parcot (c.1700-1772), Pierre Parcot (c.1664-1730) and a fieldstone which marks the grave of a person who died in 1747. A recent photo of Pierre's tombstone in the Trinity Episcopal Church Cemetery can be found on page 89.

Bottom Right: This photograph of the headstones of John Parcot, Jr. and John Parcot was taken in 1955. The Parcot-Drake house still stands today on the west side of Clove Road about 200 feet north of Eastchester Road.

94

Above Left: This photo depicts the oldest sandstone in the Huguenot Burying Ground shortly before it was removed to the Trinity Episcopal Church Cemetery.

> Here Lies the Body
> Of William Nicoll
> Son of Benj^{m} &
> Magdalene Mary
> Nicoll of New York
> Ob 17th Sep^{t} 1767
> Aged 16 Years 2
> Months & 17 Days

Above Right: The marble tomb-stone of James McBride Allaire shortly before it was removed to Trinity Episcopal Church Cemetery.

> IN
> MEMORY OF
> JAMES MCBRIDE ALLAIRE.
> Who fell
> in the Second Battle of
> Bull Run
> on the 30th day of August
> 1862
> In defense of the
> Government Constitution
> and Laws of his
> Country.
> Aged 35 Years
> *REST*

Right: This crudely inscribed fieldstone was among the tombstones removed to Trinity Episcopal Church Cemetery from the Huguenot Burying Ground in 1927. It marks the grave of John Clark, who died on May 6, 1756, at the age of 56.

> HERELI
> ESTHEB
> ODYOFIOHN
> CLARK Who
> departed th
> ISLIFON IAN
> y 6 Day of
> MAY A.D. 1
> 756 Ag 56

Top: Many of the fieldstones which marked the graves of the early residents of New Rochelle were raised and placed in the southeast portion of the Huguenot Burying Ground during the cleanup efforts of the late 1920s and 1930s. This 1955 photo is looking southeast; Division Street can be seen in the background.

Above Left: This headstone reads:

HERE·LIES·THE·BODY·OF
JONATHAN · WEYMAN
Died Sep 14 1756
Aged 42

Above: The northwest corner of the Elias Guion plot, 1955. The small fieldstone between the "72" and "71" signs reads "1760 AG". This stone marked the grave of Aman Guion (c.1690-1760), a blacksmith from whom the present Trinity Church acquired its property in 1743. Mr. Guion presented a communion table to the church which is still in its possession. Sadly, his tombstone cannot be located today.

Top: Tombstones and fieldstones from the Huguenot Burying Ground after they were removed from their original locations and before they were placed in Trinity Episcopal Church Cemetery. The fieldstone standing upright just to the left of the center of the photo marked the grave of Amon Guion and can be seen in its original location on the previous page.

Center Row: The exhumation of remains and removal of tombstones from the Huguenot Burying Ground.

Bottom Right: The tombstones lying down in the foreground were removed to Trinity Episcopal Church Cemetery in 1956, while those standing upright in the back were removed from the Huguenot Burying Ground in 1927.

Top: The photo at top left depicts the tombstone of Jean Coutant about 1955. This marker was one of only two remaining French-inscribed tombstones that were found in the Huguenot Burying Ground in 1940. Morgan Seacord told of the fate of this tombstone:

> This headstone of his was torn up in August 1956, in the progress of the total destruction of the [Huguenot Burying Ground] under the auspices of the New [England] Thruway construction. It was dumped in the rear of the Trinity Episcopal Church burying ground adjacent to the New Haven Railroad cut, and there it was tossed about from one heap of stones to another with other ancient tombstones from the old Huguenot cemetery, where it became broken in two pieces by bulldozers rolling over it. At present it lies there with other ancient tombstones awaiting with a forlorn hope that it may be assigned a final resting place; otherwise, under present conditions, it is a candidate for the rubbish heap.[115]

Today, the tombstone lies face up in the ground on the west side of the Huguenot Memorial (top right). Its inscription is given at right. Photo at top left courtesy New Rochelle Public Library Local History Collection.

M 23
VOISI · LE
COrP · DE
IEN COV
TANT
a 54

Bottom Left: The tombstones from the two Guion family plots were placed flat on the ground inside a circle near the northeast corner of the Trinity cemetery.

Bottom Right: The tombstones that were removed to Trinity Episcopal Church Cemetery from the Huguenot Burying Ground were placed flat on the ground. This fieldstone marked the grave of a person with the initials "S.S." who died in 1741. The fieldstones were placed on the west side of the Huguenot Memorial.

Lispenard Family Burial Ground
Leonard Lispenard Tomb
New Rochelle

Right: The tombstone of Elizabeth Lispenard and her daughter, Elizabeth Staple, in the Lispenard Family Burial Ground in 1940.

Location: The exact site of the Lispenard Family Burial Ground has been lost. It appears, however, that the cemetery was located in the vicinity of Kensington Oval near its intersection with Windsor Oval. The tomb of Leonard Lispenard was formerly located in the vicinity of Mt. Etna Place.

Dates of Activity: Lispenard Family Burial Ground, Pre-1819; Leonard Lispenard Tomb, 1800.

Removed: The Lispenard Family Burial Ground was destroyed during the development of the Sans Souci neighborhood about 1960. The remains of Leonard Lispenard were removed to the Lispenard Family Vault at Trinity Episcopal Church (near the southwest corner of the building) in Manhattan in 1907.

Notes: Antoine L'Espenard (1643-1696) emigrated from France to New York in 1669. First settling in Albany, he moved with his family to New Rochelle sometime after 1689.[1] Antoine's son Anthony (c.1680/83-1758) "bought from Jacob Leisler's son a half interest in present day Davenport's Neck in 1708," and "six years later he bought the other half."[2] Anthony built a stone house between 1714 and 1732 which, though heavily altered, still stands today.[3] Although the Lispenards owned a vault "in the rear of Trinity church, New York [City], near the south-west corner of the present edifice," several members of the family were interred in a plot on their property in New Rochelle, as George T. Davis noted in 1889:

> This was a small family cemetery on Davenport Neck a little east of the old stone house on the property now owned by Mr. Iselin. Here lie buried some of the original Huguenot settlers. No interment has been made here in over 70 years.[4]

The Lispenards sold the last of their land on the peninsula to the Davenport family around the turn of the 19th century, and it is unlikely that any interments were made in the cemetery after this transaction. In 1907 the *New York Times* noted that "on the Iselin estate a tombstone marks the resting place of Elizabeth, wife of David Lispenard, and Elizabeth, their daughter, who both died in 1797."[5] In 1940 the Daughters of the American Revolution gave a more specific description of the cemetery and its location:

> At the present time there is but one stone left in the burial plot. However, the location of the burial plot may still be seen, marked by an old planting of scattered pine trees. The plot is on the property of Miss Georgina Iselin, who occupies the former home of her father, Adrian Iselin, Sr. The plot is on the brow of the slope towards the Sound near the western edge of the property. It might be inferred from a first reading of the statement of Mr. Davis about this plot that Mr. Iselin owned the property on which the stone house stands. This is not what Mr. Davis meant, however. The old stone house was mentioned as a land mark – and stands now as then – on land next to the Iselin property.

The cemetery is not near the stone house, but near the line of property on which the stone house stands and much nearer the Sound. The one stone carries the following inscription:

Here lies
Interred the Bodys of
ELIZABETH
Late wife of *David Lispenard,*
who departed this life the 19
March, 1797
Aged 62 Years & 11 Months.
Also
ELIZABETH, their daughter,
late wife of *John Staple*
who departed this life the 25
Nov. 1797
Aged 39 years & 7 months;

This stone is now lying flat on the ground, but originally stood upright.[6]

As is indicated in the above inscription, Elizabeth de Klyn was the wife of David Lispenard, who was the son of Anthony Lispenard and grandson of Antoine L'Espenard.[7] Anthony Lispenard built a stone house in the early 18th century which, though it has been extensively remodeled and added to, still stands today at 180 Davenport Avenue.[8] Unfortunately, save for Elizabeth Lispenard and Elizabeth Staple, the names of the persons who were buried in the cemetery are unknown. There must have been more tombstones in this plot in the past, as the Reverend Robert Bolton stated in 1848 that "the Lispenard cemetery is located on the south side of the Neck, and contains several memorials to this family."[9] Sadly, it appears that some of the tombstones in this graveyard were taken by neighbors, as Charles W. Darling noted in his 1893 article for the *New York Genealogical and Biographical Record*:

In a communication recently received from Charles Pryer, resident of New Rochelle...it is reported that many of the old grave-stones, which in early days marked the burial-places of generations of the Lispenards, have been removed from their positions, and now form portions of walls or fences of present proprietors in New Rochelle.[10]

Unfortunately, the final remnants of the Lispenard Family Burial Ground appear to have been destroyed during the development of the Sans Souci neighborhood in the late 1950s. Interestingly, the burial ground on Davenport's Neck was not the only place of interment used by the Lispenards. In addition to the family's vault in Manhattan, David Lispenard's nephew, Leonard Lispenard, Jr., was buried on a hill near the intersection of North Avenue and Pelham Road following his death about 1800. Leonard was a prominent citizen of New York City, as Charles W. Darling noted:

[Leonard was] one of nine young men who graduated from King's College [now Columbia University] in 1762. He became a merchant, was a member of the Chamber of Commerce, and owned the property known as Davenport's Neck in New Rochelle, N.Y., where he had a summer residence. He traveled in Europe extensively, and was a person of superior culture and education. He died unmarried.[11]

Unfortunately, his resting place was forgotten over the next century and was only rediscovered by accident, as the *New York Times* reported on April 9, 1907:

The remains of Leonard Lispenard were found on March 5 on the Fisher estate in New Rochelle at the corner of Siwanoy Avenue and Cedar Road. Some workmen as they cut away a rocky hill known to the children of the neighborhood as Mount Aetna came across a skull and bones and the rusted metal ornaments of a coffin. They lay in a cavity hewn in the rock, 20 inches deep, 7 feet long by 3 feet wide, and marked by a stone at its head and its foot. It was evident that a regular burial had taken place there, and the discovery of the grave was mentioned in the newspapers. Careful inquiries were made by the children of Lispenard Stewart of this city, and it was established that the tomb contained all that was left of Leonard Lispenard, the brother of their great-grandfather.... When he died he was at his own request buried upon a favorite spot on his estate in New Rochelle.... [12]

In addition to the remains of Leonard Lispenard, "the grave contained five heavy iron casket handles and a handful of hand wrought nails."[13] The remains of Leonard Lispenard were interred in the family's vault in Trinity Church, Manhattan, on April 8, 1907.[14]

New Rochelle Presbyterian Church Cemetery

New Rochelle

Right: The 1815 Presbyterian church shortly before it was demolished in the early 20th century. The New Rochelle Presbyterian Church Cemetery was located in the rear of this building.

Location: As is indicated by the map at right, the lot on which the cemetery was located (A) was situated between Huguenot Street, Pine Court, and Pine Street (B) not far from the intersection of Huguenot Street and Main Street (C). The burials were located at the northwest portion of the lot.[15]

Dates of Activity: pre-1860.

Removed: According to historian George T. Davis, the remains for this cemetery were reinterred at Beechwoods Cemetery. However, Beechwoods Cemetery does not have any record of removals from the Presbyterian churchyard. A 1929 New Rochelle Presbyterian Church yearbook states that the cemetery disappeared in the 1920s.

Notes: The history of the New Rochelle Presbyterian Church can be traced to 1709 when a few members of the original French Calvinist Church left that congregation after the majority of the body voted to accept "the liturgy of the Church of England."[16] In 1723 the dissenting congregation built a "small wooden church" on a parcel in between present-day Huguenot Street and Pine Street, and over the next half century a number of interments were made next to this building.[17] The congregation of "Calvinist or Presbyterian French" declined in the years leading up to the Revolutionary War, and although the meeting house was removed in 1783, the burials made next to the building were not disturbed.[18]

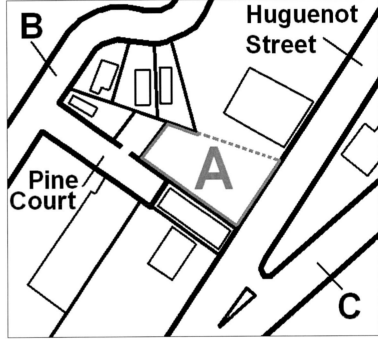

In 1808 a new Presbyterian congregation was formed, and in 1815 a wooden church was built at the triangular parcel between Huguenot and Main streets. In 1860 this building was moved to the west side of Huguenot Street so that a new church could be built. The parcel to which the 1815 church was moved was donated to the congregation by Dr. Albert Smith, founder of Beechwood Cemetery, as a parsonage lot, and coincidentally included the burial ground from the 1723 Calvinist church.

According to George T. Davis's 1889 paper on the cemeteries of New Rochelle, the interments in this burial ground "were removed to Beechwoods and other cemeteries before 1860."[19] However, Beechwoods Cemetery has no record of any removals. The 1929 yearbook of the New Rochelle Presbyterian Church gave a different explanation of the cemetery's fate:

> The old [1815] frame building was moved across the street…. In the rear of this building was an old cemetery with some very ancient graves. This cemetery has disappeared within the last ten years.[20]

The successor to the 1815 church "was greatly damaged by a fire that occurred on May 26, 1926.[21] The congregation sold its land at Huguenot and Main streets and constructed a new house of worship on Pintard Avenue.[22] The 1815 church was later demolished, and the exact fate of the burial ground that was once located behind it is unknown.

Old Catholic Cemetery
Saint Joseph's Cemetery
New Rochelle

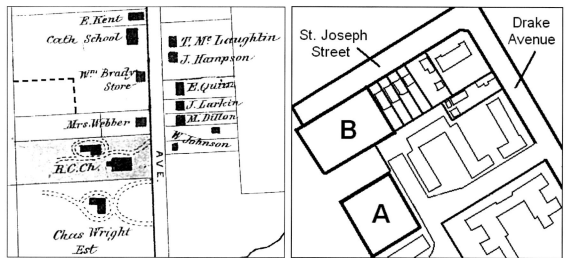

Top Left: This edited 1872 map shows the location of Saint Matthew's Church and rectory (marked "R.C. Ch."). Although it is not marked on the map, the Old Catholic Cemetery was located behind these two buildings. The location of Saint Joseph's Cemetery, then called Saint Matthew's Cemetery, is marked by the dotted lines. The two cemeteries were (and still are) separated by a house lot.

Location: The Old Catholic Cemetery (A) is located behind a series of small apartments on the west side of Drake Avenue immediately south of its intersection with St. Joseph Street. Saint Joseph's Cemetery (B) is on the south side of the dead end of St. Joseph Street.

Dates of Activity: Old Catholic Cemetery, 1845 – Unknown; Saint Joseph's Cemetery, c.1861 – 1943. Saint Joseph's Cemetery has a columbarium which is actively used.

Other Names: Blessed Sacrament Church Cemetery, Saint Matthew's Cemetery (formerly the official name of Saint Joseph's Cemetery).

Inscriptions: No listing of inscriptions was ever made for these cemeteries. The records for both of these cemeteries no longer exist.

Notes: George T. Davis described the Old Catholic Cemetery in his 1889 essay regarding burial grounds in New Rochelle:

> The Old Catholic Cemetery is situated on Drake Avenue in the rear of the old Pastoral residence. It was founded by Father O'Reilly and contains about two acres [actually slightly more than half an acre]. The first interment was made in it about 40 years ago and it is about filled. About 62 interments are made here yearly only by lot owners, as all spaces are taken up. The most prominent monuments here are the Cashman, Griffin, Cochran, Govers and Molloy.[23]

The pastoral residence mentioned by Mr. Davis was the rectory of Saint Matthew's Church. Founded in 1848, this was the first Catholic parish to be established in New Rochelle. Shortly before the establishment of Saint Matthew's, Archbishop John Hughes had purchased a parcel on Drake Avenue for the establishment of a church and burial ground on September 9, 1845.[24] Prior to the construction of the Church of the Blessed Sacrament in 1873, the church of Saint Matthew's was located on land between Drake Avenue and the old cemetery. As the burial lots in the Old Catholic Cemetery were quickly taken up, Archbishop Hughes purchased a new plot a short distance to the north of the parish lands on June 1, 1861.[25] Mr. Davis gave the following account of this later burial ground, which is presently called Saint Joseph's Cemetery:

> St. Mathew's Cemetery is situated on St. Joseph's Street, just off of Drake Avenue. It was founded by Father McLoughlin and was first used about 25 years ago. It contains about four acres [sic] and is about half taken up. About 50 interments are made here per year. No more lots are sold for two reasons, first, the opening of a new cemetery [Holy Sepulchre] farther from the village and second, on account of being so wet. Among the most prominent monuments here may be mentioned the Grogan, Burns, Consadene, Kelly, Dillon, and Baldwin.[26]

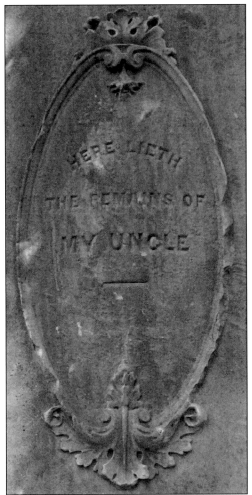

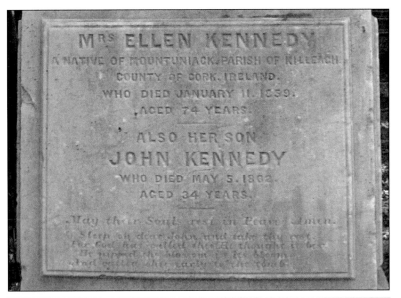

Above and Right: The vandalized memorial that was erected by Timothy and Catherine Kennedy Cashman at their family plot is the only surviving marker in the Old Catholic Cemetery. The monument is quite large compared to other mid-19th-century grave markers placed by Roman Catholics. The west face of the monument (top left) commemorates Mr. Cashman's uncle, Michael Kelly (c.1770-1840). The north face honors Catherine Cashman's mother, Ellen Kennedy, and brother, John Kennedy. The east face of the monument lists the name of Hannah Cashman, and contains a heartfelt epitaph.

[North Face]

Mrs. Ellen Kennedy
A Native of Mountuniack, Parish of Killeach
County of Cork, Ireland.
Who Died January 11, 1859,
Aged 74 Years

Also her son
John Kennedy
Who Died May 5, 1862
Aged 34 Years.

May their souls rest in Peace Amen.

Sleep oh dear John and take thy rest,
For God has called thee He thought it best,
He nipped the blossom in its bloom,
And called thee early to the tomb.

[East Face]

Erected by
Timothy and Catherine Cashman
Natives of Ballynahila, Parish of Ardach,
County of Cork, Ireland,
As a Tribute of Affection to Their Daughter
Hannah
Who Departed This Life October 27, 1865,
Aged 19 Years.

May her Soul rest in Peace Amen.

Repent Dear Parents make no delay,
Tis in my prime I was called away
You after me no sorrow take
But love each other for my sake
Dearest Daughter thou hast left us,
And thy loss we deeply feel,
But tis God who has bereft us,
He will all our sorrows heal.
The grave doth now enfold thee,
Within its narrow cell,
No more can we behold thee,
Hannah dear farewell.

Their records having vanished over time, the two graveyards were largely forgotten following the establishment of Holy Sepulchre Cemetery in 1887, and were "filled with deep holes which are completely overgrown and [could] not be seen" in 1940.[27] Ten years earlier, the WPA had found the graves of twenty Civil War veterans in the two burial grounds. Six of these veterans were interred in the Old Catholic Cemetery, and fourteen were buried in Saint Joseph's Cemetery.

By the mid-1980s each of these cemeteries had but one grave marker remaining. A resident of St. Joseph Street told the author that most of the stones were removed from the two burial grounds in the 1950s and taken to Holy Sepulchre Cemetery, where they were incorporated into a retaining wall. In 1989 the Archdiocese of New York, which was under the impression that there were no longer any remains at the site, considered selling Saint Joseph's Cemetery for development. To halt this action, several residents contacted Blessed Sacrament Church:

> Claire Sheahan Twohig...said her father was a cousin of Mary and Josie Cashin. Twohig said she witnessed the sisters' funeral in 1943 on St. Joseph Street. "I spoke with Monsignor (Eugene F.) Richard of Blessed Sacrament Church and he said there are no records of anyone being buried there," Twohig said. "I remember attending a funeral there. My father arranged the funeral. I picked out their clothes. If they're not buried there, what happened to them? The Cashin sisters died within several hours of each other and were buried in "the [Catholic] cemetery on St. Joseph's Street," according to an obituary that appeared July 15, 1943, in *The Standard-Star* of New Rochelle. Mary Cashin designated $3,000 in her will for the upkeep of the cemetery.

> The only grave marker found today on the property bears the names of the sisters' parents and brother—Martin Cashin, who died in 1884; his wife, Anne, 1896; and their son, Martin, 1896. "They're still down there—I haven't seen them take anybody out" said Lawrence F. Talt, II, who is 63 and lives across the street.... Thomas F. Specht, 70, and several other longtime residents of the street say they remember the property filled with tombstones 50 years ago. They claim tombstones were carted away years ago.[28]

Fortunately, the plans for development were dropped. Today, the Old Catholic Cemetery is unidentifiable as a burial ground except for the Cashman family monument near the southwest corner, while Saint Joseph's Cemetery contains a small columbarium used by members of the Church of the Blessed Sacrament.

Above: In this 1989 photo, a man poses in Saint Joseph's Cemetery with the tombstone that marks the grave of Martin Cashin (1830-1884), his wife, Anne (d.1896), and their son, Martin A. Cashin (d.1896). At the time, this was the only remaining tombstone in the burial ground.

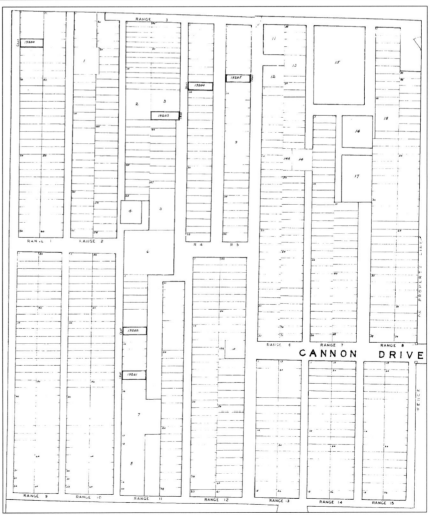

Above: Looking north from the southern edge of the Old Catholic Cemetery in 2005. The south face of the Cashman monument lists the names of Timothy and Catherine Cashman's four infant children: Thomas (1848-1849), Martin (1850-1851), John (1852) and Michael (1852-1853).

Right: This plan of the Old Catholic Cemetery was prepared by the WPA in the early 1930s. Each of the six highlighted rectangles marks the grave of a Civil War veteran.

105

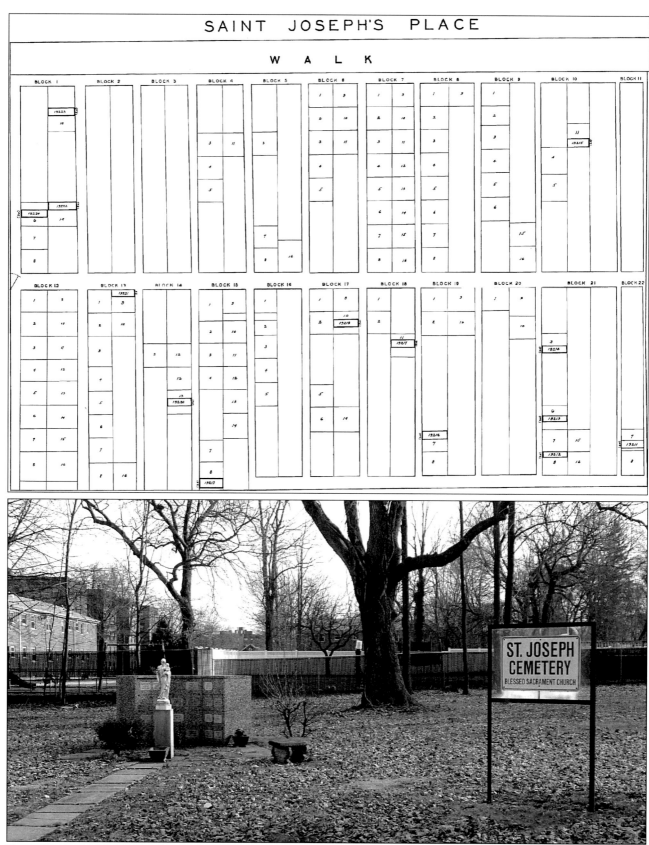

Top: This map of Saint Joseph's Cemetery was prepared by the WPA in the early 1930s. The fourteen highlighted rectangles each denote the grave of a Civil War veteran.

Bottom: Looking into Saint Joseph's Cemetery through the fence on Saint Joseph Street in 2008. The stone structure at left is a columbarium that was placed in the center of the cemetery by Blessed Sacrament Church. The Old Catholic Cemetery is located on the other side of the white fence.

106

Pugsley Family Burial Ground
New Rochelle

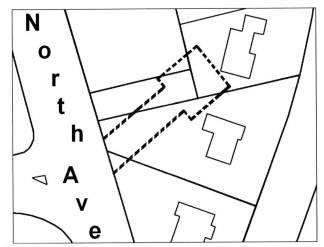

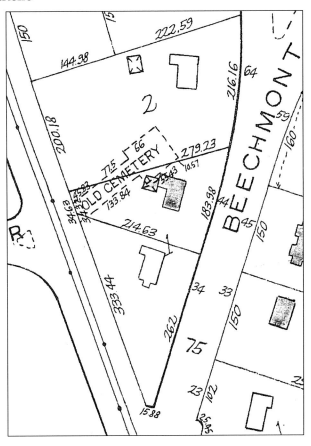

Location: The 1930 map at right depicts the site of the Pugsley Family Burial Ground, which was approached by a right-of-way leading east from the intersection of North Avenue and Eastchester Road (marked "R" on the left side of the map). The map above depicts the site of the cemetery today. Please note that the cemetery site is located on private property.

Dates of Activity: c.1789 – pre-1860.

Notes: In his work, *Historical Landmarks of New Rochelle*, historian Morgan Seacord gave a short history of the Pugsley family and their homestead:

> [James Pugsley] was a member of an old [town of] Westchester family, who had purchased [a farm in New Rochelle] in 1748. He was a Quaker and a widower at the time of the war, with an unmarried daughter, a man of considerable wealth for that period and maintained a large retinue of slaves. Upon the advance of the British Army from Pelham to New Rochelle, on October 21, 1776, General Howe established his headquarters at this house and the records show that he issued orders from New Rochelle on October 22, 23 and 24…. The Pugsleys suffered severely during the war from the disorders of the Neutral Ground. James Pugsley died in 1790 and his unmarried daughter owned it until her death in 1831, she being at that time the last of her family in New Rochelle.[29]

The following story regarding an incident at the Pugsley farm was related by Charles Pryer in *Legends, Traditions, and Superstitions of Westchester*:

> [Westchester] was destitute of armed men, with the exception perhaps of an occasional squadron of cavalry or party of skinners. The latter in some way got the idea that "Quaker Pugsley" had a large sum of money secreted in or about the house, and consequently proposed to pay him a visit that was not altogether friendly in its intentions. They accordingly appeared at his house and formally demanded of him all his money and other valuables, to which demand he very naturally refused to accede. In order to enforce their request they proceeded to first threaten and then to torture the old man in the most horrible manner, but finding they were likely to get but little out of him, they adopted a plan even more brutal. They procured a rope, and hastily making a noose, passed it around the neck of his daughter [Hannah], then a girl of some fifteen or sixteen, and dragged her to an outhouse used as a cider-mill, compelling him to follow to witness the execution. They soon proved to him that the hanging was no idle threat, got up for the purpose of terrifying him into telling his secret, but a design that they at once proceeded to accomplish, for after passing the rope around a beam they actually suspended the girl in mid air.[30]

Fortunately, one of the Pugsley slaves was able to find a detachment of British cavalry, who rushed to the scene and drove off the skinners. Upon returning to the cider mill, the slave took Hannah down and successfully revived her.[31]

James Pugsley set out the boundaries of a cemetery for his family in his will, written on September 10, 1789, where he reserved "four Rods of Land for a burying place and a Road to the same for that use to pass and repass" while bequeathing the remainder of his property to his daughter, Hannah. Charles Pryer described a visit to Hannah Pugsley's grave in 1890:

> …we visited her grave, which is only a few minutes' walk from the [Pugsley] house and is marked by a small head-stone bearing no inscription whatever. There are several other graves in the vicinity of apparently much greater age, which probably are those of her parents, and like hers are marked simply by a common stone after the Quaker custom.[32]

Above The dilapidated Pugsley house as Charles Pryer would have seen it in 1890.

The Pugsley family freed their slaves sometime after the close of the Revolutionary War. Nevertheless, several of the freed slaves continued in the employ of the Pugsley family, and it is believed that they and their descendants used this cemetery. After Hannah's death, her will directed her executors to use 150 acres of her property for "the Support and Maintainence of [Ms. Pugsley's] three Servants, (that is to say) Lewy, Caty, and Plato (Colured Persons)...as they shall think they stand need of as long as they or any of them shall live."[33] Additionally, Hannah reserved "Rooms in the house" for "Lewy and Caty and Mary Guion and Eliza Guion.[34] Upon the death of the three servants, Hannah's executors were instructed to sell the land with the exception of the "family Burying ground in the Orchard near the road."[35] Author Benson Lossing visited the "very much dilapidated" Pugsley house while preparing his work, *The Pictorial Field-Book of the American Revolution*, in the early 1850s. At that time, he found the home "occupied by a colored family," which was most likely that of Eliza Guion and her husband, Henry Everson.[36] Lewy (whose name is also given as Leroy) and Plato died prior to Hannah's death, while Caty must have survived until 1860, when the remaining portion of the Pugsley homestead was sold to Romanzo W. Montgomery.[37] The deed which transferred Hannah's property to Mr. Montgomery contained the following provision for the family cemetery:

> <u>Nevertheless it is expressly understood</u> that four rods square of land in the orchard near the highway aforesaid for a family burying ground as the said burying ground is now staked out and a right of way two rods wide from the highway to said burying ground are hereby excepted and reserved from said premises above described.[38]

The Pugsley house, which was located a few hundred feet north of the cemetery just east of North Avenue, stood until the turn of the 20th century. The Montgomery family sold the land to the City Realty Company in 1901, unfortunately without any mention of the burial ground in the deed.[39] The above-ground remains of the burial ground disappeared sometime after this sale when the farm was subdivided to create the neighborhood of Beechmont. No removals appear to have been made from the cemetery.

Saint John's Methodist Church Cemetery

New Rochelle

Above: The view in this postcard of Saint John's Methodist Church from the early 20th century is looking northwest from the southeast corner of the church property. The monuments visible on either side of the tree mark the burials of members of the Anderson family. The base of the tall monument at right was among the tombstones brought to Christ Episcopal Church Cemetery in 1965, and can be seen at the head of the plot in the photo at bottom left on page 73.

Location: The church and cemetery were formerly located at the northeast corner of the intersection of LeCount Place and Main Street. The map at right is taken from a 1930 atlas. Originally, the cemetery comprised all of the church property on the east side of the dotted line. This rectangular parcel was also the site of the original meeting house, and had been acquired by the congregation on May 5, 1810.[40] In the early 20th century, nearly all of the graves were consolidated in the northern portion of the cemetery (A) to make room for a parish house. Only the graves of the Anderson family (B) were left in their original place.

Dates of Activity: 1811 – 1910.

Removed: To Christ Methodist Church Cemetery in July 1965.

Other Names: Methodist Episcopal Burying Ground.

Inscriptions: *WCHS* Books #18 (p.130-146) and #19 (Part I, p.77-86).

Notes: An "outgrowth of the First Methodist Church on North Avenue," Saint John's Methodist Church was established for the members of the former congregation who found it difficult to travel to services in northern New Rochelle.[41] Although the original church building on the site was constructed in 1810, the congregation was not formally incorporated as a separate entity until 1858. A portion of the half-acre rectangular plot on which the original meeting house was constructed was used as a graveyard as early as 1810. Although the church building was located on Banks Street from 1844 to 1890, the cemetery itself continued to be used during this time.[42] The number of interments in the cemetery decreased in the latter half of the 19th century. In 1889 George T. Davis wrote that "but one interment [had] been made during the past year and [the cemetery] is but little used."

The construction of a parish house in the early 20th century caused a consolidation of the graves in the cemetery. This change was noted in the DAR's appraisal of the burial ground in 1940:

> A few of the graves are in their original positions [but] most of the graves, however, were removed before the time the Church House extension was built. They are now located in a small yard at the back of the Church House. At present the stones stand close together and more or less in rows. Their arrangement is not always regular and many foot stones are out of place. They do not represent actual burials in their present position, but each stone does represent an interment in the cemetery.... [The cemetery] is not kept up. In the little grave yard burdocks and other weeds [have] been allowed to grow unchecked for years. At the back of this yard there is a pile of pathetic stones, some of them, no doubt, to the memory of the founders of the Church. They were too heavy to be moved and read, but many of them seemed to be in good condition.[43]

The church's membership had declined significantly by 1960, and its property had become prime real estate for New Rochelle's proposed urban renewal project. In 1962 Saint John's decided to merge with its former parent congregation, the First Methodist Church. Together, the new congregation formed Christ United Methodist Church.[44] The interments and headstones from Saint John's were removed to Christ Church Cemetery in 1965, where they lie in a plot on the southern side of that graveyard.[45]

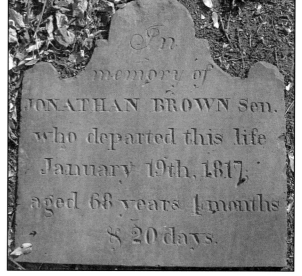

Above and Right: Three of the headstones that were removed from Saint John's Methodist Church Cemetery to Christ Methodist Church Cemetery. The headstone at top left is the oldest surviving headstone from Saint John's. It reads: Here lies the body of ANN, Wife of Stephen Odell, who departed this life March 5th, 1815, aged 69 years."

The second-oldest surviving headstone is that of Jonathan Brown, Sr. (top right), who died on January 19, 1817, at the age of 68 years, 4 months and 20 days. The marble tombstone at bottom right marked the grave of John and Eliza Taylor's daughter, Jane Ellenor, who died on December 20, 1854, at the age of five years, six months and one day. The verse at the bottom of this headstone reads:

> She was the sunshine of our home
> An angel to us given
> But as we learned to love her most
> God called her back to Heaven.

Shute Family Burial Ground

New Rochelle

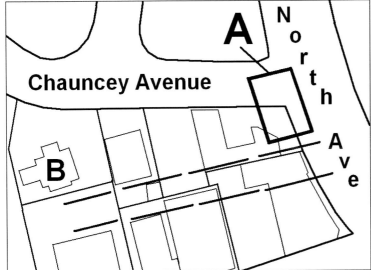

Above Right: Only a portion of Elizabeth Shute's headstone is still visible. It reads:

IN MEMORY OF
ELIZABETH SHUTE
consort of the Late
Peter Shute

Bottom Right: The worn headstone of Peter Shute in 2007.

In
Memory of
PETER SHUTE ESQ.
who departed this Life
February 8th 1808
Aged 51 Years
10 Months & 15 Days

Location: The burial ground (marked "A" in the map at top left) was formerly located at the southwest corner of the intersection of North and Chauncey avenues. The dashed lines on the south side of the cemetery mark the approximate location of the driveway to the Shute house (B). The intersection of this driveway and North Avenue formed the "corner of the road" mentioned by Peter Shute in his will.

Dates of Activity: pre-1803 – 1835.

Removed: To Beechwoods Cemetery (Section 24, about 15 yards in front of the railroad fence) on October 25, 1886. [46]

Notes: Peter G. Shute (1756-1809) was the great-great-grandson of Richard Shute, a native of England whose grave at Saint Paul's Church Cemetery in Mount Vernon is marked by the oldest surviving identifiable tombstone in Westchester County.[47] Peter Shute moved to New Rochelle from Eastchester in 1785, and over the following 10 years purchased land on both sides of North Avenue between present-day Mayflower and Lincoln avenues.[48] Mr. Shute, whose will requested that he be "buried in a decent but not expensive manner," set out a family cemetery in that same document, which was written on February 4, 1803: "I hereby reserve before the Execution hereof a burial spot of ground at the corner of the road where I have one child already buried to be for the use and burial of all my children and family."[49] The "one child" mentioned by Mr. Shute was probably his daughter Ann, and the corner was made by North Avenue, then called North Street, and a lane which led to his farmhouse. Unlike his ancestor's crudely inscribed marker, Peter's tombstone, which stands alongside that of his wife and has been made almost completely illegible by the elements, was a finely cut marble slab.

Only a few burials appear to have been made in the Shute plot, with all of them being of members of Mr. Shute's immediate family. In addition to Ann and Peter Shute, these interments include his wife, Elizabeth Bailey (1759-1835), and their daughters, Louisa (1784-1810), and Mary, the wife of Peter Underhill. After removing the interments and tombstones in the graveyard to Beechwoods Cemetery, Peter Shute's heirs sold the plot to the estate of Elihu Chauncey on October 11, 1886, for the price of $150.[50] The deed recording this sale gives a brief description of the small cemetery and its location:

> Commencing at a point on North Street aforesaid at the distance of about one hundred and twenty-six feet more or less Northward from Coligni Avenue so called and containing sixty feet more or less on North Street and the same on the Westerly side and forty feet more or less on each of the Northerly and Southerly sides and being enclosed with a stone wall.[51]

The Shute house, which is usually referred to as the Shute-Carpenter house, still stands today at 26 Chauncey Avenue.

Above: The Shute plot at Beechwoods Cemetery, 2011. Mr. Shute's footstone, marked "P. S." can be seen on the bottom left corner. From left to right are the tombstones of Mary Shute Underhill, Peter Shute, Elizabeth Shute, and Louisa Shute. This plot also contains the unmarked grave of Ann Shute.

112

Thomas Paine Burial Plot

New Rochelle

Above: Thomas Paine's abandoned burial plot in 1868. The following description of the site was written in 1866: "The remains of the wall which surrounded the grave of the old man, in the midst of which stands a thrifty young hickory, alone continue, to tell the romantic story. There is no longer a headstone to tell of him who was laid there.[52]

Location: Formerly at the southeast corner of the intersection of North and Paine avenues.

Date of Activity: 1809.

Removed: The remains of Thomas Paine were stolen from his grave by William Cobbett in 1819.

Notes: On May 12, 1784, the State of New York awarded Thomas Paine a 300-acre farm in New Rochelle "in consideration for the eminent services rendered to the United State in the progress of the late war...[and] as a testimony of the sense which the people of this State entertains of his distinguished merits."[53] In his will, Paine gave the following instructions regarding his burial on this farm:

> I know not if the Society of people called Quakers, admit a person to be buried in their burying ground, who does not belong to their Society, but if they do, or will admit me, I would prefer being buried there; my father belonged to that profession, and I was partly bought up in that. But if it is not consistent with their rulers to do this, I desire to be buried on my own farm in New Rochelle. The place where I am to be buried, to be a square of twelve feet, to be enclosed with a row of trees, and a stone or post and rail fence, with a headstone with my name and age engraved upon it, author of Common Sense.

Paine died in New York City on June 8, 1809.[54] His deist convictions prevented him from being buried in a Quaker cemetery. These beliefs, coupled with his other unpopular opinions including opposition to slavery, resulted in a lack of tribute paid to him at his death by his adopted country:

> At his funeral, no pomp, no pageantry, no civic procession, no military display. In a carriage, a woman and her son who had lived on the bounty of the dead – on horseback, a Quaker, the humanity of whose heart dominated the creed of his head   and, following on foot, two negroes filled with gratitude – consisted the funeral cortege of Thomas Paine.[55]

Madame Margaret Brazier Bonneville, Paine's good friend from his days in France and the woman mentioned in the previous passage, described the situation of the burial plot and mentioned its dubious distinction as one of the earliest vandalized burial places in Westchester (which she does not appear to condemn, apparently viewing the vandals as acting out of a strange sense of respect for her friend), as well as the funeral that was conducted on that spot:

It was my intention to have him buried in the Orchard of his own farm; but the farmer who lived there at that time said, that Thomas Paine, walking with him one day, said, pointing to another point of the land, he was desirous of being buried there. "Then," said I, "that shall be the place of his burial." And, my instructions were accordingly put into execution. The head-stone was put up about a week afterwards with the following inscription: "Thomas Paine, Author of 'Common Sense,' died the eighth of June, 1809, aged 72 years." According to his will, a wall twelve feet square was erected round his tomb. Four trees have been planted outside the wall, two weeping willows and two cypresses. Many persons have taken away pieces of the tombstone and of the trees, in memory of the deceased; foreigners especially have been eager to obtain these memorials, some of which have been sent to England. They have been put in frames and preserved. Verses in honor of Paine have been written on the head stone. The grave is situated at the angle of the farm, near the entrance to it.

The interment was a scene to affect and to wound any sensible heart. Contemplating who it was, what man it was, that we were committing to an obscure grave on an open and disregarded bit of land, I could not help feeling most acutely. Before the earth was thrown down upon the coffin, I, placing myself at the east end of the grave, said to my son Benjamin, "stand you there, at the other end, as a witness for grateful America." Looking round me, and beholding the small group of spectators, I exclaimed, as the earth was tumbled into the grave, "O! Mr. Paine! My son stands here as testimony of the gratitude of America, and I, for France!" This was the funeral ceremony of this great politician and philosopher![56]

After he was refused the possibility of burial in a Quaker cemetery, Paine sadly remarked: "…the farm will be sold, and they will dig my bones up before they be[come] half rotten."[57] This prediction would come true due to an admirer of Paine's who was not content to have only a small relic such as a piece of tombstone. William Cobbett, a British journalist who felt that Paine's burial place "seemed unworthy" made clear his plan to bring the remains of Thomas Paine to the United Kingdom:

Paine lies in a little hole under the grass and weeds of an obscure farm in America. There, however, he shall not lie unnoticed, much longer. He belongs to England. His fame is the property of England; and if no other people will show that they value that fame, the people of England will.[58]

Cobbett successfully carried out his plan in September 1819. The incident was described by the Reverend Charles E. Lindsley in Scharf's *History of Westchester County, New York*:

…in the year 1819, [Paine's] remains were disinterred by William Cobbett, and conveyed to England. I once met with an aged man, who informed me that he was a small boy at the time, living in a house almost directly opposite the place where Paine was buried. At a very early hour one morning, when going to the pasture to drive up the cows for milking, he discovered several men hard at work digging near the road. He was alarmed and watched them from a distance. They placed something in a box, in a wagon, filled up the empty grave and drove rapidly away. That was the last of the mortal remains of the author of "Common Sense" ever seen in this country.[59]

"After some delay," a party was organized to pursue Cobbett, but gave up after it was learned that he had crossed King's Bridge.[60] Cobbett proudly described his successful exploit:

I have just done here a thing which I have always since I came here vowed I would do; that is, taken up the remains of Thomas Paine…. I found him laying in the corner of a barren, rugged field…. Our expedition set out from New York in the middle of the night, got to the place–twenty-two miles off– at the peep of day; took up the coffin entire, and just as we found it it goes to England.[61]

Corbett successfully conveyed his macabre baggage to England, whereupon he proudly declared at the customs house, "Here are the bones of the late Thomas Paine."[62] Rather than serve to inspire the people of England, Cobbett's deed was mocked in the British press, and "he and his imported bones were met with shouts of derision:"

Finding that the bones aroused ridicule rather than enthusiasm, Cobbett, after a short time ceased to exploit them, but they remained in his possession until his death in 1835. In January 1836 his effects were publicly sold to pay his debts. The auctioneer refused to offer the bones for sale, and the Lord Chancellor, on reference being made to him by the official receiver, declined to recognize them as part of the estate or to make any order in regard to them. They, therefore, remained at the receiver's office until 1844, when they were given to Mr. Tilly of 13 Bedford Square, East, London.[63]

Despite the loss of Paine's remains, his gravesite remained in existence for some time after the theft. Paine's will deeded the southern part of his farm for the benefit of Madame Bonneville, so that she would have ample resources to provide for herself and her two sons. One of these young men, Benjamin (who would later gain national fame as an explorer of the West), inherited the land and sold it in 1824 with the provision that the burial site would be maintained.[64] On July 4, 1837, Gilbert Vale, a biographer of Paine, paid a visit to the desecrated gravesite:

> The tomb is close by the road side, but over a stone fence, and now consists of a low, broken, rough, dry stone wall, of oblong shape, of about eight feet by four feet, with loose stones, grass, and earth, in the centre; the upright slab...no longer exists. After Cobbett violated the grave, and removed the bones from the remains of Mr. Paine, the headstone was broken, and pieces successively removed by different visitors; one large fragment was preserved by a lady in an opposite cottage, in which Mr. Paine had sometimes boarded...but this fragment gradually suffered diminution, as successive visitors begged a piece of what they could no longer steal. To preserve the last remnant, this lady has had it plastered up in a wall. We discovered that the lady mentioned, the nearest neighbor to the tomb, would be favorable to the repair of the tomb, and we learned that she believed that such repairs would be popular among the neighbors; and on this understanding, in which we have not been deceived, we determined to commence a subscription to repair the tomb, or put up a monument; and before we left the village we obtained from Mr. James, who had then marble saw-mills in New Rochelle, a promise to be at the expense of putting up a heavy block of marble, instead of a head-stone, if purchased by subscription; subsequently Mr. Frazee, an eminent architect, offered in conjunction with some friends to give the work on a monument, if the materials were procured, and other expenses paid. This has now been accomplished, and paid for.[65]

The monument discussed in the above passage is not actually located at the burial plot itself, but is situated a few yards to the north at the intersection of North and Paine avenues. "The remains of the wall" around Paine's gravesite "were removed in 1874 by Simeon Lester who set four locust posts in the ground to mark the corners of the plot."[66] These last remnants of the Paine plot were later removed and replaced by a sidewalk as a result of the widening of North Avenue.[67]

In 1900 Paine biographer Dr. Moncure Daniel Conway "conducted a persistent search for whatever fragments of the *introuvable* remains of Paine he could recover," and "succeeded in collecting...only two locks of hair and a fragment of the brain. One of the locks was given to him by Edward Smith, Cobbett's biographer [and] the other lock of hair and the brain fragment were purchased for £5 from Charles Higham, a second-hand bookseller in London, who had obtained them from the Rev[erend] George Reynolds."[68] These remains were placed in a box and buried beneath the Paine monument during the rededication of that memorial on October 14, 1905.[69] In May 1914, two more locks of Paine's hair as well as a wax death mask were acquired by the Thomas Paine Historical Association. These items were sent in the mail to the association in a box labeled, "Of no commercial value."[70] A plaque donated by Rowena Stillman, which indicates the site of Paine's grave, was placed on the wall next to the sidewalk in 1952.

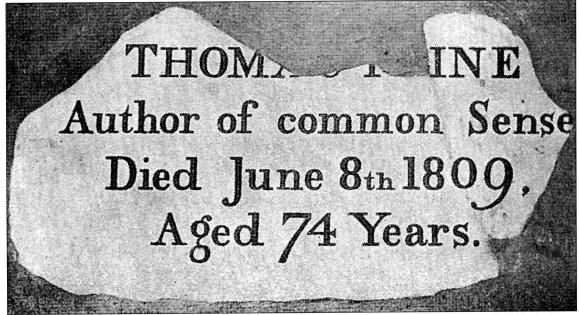

Above: The remnant of Thomas Paine's tombstone in the 1930s. Paine was actually 72 years old at his death.

Trinity Episcopal Church Cemetery
New Rochelle

Right: Looking southeast in Trinity Episcopal Church Cemetery in 1956. The two rows of headstones in the foreground were removed to the Trinity churchyard when the southern portion of the Huguenot Burying Ground was sold for the Pelham-Port Chester Parkway right-of-way in 1927. The stones lying flat on the ground in front of the two cars were placed in the churchyard in 1956 after the remainder of the Huguenot Burying Ground was sold for the construction of the New England Thruway.

Location: 311 Huguenot Street (northwest corner of the intersection of Huguenot and Division streets).

Dates of Activity: 1808 – Present.

Inscriptions: *WCHS* Books #8 (p.134-157), #18 (p.23-53) and #19 (Part I, p.2-26).

Notes: The origins of Trinity Church can be traced back to the purchase of what is now New Rochelle by the representative of the Huguenots, Jacob Leisler, from Thomas Pell. This grant included a gift of "One hundred Acres of Land...for the French Church erected or to be erected" by the residents of the new settlement.[71] The first house of worship to be erected in New Rochelle was constructed on this glebe in 1692 or 1693, and served the community until 1710, when a small stone church was built at the present intersection of Huguenot and Division streets.[72] Known as the "Stone Jug" due to its shape, this church served as the burial place for the first three rectors of the building: the Reverends Daniel Boudet (d.1722), Pierre Stouppe (1690-1760), and Michael Houdin (1705-1766), all of whom were interred "beneath the chancel."[73] The Reverend Stouppe's wife, Magdalene (d.c.1771), was interred here as well.[74] Upon the construction of a third church building in 1827, the remains of these ministers "were placed somewhere without a stone to mark the spot [and] it is even believed they may have been located somewhere under what is now the sidewalk or street."[75] The Reverend Robert Bolton supported the latter theory and claimed that "the ashes of these worthy and laborious missionaries repose in the highway."[76] Unfortunately, there is no real proof of exactly where these early clergymen lie. In 1908 historian C. H. Augur noted that "some chroniclers assert that beneath the busy highway where your vehicle stops the remains of the earlier pastors of the church lie buried; others dispute this, and you may choose between a conflict of testimony offered without satisfactory proof on either side."[77] The early rectors of Trinity are commemorated by stained-glass windows within the third and present church, which was completed in 1864.

With the exception of the three ministers, the members of the church were mostly interred in the Huguenot Burying Ground until the early years of the 19th century. In 1747 a "small parcel of land containing one acre & three quarters more or less" was donated to the French Church by Aman Guion.[78] This plot contains the land on which the present Trinity Church and its cemetery now stand. The French Church was formally chartered as Trinity Church in 1762, and nearly half a century later a new burial ground began to spring up on the parcel that had been donated by Mr. Guion. The vestry of Trinity Church laid out plots in this cemetery in April 1809.[79] The vestry also ordered that "no part of the said church land be broken up for the interment of any person known to hold Atheistical or Deistical principles."[80] A price ranging from four to eight dollars was charged for burial in the churchyard during the mid-19th century, with "one extra dollar" required "for tolling the bell."[81] The deeds which accompanied the sale of plots contained the following stipulation:

> If there be the performances of any Funeral services upon [the plot] the services shall be under the exclusive control or by the permission of the Rector or Minister of the Parish.... ALSO that no grave stone or stones memorial or memorials or any other object of a kind or character offensive to good taste or contrary to the Christian Religion shall be put or erected on said lot; that no inscription mark or design whatever shall be placed on said lot or any part of its enclosure which shall conflict with the doctrines, teachings order or established principles of the Protestant Episcopal Church.[82]

116

Above: This 1910 photo shows the monument at the grave of the Reverend Theodosius Bartow (1747-1819), who served as rector of Trinity Church from 1790 to 1819. Interestingly, this monument, which was imported from Italy, primarily depicts pagan rather than Christian symbols.[83] Note the upside-down torch which is about to be extinguished, as well as the winged hourglass which symbolizes the flight of time.

The third Trinity Church building stood on the site of the present parish house from 1823-24 to 1864, at which time the fourth and final edifice was completed.[84] Prior to the construction of the New York & New Haven Railroad in the late 1840s, there was no delineation between the Trinity Cemetery and Huguenot Burying Ground, resulting in many contemporary accounts referring to the two as one entity. The number of interments in the Trinity churchyard declined after the founding of Beechwoods Cemetery in 1854. However, all of the interments in the Huguenot Burying Ground and the Allaire Family Burial Ground were relocated to the churchyard between 1927 and 1956. The church and cemetery were added to the National Register of Historic Places in 2006.

Above: The second Trinity Church (1710-1827) under which the Reverends Boudet, Stouppe and Houdin were buried.

117

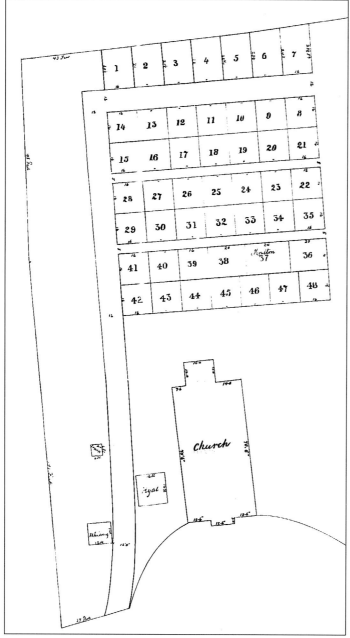

Top Left: The three headstones in the foreground mark the graves of (left to right) Joseph (1777-1816), Sarah (c.1741-1819), and Susan Bayley (c.1799-1833). Sarah was the grandmother of the Reverend William Hague, who recounted a visit to her grave for Scharf's *History of Westchester County, New York*: "I turned my steps toward the church burial-ground, seeking the graves of my grandparents. Long slumbering memories were aroused...by the sight of the marble that marked the grave of my grandmother—Sarah Pell, widow of Captain William Bayley—whose funeral service, ministered in the church-yard by her aged relative, the rector, Rev. Theodosius Bartow, I had attended with a large family gathering in the month of March, 1819, being then eleven years of age. The form of the venerable clergyman in his official robes at the grave, his bald head uncovered despite the chill of a heavy snow-fall, is vividly remembered now as if it had figured in a scene of yesterday."[85]

Bottom Left: This map of Trinity Episcopal Church Cemetery was drawn in 1854. The building marked "Church" identifies Trinity's third house of worship, which was used from 1823-24 to 1864. Today, the parish house occupies the site of the third church. (Westchester County Clerk Map #254).

Next Page: This c.1910 photo depicts the monument at the grave of William Leggett. The monument is inscribed:

TO
WILLIAM LEGGETT,
THE ELOQUENT JOURNALIST
WHOSE GENIUS, DISINTERESTEDNESS
AND COURAGE ENNOBLED HIS PROFESSION
WHO LOVED TRUTH FOR ITS OWN SAKE,
AND ASSERTED IT WITH MOST ARDOR
WHEN WEAKER MINDS WERE MOST DISMAYED
WITH OPPOSITION;
WHO COULD ENDURE NO FORM OF TYRANNY,
AND RAISED HIS VOICE AGAINST
ALL INJUSTICE
ON WHOMSOEVER COMMITTED,
AND WHOEVER WERE ITS AUTHORS.

THE DEMOCRATIC YOUNG MEN
OF NEW YORK,
SORROWING THAT A CAREER SO GLORIOUS
SHOULD HAVE CLOSED SO PREMATURELY,
HAVE ERECTED THIS MONUMENT.

William Leggett was born in New York City on April 30, 1801. After resigning from the United States Navy in 1826, Leggett published a book of poetry. In 1828 he became the editor of *The Critic*, "a weekly literary periodical," and moved to New Rochelle with his wife, Elmira, who was a native of the city.[86] From 1829 to 1836 he edited *The Evening Post* with William Cullen Bryant. After leaving the *Post*, Leggett became the editor of *The Plaindealer*, a weekly newspaper. Leggett's editorials reflected his strong support of the Democratic Party, and his "mildness of manner surprised those who had known him through his fiery writings."[87] Leggett died in New Rochelle on May 29, 1839, shortly after he received an appointment from President Martin Van Buren as "Diplomatic Agent to the Republic of Guatemala."[88] Leggett's friends met at New Rochelle "in the summer of 1840...to make arrangements" for the placement of this monument at his grave.[89]

Trinity Episcopal Church African Cemetery
New Rochelle

Location: Presently covered by 733 Pelham Road (north side of Pelham Road about 1,000 feet east of its intersection with Pelhamdale Avenue). Although the cemetery has been built over, the boundaries of the lot (A) have remained intact to the present day.

Dates of Activity: Unknown – 1824.

Other Names: Deveautown Cemetery.

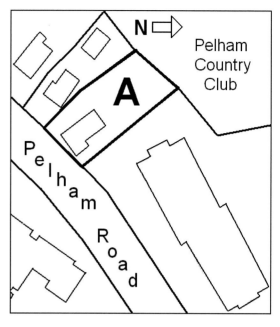

Notes: In 1689 John Pell deeded the French Church a parcel of 100 acres as a gift to accompany the Huguenots' purchase of the land that would soon become New Rochelle. This glebe was transferred to the Anglican Church when a majority of the Huguenots became a part of that body in 1709 and joined the parish that would later become Trinity Church.[90] The glebe consisted of "a part of the undivided lands on Pelham Road, west of Weyman Avenue" and south of Morgan Street.[91] Over the century that followed the Anglican Church's acquisition of the land, all of this parcel was sold off by Trinity Church save for a small piece of land on the north side of Pelham Road. This plot, which "had been set apart at an early date by Trinity," was used as a burial ground for the slaves and free Blacks who lived in the vicinity of Trinity Church.[92] The specifications for this cemetery were contained in an 1805 deed transferring the surrounding land to Moses Ward:

> ALWAYS EXCEPTING and reserving to the Minister & members of Trinity Church in [New Rochelle] and their successors forever ONE QUARTER OF AN ACRE adjoining Pelham Road & Davoe's barn.[93]

Unfortunately, little else is known concerning this cemetery. Trinity Church sold the burial ground to Joseph Thomas on July 27, 1824, three years before the final abolition of slavery took place in the state of New York. This act marked the end of the parcel's use as a cemetery.[94] Joseph Thomas, who later adopted the surname Turpin, was, in fact, a former slave himself. In his will he mentioned owning a "portrait of my own late lamented Master and Benefactor William Turpin deceased."[95] William Turpin was a native of South Carolina who freed his slaves and moved to New York several years before his death. The *African Repository and Colonial Journal*, a publication of the American Colonization Society, noted that "the circumstances of [Turpin's] dying...excited a general curiosity concerning his will," as he left much of his fortune to his former slaves. William bequeathed four properties in Manhattan that were worth a total of "fifty or sixty thousand dollars" to Joseph, whom he referred to as his "friend and freed black man."[96] Joseph was interred at Saint Paul's Episcopal Church Cemetery in Mount Vernon following his death in 1835 at the age of 35.

No records have been found regarding exhumations and re-interments from this cemetery, and the boundaries of this parcel have remained intact to the present day. The closing of this cemetery led to the opening of the Carpenter Cemetery in northern New Rochelle, as the Daughters of the American Revolution noted:

> In 1838 the Vestry [of Trinity Church] made inquiry as to what provision was being made for colored burials. A committee was appointed and, after investigation, reported that the colored people had been provided for in Upper New Rochelle. The burial place referred to here is the Carpenter Cemetery.[97]

Town of Pelham

Above: The photo above depicts the Roosevelt family vault in Beechwoods Cemetery in New Rochelle in 2010. The remains which were originally interred in the Roosevelt family vault beneath Christ Church in Pelham were removed to this vault in the late 19th century. The Roosevelt family owned a significant amount of land along Pelham Road in Pelham and New Rochelle. Like Presidents Theodore and Franklin Delano Roosevelt, Elbert Roosevelt (1767-1857) was a descendant of Claes Martenzsen Rosenvelt (d.1658), a native of Holland who settled in the Dutch colony of New Amsterdam. The monuments to the right of the vault commemorate the members of the Roosevelt family who are entombed there.

Prior to 1896, City Island and most of the land which encompasses Pelham Bay Park in the Bronx were part of the Town of Pelham. When this portion of the town was annexed by New York City, the town lost its two cemeteries, the Pell Family Burial Ground in Pelham Bay Park and Pelham Cemetery on City Island. Nevertheless, there are a few burial places in the present Town of Pelham. Christ Episcopal Church, the home of the Parish of Christ the Redeemer, contains the private vault of the Bolton family. As is mentioned in the Appendix, a single grave is located on the grounds of the Bolton Priory, home to the founders of Christ Church. Additionally, both Christ Church and the Huguenot Memorial Church have columbaria for the interment of cremated remains.

Christ Episcopal Church Vaults

Pelham (Pelham Manor)

Location: 1415 Pelhamdale Avenue (at the corner of Shore Road).

Dates of Activity: 1843 – 1877.

Removed: The interments in the Roosevelt and Schuyler family vaults were removed to Beechwoods Cemetery in New Rochelle about 1881.

Notes: The Reverend Robert Bolton (1788-1857), an Episcopal priest and native of Savannah, Georgia, built Bolton Priory, a Gothic home, in present-day Pelham Manor in 1838.[1] The Reverend Bolton held Episcopal services in the Priory until 1843, when he had a church constructed at the south end of his property. The Reverend Robert Bolton, Jr., son of the founder of Christ Church, wrote *History of the Several Towns, Manors, and Patents of the County of Westchester*, the first history of Westchester County, in 1848.

The construction of Christ Church included three family burial vaults. One vault was intended for the use of the Bolton family, while the other two were reserved for the families of Elbert Roosevelt and Philip Schuyler. The elder Reverend Bolton deeded the Roosevelt family vault to Elbert Roosevelt on September 13, 1853.[2] On May 22, 1857, the Reverend Robert and Anne Bolton transferred land on which the church stood, "excepting and reserving thereout the two vaults...with the privilege of opening and using the same for the burial of their dead or other necessary purposes," to Christ Church.[3] In 1855 the Reverend Robert Bolton, Jr., identified the persons who had been interred in the two vaults:

> In a vault beneath the chancel repose the mortal remains of William Matthew Evans, Esq., son of William Evans and Sarah, (second daughter of Robert Bolton, Esq. of Savannah, Geo[rgia] and Susannah Mauve) who departed this life in Eastchester, on the 18th of November, 1837, aged sixty-three. Also, Abby Bolton, fifth daughter of the Rev. Robert Bolton and Anne Jay, his wife, who was born at Henley upon Thames, Oxfordshire, England, February 3rd, 1827, and died in Pelham, June the 16th, 1849. Also, her sister-in-law, Elizabeth Rebecca, wife of Robert Bolton, Jun. and second daughter of James Brenton, Esq., of Newport, R.I., who was born at Pittstown, in this State, on the 2nd of August, 1814, and died in New Rochelle on the 12th of March, 1852.
>
> In the Roosevelt family vault are the following: Elizabeth Curtenius, daughter of Peter T. Curtenius, (Commissary during the Revolution) who died May, 1837, aged 80 years. Jane Roosevelt, wife of Elbert Roosevelt, and sister of the above, who died in Pelham, January 31st, 1846, aged 75. Elizabeth Roosevelt, daughter of Cornelius Roosevelt, who died April 25th, 1850, aged 84. Mary Eliza Roosevelt, daughter of the Rev. Washington Roosevelt, and granddaughter of Elbert Roosevelt, who died August 13th, 1851, aged 7 years.[4]

The remains of four other persons were entombed in the Bolton family vault: the Reverend Robert Bolton, Jr. (1814-1877); Richard Woodhull Bolton (1864-1868), son of Robert Bolton, Jr., and Josephine Woodhull; an infant son of the Reverend John Bolton, who in turn was a brother of Robert Bolton, Jr.; and Ann Griffin (c.1801-1852), the "English nurse of the Bolton family."[5] The following description of the Schuyler vault was provided in 1881:

> In the Schuyler family vault are the following: Philip Schuyler, Esq., born October 26, 1788, died Feb. 12, 1865; Grace Hunter Schuyler, born April 10, 1790, died Dec. 23, 1855; Harriet Schuyler, daughter of the above, born Oct. 26, 1823, died Nov. 22, 1877.[6]

The Roosevelts transferred the remains in their vault to Beechwoods Cemetery in New Rochelle about 1857, and the Schuylers did the same sometime thereafter. The Bolton vault is located beneath the "floor of the south aisle" of the church, and is marked by a stone.[7] In the mid-20th century the church established the Garden of Resurrection, which contains the parish's columbarium. The following passage by the Reverend Lawrence Bernard Larsen was written about the columbarium, but can easily be applied to any of the burial places in Westchester County:

> There are sermons in stones if one has the eye to see them and the ears to hear them. They speak of spiritual things to men and they do point the way to where man's search for God may end in fruition and where his deepest hopes may find fulfillment.

City of Rye

Above: This sandstone is located in the Blind Brook Burial Ground. It reads: "In Memory of Jamima Theall wife of Charles Theall who Died Sep^br. 29th, 1768 Aged 64 Years." Photo courtesy Gray Williams.

African Cemetery	124	Jay Family Cemetery	142
Blind Brook Burial Ground	126	Miriam Osborn Memorial Cemetery	145
Budd Family Burial Ground	132	Purdy Family Burial Ground	146
Christ's Church Burial Ground and Tomb	133	Rye Presbyterian Churchyard	148
Christ's Church Rectors' Burial Ground	133	Saint Mary's Cemetery	149
Greenwood Union Cemetery	138	Theall Family Burial Ground	150
Christ Church Cemetery	138	Town Field Burying Ground	150
Hart Family Burial Ground	141		

The City of Rye contains an interesting variety of burial grounds, including the family cemetery of one of America's Founding Fathers as well as the only cemetery connected with a retirement home in Westchester County. Prior to becoming a city in 1942, this municipality was an incorporated village that was a part of the Town of Rye. As such, the Blind Brook Burial Ground, a community cemetery that dates to Colonial times, served the residents of both the present Town and City of Rye. As this cemetery became nearly full by the mid-19th century, the Christ Church and Greenwood Union cemeteries were founded in 1837 and 1855, respectively. Greenwood Union Cemetery began as a Methodist graveyard, but became a non-denominational cemetery in 1902. The City of Rye boasts two other incorporated burial grounds: the Jay Family Cemetery, which serves as the final resting place of America's first chief justice of the Supreme Court, and the Miriam Osborn Memorial Cemetery, the place of interment for a number of women who lived out their final days in the Osborn Home. The African American residents of Rye interred their friends and family in two graveyards which no longer exist, the Mead Farm and Town Field burying grounds, until the opening of the African Cemetery in 1860. The latter burial ground, which belongs to the Town of Rye, was used for more than 100 years and was restored in the 1980s.

African Cemetery
Rye City

Above: Looking southeast into the African Cemetery from Greenwood Union Cemetery in 2006.

Location: The African Cemetery is bordered by the New England Thruway on the east and south and Greenwood Union Cemetery on the west and north. The burial ground can be accessed by following Cemetery Road south through Greenwood Union Cemetery for a quarter-mile from its intersection with North Street.

Dates of Activity: 1860 – 1964.

Other Names: Colored Peoples Burying Ground, Rye Colored Cemetery.

Notes: The burial ground known as the African Cemetery originated in 1859 when Benjamin Mead transferred a piece of land to Underhill Halstead "to be held in trust for persons of Color residing in the Town of Rye."[1] Mr. Halstead in turn deeded the parcel to the Trustees of the Town of Rye and "their successors in office forever" on June 27, 1860.[2] This land was to "be forever hereafter kept, held and used for the purpose of a cemetery or burial place for the colored inhabitants of the said Town of Rye, and its vicinity free and clear of any charge therefore."[3] For more than a century, the African American residents of Rye used this burial ground, usually referred to as the African Cemetery, as a final resting place. While most of the burials here were made in single graves, a number of family plots were also established.

More than two dozen Rye residents who served in America's armed conflicts are buried in the African Cemetery, including veterans of the Civil War, the Spanish American War, and both World Wars. Among the Civil War veterans interred here is Edwin Purdy, a member of the United States Navy, who served aboard the famed *USS Monitor*. The African Cemetery was used on a regular basis until the last interment was made there in 1964. The cemetery was neglected over the next 20 years, but in May 1986 it was rededicated after two years of cleanup and restoration.[4] Although the cemetery has been part of the City of Rye since the incorporation of that municipality in 1942, the Town of Rye still holds title to the burial ground.

Above: This 2007 photo shows the Francis family plot in the African Cemetery.

Top Left: Marked "Cold'd Cem," the African Cemetery can be seen south of Greenwood Union Cemetery on this c.1870 map. The home of Benjamin Mead, the donor of the cemetery, is marked "B. Mead" on the east side of the railroad tracks.

Top Right: This tombstone marks the grave of Edwin Purdy, a naval veteran of the Civil War who served on the *USS Monitor*.

Center Left: This view of the African Cemetery from the early 1980s indicates the amount of overgrowth that existed in the burial ground at that time.

Center Right: The veteran's headstone of Corporal Amos Williams (c.1843-1887), who served in the 31st United States Colored Infantry Regiment during the Civil War.

125

Blind Brook Burial Ground
Rye City

Above: Looking west into the Blind Brook Burial Ground on August 5, 1907. **Right:** The tombstone of Lydia Hawser lies flat on the ground near the northern boundary of the Blind Brook Burial Ground.

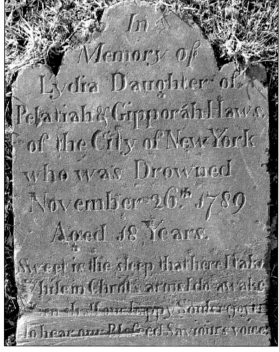

In
Memory of
Lydia Daughter of
Pelatiah & Gipporah Haws[er]
of the City of New York
who was Drowned
November 26th, 1789
Aged 18 Years.

Sweet is the sleep that here I take
While in Christ's arms I do awake
When shall our happy Souls rejoyce
To hear our Blessed Saviours voice.

Location: East side of Milton Road about 600 feet south of Playland Parkway.

Dates of Activity: c.1750 – c.1931.

Other Names: City of Rye Cemetery, Milton Cemetery, Old Rye Cemetery, Rye Public Cemetery.

Inscriptions: *WCHS* Books #15 (p.52-58) and #34 (p.261-283).

Notes: Rye's public burial ground was created as a place for interment for all residents of the town, regardless of creed. As none of Rye's Colonial-era churches had a burial place for their congregants, those residents who did not have a family graveyard of their own chose to use the Blind Brook Burial Ground as a resting place for their loved ones. The Reverend Charles W. Baird of the Rye Presbyterian Church described the history of the burial ground as well as its physical appearance as he saw it in 1871:

126

The visitor on his way to our Beach may notice at the turn of the road above Milton, the little burying-ground by Blind Brook; not as differing from other country grave-yards in its aspect of seclusion and neglect, but for the quiet beauty of the scene in which it lies. Just here the outlet of the stream, whose meanderings have proceeded through the low meadow lands, becomes visible toward the south, and the waters of the Sound appear beyond the higher banks that skirt the creek. It is a spot well chosen for its suggestions of rest and of hereafter. The oldest legible inscription in this cemetery is to be found on a tombstone near the entrance. It reads thus:

Here
Lyeth the Body of
Nehemiah Webb
Son to the Rev^d M^r
Joseph Webb of Fairfield
who Dyed at Rye April y^e
22^d A^d 1722 In the 28 Year
of his Age.

The preservation of this epitaph for so long a time is doubtless due to the fact that the face of the tombstone has become much inclined, so as to be sheltered from the weather. There are many time-worn slabs around it that are probably much less ancient, but their records cannot be deciphered.... The earliest mention of this burying-ground in our Town Records, occurs in a deed dated 1753. It speaks of "ye boring [burying] place in Rye neck," opposite a certain tract of land on the west side of the mill creek, which Samuel Purdy conveyed to his sons, Samuel and Caleb.... It seems likely that the Blind Brook Cemetery was laid out about the year 1750. An aged person has informed me that the land was given to the town for this purpose by Joseph Lyon, who lies buried here, and who died in 1761. The fact that older inscriptions, like that of Mr. Webb, are to be found, may be accounted for by the supposition that bodies were removed to this place from other localities, after the opening of a common burying ground. [5]

Above: The headstone (top) and footstone of Nehemiah Webb, 2007. The footstone is as tall as the headstone and contains the letters "N W" within a heart.

The Reverend Baird also mentioned an interesting entry from the records of the Town of Rye regarding the maintenance of this cemetery, which was the work of both humans and animals:

In 1761, "Jonathan Brown iuner [junior] is aloud [allowed]" by the town "the priviledge of pastring the Buring yard upon the Conditions that he mackes a Geat [gate] and Cuts the Brush and Keeps it Clear." This permission was renewed yearly until 1770.[6]

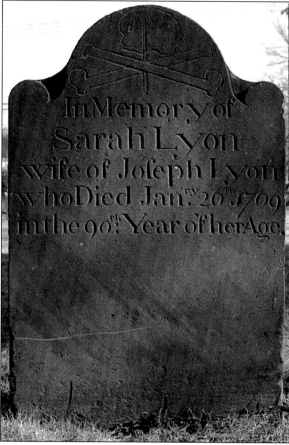

Above and Bottom Right: The photo at top left depicts the damaged headstone of Joseph Lyon, the gentleman who donated the land for the Blind Brook Burial Ground. Note the elaborate borders along the edges of the tombstone as well as the soul effigy at the top. Near Mr. Lyon's tombstone is that of his wife, Sarah (top right), which features a skull, crossbones and arrow (bottom right). Photos courtesy Gray Williams.

In Memory of
M^r. JOSEPH LYON
Who deceased
February 21st
A.D. 1761
in the 84th year of
his age.

In Memory of
Sarah Lyon
wife of Joseph Lyon
who Died Jan^{ry}. 26th 1769
in the 90th Year of her Age.

The northwest portion of the Blind Brook Burial Ground is occupied by an enclosed plot belonging to the Halsted family. Among those buried in this plot is Ezekiel Halsted, who owned the Knapp house across the street from the cemetery from 1749 to 1757 and went to his grave "after a fall from a tree" at the age of 49.[7] Gradually, the use of the cemetery declined in the 19th century following the establishment of Christ Church and Greenwood Union cemeteries in Rye. However, the cemetery proved to be useful to the government of Rye as a cemetery for indigent persons. A 1934 article in the Mount Vernon *Daily Argus* stated that the "Town of Rye has used [this] burial place as a 'Potter's Field' on occasion, as recently as 1931."[8] The cemetery is well maintained today, and the Rye Historical Society has placed small markers that identify the name of the deceased, as well as his or her years of birth and death, in front of each of the older tombstones.

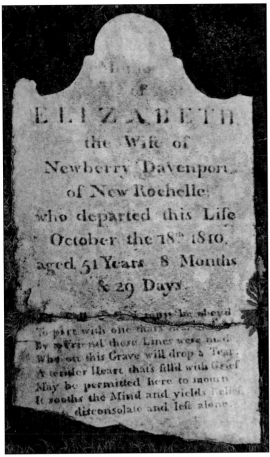

Top Left and Top Right: These two marble tombstones now lie on the ground in the Blind Brook Burial Ground. The tombstone at top left was placed "In Memory of ELIZABETH the Wife of Newberry Davenport of New Rochelle, who departed this Life October the 18th, 1810, aged 51 Years 8 Months & 29 Days." The legible portion of Mrs. Davenport's epitaph reads:

> By a Friend these Lines were made,
> Who on this grave will drop a Tear,
> A tender Heart that's fill'd with grief
> May be permitted here to mourn;
> It sooths the Mind and yields Relief,
> ---- disconsolate and left alone.

The tombstone at top right marks the grave of Dr. Charles McDonald, a "Soldier of the Revolution," who died on September 12, 1841, at the age of 82 years, 11 months and 8 days. His epitaph reads:

> God my Redeemer lives
> And ever from the skies
> Looks down and watches all my dust
> Till he shall bid it rise.
>
> Arrayed in glorious grace
> Shall these vile bodies shine
> And every shape and ev'ry face
> Be heavenly and divine.

Above: This tombstone reads: In Memory of Eme Budd formerly the wife of John Sutton who Died Jan[ry] 24th 1771 Aged 59 Years. Photo courtesy Gray Williams.

129

Top Left and Top Right: James and Mary Hains buried their infant daughters Martha and Sibbey (top left) in the Blind Brook Burial Ground in 1769. Five years later, they buried another daughter, also named Martha, in the cemetery (top right). Right photo courtesy Gray Williams.

Here Lies
Martha & Sibbey
Infant Daughters of
James & Mary Hains
Obit Anno 1769

Here Lies
the Remains of Martha
Dau^{tr}. of James & Mary
Hains
who Died May 4th 1774
Aged 3 Years.

Bottom Right: This tombstone reads:

In
Memory of
SARAH,
Consort of Joseph H. Horton
who departed this Life
September 20th, 1816
aged 27 years and 1 month.

She is no more! In silence we express
Lo! Here she lies, her soul has gone to rest
She bid adieu to friends, triumph'd in pain
And said rejoice, we soon shall meet again

Photo courtesy Gray Williams.

Next Page: The photos at the top of the page depict the matching headstone (top right) and footstone (top left) of Anne Budd. Mrs. Budd was the daughter of Joseph Lyon, the gentleman who donated the land for the Blind Brook Burial Ground, and his wife, Sarah. Mrs. Budd is interred alongside her parents and her husband, Elisha. Elisha Budd was the son of Joseph Budd (the last person buried in the Budd Family Burial Ground in the City of Rye) and the brother of Underhill Budd (the first person to be interred in the Budd Family Burial Ground in Mamaroneck). Although only the base (bottom left) of Mr. Budd's headstone remains intact today, his footstone (which matches that of his wife) is still intact. The 1982 photo at bottom right shows the intact tombstone of Elisha Budd. Right column photos courtesy Gray Williams.

In Memory of
Mrs ANNE BUDD
Wife of
Mr. ELISHA BUDD
Who died
Dec 6th, 1760.

In Memory of
Mr ELISHA BUDD
who died Sept
y^{e} 21st 1765
In the 60th year
of his Age.

130

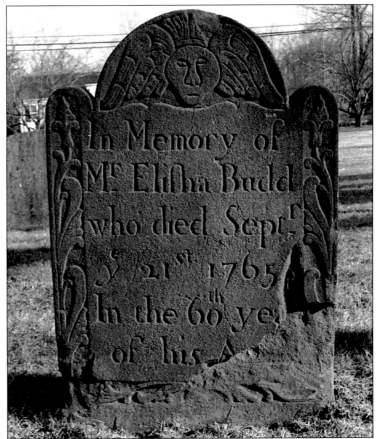

131

Budd Family Burial Ground
Rye City

Above: Looking at Hen Island from the shore of the Marshlands Sanctuary in 2009. During the time that the Budd family owned this land, Hen Island was accessible from the mainland by a sand bar which appeared at low tide. Therefore, the family did not need to use boats to visit their burial ground on the island.

Location: At an unknown part of Hen Island.

Dates of Activity: Early 18th century.

Notes: John Budd, "one of the first planters" of New Haven, Connecticut, purchased a piece of land that would become known as Budd's Neck from the Indians in 1661. Budd's Neck included the land between Guion Creek, Beaver Swamp, and Blind Brook.[9] Although John was not able to obtain a royal patent for this land, his grandson Joseph Budd (1669-1722) was awarded one in 1720. Following his death two years later, Joseph was interred in a plot on Hen Island, a piece of land which is located just west of Milton Point and separates Mamaroneck and Milton harbors.[10] Joseph's son John Budd sold his 250-acre portion of Budd's Neck to Peter Jay, father of John Jay, on March 26, 1745:

> ...except[ing] and always reserve[ing] out of this present grant...the liberty and privilege to and for John Budd and his heirs [the right of way] in and to the said premises at seasonable and reasonable times to the usual burial place on the said premises where his father is buried in order to bury the dead of his the said Johns family which said burial place contains by estimation a quarter of an acre of land, and is hereby declared and agreed to be and remain a burial place. [11]

According to Alison Beall, curator of the Marshlands Sanctuary, the Budd Family Burial Ground is located on Hen Island. Unfortunately, the exact location of this cemetery has been lost to history. Two of Joseph Budd's sons, Underhill (1708-1755) and Gilbert (1718-1805), were interred in the Budd Family Burial Ground in Mamaroneck. Another son, Elisha (c.1705-1765), is interred in the Blind Brook Burial Ground in the City of Rye.

Christ's Church Rectors' Burial Ground
Christ's Church Burial Ground and Tomb
Rye City

Above and Right: The tombstone (right) of the Reverend James Wetmore in Christ's Church Cemetery in 2008. Wetmore (above) led the parish at Rye from 1726 to 1760. As is alluded to by his epitaph, he was an ardent and frequent defender of his Church against the Quakers and "Dissenters" who competed for the attention of the residents of Rye.[12] In reporting the death of "this worthy clergyman," the *New York Mercury* noted that "in the important discharge of his ministerial office he was zealous, constant, and unwearied."[13]

> SACRED to the MEMORY of
> The Rev[d] M[r] JAMES WETMORE
> the late worthy learned & faithful
> minister of this PARISH of RYE
> for above 30 Years, Who having
> strenuously defended the Church
> with his pen & adorned it by his life
> & Doctrine, at length being seized
> by the Small-pox, Departed this
> Life May 15 1760 AEtatis 65.
> Cujus memoriae sit in
> Benedictione sempiterna.

Location: The Christ's Church Rectors' Burial Ground (A) was accessed through a right-of-way leading from present-day Walnut Street (B) about 128 feet south of present-day Orchard Avenue (C). Christ's Church itself is located at the northwest corner of the intersection of Milton Road and Rectory Street.

Dates of Activity: Rectors' Burial Ground, 1758 – 1837; Christ's Church Burial Ground and Tomb, 18th century.

Removed: The interments in the Rectors' Burial Ground were removed to Christ Church Cemetery (Lots 5 and 6) in 1893 while the land which surrounded it was being subdivided for residential development.

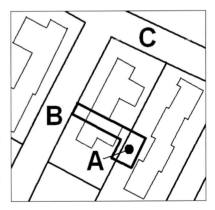

Inscriptions: See G.H. Van Wagenen. "Inscriptions From Tombstones in a Cemetery at Rye, Westchester County, N.Y." *The New York Genealogical & Biographical Record*, Vol.16 No.3 (July 1885) 137-138.

Notes: An active worship community in five different centuries, Christ's Episcopal Church traces its origins back to March 24, 1693, when the General Assembly of the Colony of New York created a parish "to have the care of Rye, Mamaroneck, and Bedford, &c."[14] The earliest known burials of persons identified with this congregation actually took place underneath the house of worship itself, as the Reverend Robert Bolton noted in his 1848 history of Westchester County:

> Beneath the floor of the church, lie pillowed in the darkness of the grave, the Rev. George Muirson, who died rector of this Parish in 1708, and his successor, the Rev. Christopher Bridge, who departed this life, A.D. 1719.[15]

A newly ordained minister when he arrived at Rye in 1705, the Reverend Muirson was instrumental in the construction of the first Episcopal Church in Rye in 1706. Fittingly, he was buried beneath the building following his death on October 12, 1708. The Cambridge-educated Reverend Christopher Bridge led the congregation at Rye from 1710 until his death on May 22, 1719. In reporting on his death, the *Boston News-Letter* noted that the Reverend Bridge was "a religious and worthy man, a very good scholar and a fine, grave preacher, his performances in the pulpit were solid, judicious, and profitable."[16] It appears that these two ministers were the only persons buried beneath the church. Today, the fourth church building, which was constructed in 1868, stands on the location of the original edifice.[17]

The Episcopal Church in Rye was officially chartered as Christ Church on December 19, 1764. Four years previously, a small burial ground had been established for the rectors of this parish. In 1885 G. H. Van Wagenen gave a short history and description of the Rectors' Burial Ground for the *New York Genealogical & Biographical Record*:

> In the village of Rye, Westchester County, N.Y., on the west side of Blind Brook, behind the store belonging to David Strang and now occupied by Charles Field, lies a small cemetery belonging to the Protestant Episcopal Church of Rye, and which from its secluded situation is not likely to attract the attention of passers-by on the highroad. Here rest five of the former rectors of the church, whose rectorships cover a period of about forty-five years in the history of this ancient parish. The plot of ground on which this cemetery is located formerly belonged to the Rev. James Wetmore, and was given by him to the parish church of Rye about the year 1759. This plot contained about twenty acres, and of this a small piece was set apart as a burial place for the rectors of the church.[18]

Right: The tombstone of Hannah Avery now lies flat on the ground in Christ's Church Cemetery in Rye. It reads:

SACRED
to the Memory of Mrs Hannah
late Consort of
the Revd Ephraim Avery
who having lived greatly
beloved, Died universally
lamented after six Weeks
excruciating Pain on ye 13th
Day of May AD. 1776 in y^{e}
39th Year of her Age.

Blessed are the Dead
who die in the Lord

134

The first person known to have been interred in the Rectors' Burial Ground was the Reverend Wetmore's grandson, whose tombstone featured "a figure curiously carved in the similtude of a cherub, surrounded with a rich foliated border" and read: "SACRED TO the dear Memory of JAMES, beloved son of Timothy and Jane Wetmore, who changed this Life for a better, Nov. the 25th, 1758, Aged 13 months and 4 ds."[19] The Reverend followed his grandson to the grave two years later.

In 1765 the young Reverend Ephraim Avery (1741-1776), a graduate of both Yale and King's colleges, was installed as the minister of the Rye church. Although his stepfather was the patriot General Israel Putnam, Avery remained a staunch supporter of the British crown at the outbreak of the Revolutionary War. Avery's wife, Hannah, died on May 13, 1776. Her obituary appeared in the *New York Gazette and Mercury:*

> On Monday the 13th Instant died at Rye, in the 39th Year of her Age, MRS. AVERY, the wife of the Revd. Mr. Avery, Rector of that Parish. She endured a most distressing Illness of six Weeks, with the greatest Patience, sustaining the most excruciating Pains without on repining Expression, and submitted to her Dissolution with the most placid Resignation to the Will of her heavenly Father, exhibiting a most striking Instance of that Fortitude in the most trying Scene, that human Nature is exposed to, which nothing but a well spent Life, and a firm Trust in the Mercies of God through the Redeemer of the Word can inspire.... By her Death the Husband and five Children are deprived of a most excellent Wife and Mother, and all her Acquaintance of a most sensible, agreeable, and cheerful Companion.

The Reverend interred his wife in the Rectors' Burial Ground and had a tombstone cut for her which mentioned the "six weeks of excruciating pain" which she had suffered. "On account of his political faith" and his "refus[al] to pray for the [Continental] Congress," the Reverend Avery "was subjected to persecution [and] destruction of his private property" as the Revolutionary War intensified."[20] The Reverend had also suffered a stroke shortly before his wife's death. These misfortunes were "supposed to have unbalanced his mind," and he was found dead with his throat cut, the result of either suicide or murder, on November 5, 1776.[21] Although he was apparently interred in the Rectors' Burial Ground, no tombstone has ever been found for this ill-fated minister.

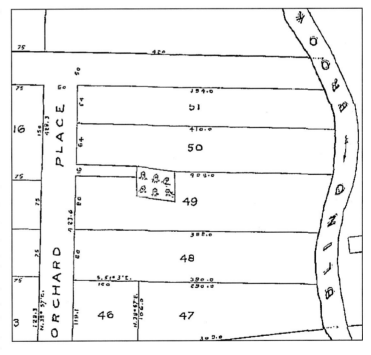

Right: This 1883 map, prepared for the subdivision of the Halstead estate, shows the location of the Christ's Church Rectors' Burial Ground just east of Orchard Place (now Walnut Street). Westchester County Clerk Map #679.

The Rectors' Burial Ground was used sparingly as an active graveyard for 77 years, with the last of the 11 interments in this small cemetery being made in 1837. Christ's Church sold the glebe to James D. Halsted through John C. and Laura Jay in 1846, "saving and excepting the burying lot fifty feet square...and also reserving the right of way for passing to and from the said burying lot."[22] Unlike the majority of the early houses of worship in Westchester County, Christ's Church did not have an extensive cemetery adjoining its parish holdings. A portion of the area which surrounds the church may have been used for a time as a place of interment. In addition to the tombstone of Mrs. Martha Marven (d.1767) which the Reverend Bolton found "in the wall on the west side of the church," Bolton noted that he had been "credibly informed" that "many other persons were interred near the church."[23] It appears that most of the parishioners were interred in the Blind Brook Burial Ground, and the Reverend Charles Baird of the Rye Presbyterian Church believed that "it [was] not probable that many persons were buried [in the churchyard], as the nature of the soil would render it unsuitable for this use."[24]

As the 19th century drew to a close, the Halsted family wished to sell their land for a subdivision. To do so, they arranged for the relocation of the interments in this small burial ground by purchasing two adjoining plots in Christ Church Cemetery on July 7, 1893.[25] Today, the stones from the Rectors' Burial Ground lie flat in the ground, a position that hinders the deciphering of the epitaphs, an unfortunate occurrence as these markers are among the largest Colonial tombstones in Westchester County. Among these stones is a footstone inscribed "MM 1767," a marker which is presumably the footstone of Martha Maven.

Above: The Reverend Ebenezer Punderson, who served as rector of Christ's Church from 1763 to 1764, was a native of New Haven, Connecticut, and was educated at Yale and King's College, now Columbia University.[26]

> Sacred to the Memory of the
> Rev[d] Ebenezer Punderson Late
> Missionary to the Rev[d] Society for
> ProPagating the GosPel in foreign
> Parts who Died 22 SeP A.D. 1764
> Being 60 Years of Age.

> With Pure Religion Was his SPrit fraught
> Practisd Himself what he to others Taught.

Right: This sandstone reads:

> Sacred
> To the memory
> Of Ann the Wife of
> Jacob Moore, of the
> City of Newyork who
> Fled from the Pestilence
> Raging in that city and
> who died and was Intered
> Here on the 26th day of
> September 1798 aged
> 33 years 22 days.

136

Above Left: This small stone reads, "M M 1767." It is probably the footstone of Martha Maven, who died in 1767. According to the Reverend Robert Bolton, Mrs. Maven's tombstone was located "in the wall on the west side of [Christ's] church." The tombstone read:

> Sacred to the Memory
> of Mrs. Martha Marven
> late consort of Mr. Lewis
> Marven, of Rye, who exchanged
> this life for a better, Feb'y 5th, 1767,
> in the 39th year of her age.
>
> Let us since life can little more supply–
> Than just to look about us and to die,
> Hope humbly, and with trembling pinions sore,
> Wait the great teacher, death, and God adore.

Above Right: The Reverend David Foote served as pastor of Christ's Church from 1790 until 1793. In his *History of the County of Westchester*, the Reverend Robert Bolton noted that Foote "was called from the field of labor to reap an eternal reward" following his "many judicious and efforts to restore order and promote both the spiritual and temporal prosperity of the Parish."[27] His tombstone reads:

> In memory
> of
> the Rev[d] M[r] DAVID FOOTE
> late Pastor at
> Rye & White Plains
> who departed this life the 1st of August
> 1793
> aged 32 years.
> Blessed are the dead who
> Die in the Lord.

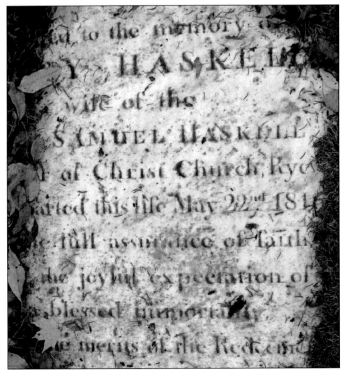

Left: The Reverend Samuel Haskell (1762-1845) served as rector of Christ's Church from 1809 to 1823. He interred his wife, Mary, in the Rectors' Burial Ground and had a tombstone cut with the following inscription:

> Sacred to the memory of
> MARY HASEKLL
> Wife of the
> REV. SAMUEL HASKELL
> Rector of Christ Church, Rye
> Departed this life May 22nd 1816
> In the full assurance of faith
> And the joyful expectation of
> A blessed immortality
> Through the merits of the Redeemer.

The portion which is not shown reads:

> Oh, Death, thou victor of this mortal frame,
> The race of Adam trembles at thy name
> How long shall man be doomed to dread thy sway
> And mourn for those whom thou dost take away.

The Reverend Haskell later served as rector of Trinity Episcopal Church in New Rochelle from 1823 to 1845. He is buried in the churchyard at that place.

Greenwood Union Cemetery
Christ's Church Cemetery
Rye City

Above: The Grand Army of the Republic plot in Greenwood Union Cemetery in 2006. The veterans' plot owned by the Town of Rye is visible in the background.

Location: South side of North Street between Locust and Theodore Fremd avenues.

Dates of Activity: Christ's Church Cemetery, 1837 – Present; Greenwood Union Cemetery, 1855 – Present.

Mailing Address: 215 North Street, Rye, NY 10580.

Notes: From its inception in the late 17th century until the late 1830's Christ's Episcopal Church had no suitable place of interment for its parishioners. The congregation was limited to the use of the Blind Brook Burial Ground and private family burial grounds as a result of the poor terrain on which their house of worship was located. In order to secure a more modern burial place for the congregation, James Barker and David Brooks donated a piece of land to the church on May 4, 1837. This parcel had been purchased from Benjamin Mead on the previous day. Christ's Church Cemetery was laid out to contain 141 burial plots for sale, "besides two stripes of ground on the easterly and westerly sides thereof, which are not divided or numbered and are set apart for the interment of poor persons."[28] These two free burial places were not available to all, as the deed for the property noted that the "Public Cemetery" was to be "for the burial of poor persons (not of Colour) who may wish to bury therein."[29] Additionally, the deed specified that 75¢ and 50¢ should be charged for the opening of large and small graves respectively, while no charge was to be made for interments removed to Christ's Church Cemetery from other burial grounds.[30] In September 1839 the Vestry of Christ's Church gave David Brooks the authority "to Sell Burial Plots in the New Cemetery."[31]

Christ's Church was not the only congregation which found the land next to Beaver Swamp to be an ideal place for a cemetery, as the Reverend Charles Baird wrote in 1871:

In [1855], the trustees of the Methodist Episcopal Church of Rye bought eight acres contiguous to [Christ's Church Cemetery]; and in 1864-68, they added more than six acres, making fourteen and a quarter in all. The grounds thus owned by the two congregations have been graded, enclosed, and laid out uniformly, with no visible separation between them; and they form one of the most beautiful cemeteries in this part of the country. To this spot many of our families have brought the remains of relatives buried in other localities; and here, too, many a stranger is borne from the city.[32]

Although this burial ground was incorporated as Greenwood Union Cemetery on November 23, 1855, the individual plots were actually sold by the Rye Methodist Church.[33] Over the next 50 years, the Methodist Church gradually opened four sections for burial. By the turn of the 20th century, the need to establish a more suitable burial ground for Rye and its surrounding area resulted in the reincorporation of Greenwood Union Cemetery on October 10, 1902. The Methodist Church transferred the cemetery lands to that corporation on November 21st of that year.[34] This new corporation embarked upon a lengthy upgrade of its property, transforming it into a modern rural cemetery. In 1912 the association reported on the work it had completed:

During ten years this corporation with its squad of men has toiled. Money has been expended with generous wisdom and foresight. No words are necessary to carry this message to the man who, having known the Cemetery then, sees it now. Here is a brief of our work. Fifty acres drained perfectly. Twenty acres graded. Ten acres top-dressed. Two miles of road built or reclaimed. New buildings erected. Old walls removed. Open land made gently-rolling grass knolls. New gateways, walls, entrances built. Shrubbery beds and trees planted for landscaping and forestation. Fifteen acres of old cemetery continually cared for. Entire property put under perpetual care.[35]

One of the most interesting plots in the cemetery is located south of the cemetery office and features an impressive statue of a Civil War soldier. Purchased by the Charles Lawrence Post of the Grand Army of the Republic in 1887, this plot serves as the final resting place of several veterans who belonged to that organization.[36] On the west face of the monument is a plaque dedicated to Newell W. Rising, a sailor who lost his life in the explosion of the USS Maine.[37]

Above: This plaque is visible in the photo on the previous page; it reads: "In Memoriam Newell W. Rising Son of Comrade Elihu Rising who lost his life on the U.S. Battle Ship Maine in the harbor of Havana Cuba February 15th 1898. May the rising sun for ever shine o'er a freed American main." Rising served aboard the Maine as a coal passer. A monument which features a shell raised from the ship was erected to his memory in Port Chester's Summerfield Park.

Immediately east of the GAR plot is a section purchased by the Town of Rye in 1940 "as a place of burial [for] the remains of veterans of the federal forces of the United States."[38] Today, Greenwood Union Cemetery contains 54 acres of land and continues to be a popular place of interment for the residents of the Sound Shore area. The cemetery is operated by "an independent, elected Board of Trustees" which consists of "lot owners and community leaders."[39]

Above Left: The tombstone at the grave of Mary L. Horton (1817-1841) was moved to Greenwood Union Cemetery from another burial ground. Note the image of a woman mourning at a monument beneath a weeping willow. A line at the bottom of the tombstone notes that it also marks the grave of Mrs. Horton's infant son.

Above Right: This tombstone in Christ's Church Cemetery reads: "In memory of Rev. Elisha Andrews, member of the M.E. Church who was lost from on board the steamboat Columbus on her passage up the Hudson River to Camp Meeting on the 6th of Sep 1845. His body was found on the 9th inst. and intered. Born May 4, 1800 near Glens Falls." The Reverend Andrews was interred in an Episcopal cemetery as the Methodists of Rye had yet to acquire a burial place of their own.

Bottom Left: The grave of Joseph Churchwell is located in the section of Christ's Church Cemetery reserved for "the interment of poor persons." The legible portion of the tombstone reads: "A member of Co. C, 49th Regt. N.Y.V. 6th Army Corps. Died July 18, 1864 of wounds received at the Battle of the Wilderness, aged 19 years & 8 mo's, having served his country faithfully for 2 years & 8 mo's. Our young hero gave his life to save his nation's honor. Heaven's treasure, too good for Earth. His last words were: Tell my Mother I will meet her in Heaven."[40]

Bottom Right: The monument over the grave of Captain John Hyer (c.1791-1866) features depictions of an anchor and a lighthouse.

Hart Family Burial Ground

Rye City

Location: The cemetery is surrounded by private property off of Norman Drive.

Dates of Activity: 1826 – 1856.

Other Names: Brevoort Cemetery, Emma Bizallion Plot.

Inscriptions: *WCHS* Book #17 (p.154).

Notes: Jonathan Hart, a native of Flushing, Queens, moved to Rye about the year 1685. Sometime after his arrival in Westchester, he married Hannah Budd, a daughter of John Budd, and acquired land in the present neighborhood of Greenhaven.[41] At some point thereafter, the Hart family established a burying ground on their property. Although the oldest surviving tombstone dates from 1826, it is possible that the cemetery is older. Jonathan Hart's great-grandson James deeded this burial ground to his descendants in 1830:

> I the said James Hart...sell unto ELIZA HART, of the City of New York, widow of my son PETER G. HART, deceased and unto MARGARET ANN BARKER, MARY ELIZA HART, ANTOINETT HART AND CORDELIA HART, their children and unto Benjamin Hart, John Hart, Betsey Hart, Sally Ann Hadden, daughter of Betsey Hadden, deceased my children and grandchild and to the survivor of them and the heirs and assigns of such survivors, ALL that certain piece of land used and intended for a Family burying place...near the dwelling house which I now occupy, bounded and butted as follows: namely lying off the southerly side of the turnpike and off the west of a lane leading therefrom to my dwelling house, and being about twenty two rods from said house, in a northwesterly direction and about twenty three rods from a barn standing on said lane in a southwesterly direction bounded as follows: BEGINNING at the southwesterly corner of the land hereby intended to be granted, between a flat rock and a large Apple tree thence running northerly three rods and a half; thence easterly three rods and a half thence southerly three rods and a half and thence westerly three rods and a half to the place of beginning.... The same shall be devoted to the purpose of a burial place for myself and my children and descendants and their relatives and to no other purpose whatever.... AND furthermore I do grant unto the grantees above named to have and use the right of passage and repassing for the purpose of any burial over and upon the land and the land adjacent to the said Burial Place, with all their friends and connexions [sic] in carriages and on foot at all reasonable times to and from the aforesaid burial place.[42]

Peter G. Hart's tombstone notes that he died on December 21, 1827, "in his 44th year at the Island of St. Croix in the West Indies where he had gone for the restoration of his health." Following his death, Mr. Hart's executors sold his 141-acre estate on November 14, 1838.[43] The cemetery was not extensively used by the Hart family, as only 12 people were interred there over a period of 30 years. The Hart estate became a part of Greenhaven, a garden suburb which was developed in the 1920s.

Jay Family Cemetery
Rye City

Above: The monument at the grave of John Jay on August 19, 1908. The inscription on this monument is given at right.

Location: Within the Marshlands Sanctuary near the eastern border of the reservation. The first 350 feet of the Marshlands Sanctuary entrance road coincide with the Jay Cemetery right-of-way. However, the cemetery as well as the remainder of the right-of-way are fenced-in and locked. The burial ground itself is located about 500 feet southeast of the Sanctuary's interpretive building.

Dates of Activity: 1805 – Present.

Inscriptions: *WCHS* Book #17 (p.66-71).

IN MEMORY OF
JOHN JAY,
EMINENT AMONG THOSE WHO ASSERTED THE LIBERTY
AND ESTABLISHED THE INDEPENDENCE
OF HIS COUNTRY
WHICH HE LONG SERVED IN THE MOST
IMPORTANT OFFICES
LEGISLATIVE, EXECUTIVE, JUDICIAL AND DIPLOMATIC
AND DISTINGUISHED IN THEM ALL BY HIS
ABILITY, FIRMNESS, PATRIOTISM AND INTEGRITY,
HE WAS IN LIFE AND IN HIS DEATH
AN EXAMPLE OF THE VIRTUES,
THE FAITH AND THE HOPES
OF A CHRISTIAN.
BORN DEC. 12, 1745;
DIED MAY 17, 1829.

Notes: The origins of the Jay Family Cemetery were recounted in a 1947 volume published by the members of the family of John Jay, the first Chief Justice of the United States Supreme Court:

> In 1745 [John Jay's father] Peter Jay (son of Augustus, the first Jay to come to America, in 1685) retired from business in New York City to live in the country. This move is believed to have been due to the threat of another smallpox epidemic in the city and to his desire to provide a country life for two of his

children who had earlier become blind through smallpox. He bought a farm of 400 acres in Rye, Westchester County. The farm remained intact through four generations until 1905 when the then heirs of the property sold it....

In the latter years of the 18th century, members of the family used to be buried in a family vault believed to have been at, or close to, the church of St. Marks-in-the-Bouwerie, near 10th Street and 2nd Avenue, New York City. But in 1805 the young son of Goldsborough Banyer, who married John Jay's daughter Maria, died and was buried in a lot in the "East Meadow" of the farm at Rye. A year later the father also died and was buried beside his son. This appears to have been the beginning of the Rye cemetery. Apparently, it was a definite decision, for a year later, in 1807, the remains of those who had been buried in the vault in New York City were brought to the same lot in Rye and there interred, but without individual grave stones; merely one stone having the inscription: *Remains from the Family Vault in New York 1807*. In 1808 and 1810 there were further burials; and in 1815 the remains of Peter Jay and Sir James Jay, brothers of John, were buried there. In 1815, John Jay upon inheriting the farm from Peter, set aside, as a family cemetery, the lot where these burials had occurred. He himself was buried there in 1829.[44]

In his 1853 article which described the Jay homestead for the book *Homes of American Statesmen*, William S. Thayer explained why John Jay preferred a cemetery to a church vault for his own burial:

> According to his expressed desire, the body of Mr. Jay was not deposited in the family vault, but committed to the bosom of the earth. He always strenuously protested against what he considered the heathenish attempt to rescue the worthless relics of mortality from that dissolution, which seems to be their natural and appropriate destination.[45]

Right: The original portion of the Jay Family Cemetery from the south end about 1886.

On December 21, 1815, John Jay transferred the burial ground to his son Peter Augustus Jay and nephew Peter Jay Munro as trustees in a deed which specified which persons may be buried in the cemetery:

> As and for a burial place for all and every of the descendants of my father and the said Peter Jay, deceased and for the husbands, wives and widows of such descendants and each and every one of them from time to time at his, her or their free will and pleasure to make such repairs and monumental fixtures to said burial place and to plant and replace such trees on the above described circumjacent ground and to do every such acts concerning the said burial place and ground.... And I do also for the consideration aforesaid further give and grant to the said Peter Jay Munro and Peter Augustus Jay, and their heirs forever a privilege or right of way over a road from the said burial ground of two rods wide, close along the easterly line of the said farm to the public highway, but on the special trust to permit all and every of the descendants to pass and repass by the said way or road to and from the said public highway and the said burial place...with attendants and horses and carriages of every kind, at his her or their free will and pleasure.[46]

The family history of the cemetery notes that two exceptions have been made to the rule of eligibility for burial: "In 1843 Judith Livingston Watkins, sister of Mrs. John Jay and an intimate in the Jay family, was buried in the cemetery. In 1810, before the cemetery trust was created, three children [from the Titford family], who were drowned in the Sound at the foot of the farm, were buried there."[47] The cemetery was maintained by the owners of the Jay estate following the deaths of Peter Jay Munro and Peter Augustus Jay in 1833 and 1843, respectively. However, the sale of the estate in 1904 necessitated the formation of a family cemetery corporation in 1906.[48] The incorporation of the Jay Family Cemetery provided that the burial ground and right-of-way "shall be maintained by three Trustees, each of whom shall be a descendant of Peter Jay, father of John Jay."[49] The heirs of John Jay transferred the graveyard and a right-of-way to that organization on February 15, 1906.[50] By the mid-1940s, most of the burial space within the original cemetery plot had been taken up. To expand the graveyard, Elizabeth S., Louise K., Susan and Mary R. Jay purchased a piece of property from the Devereux family on February 1, 1946. The size of the cemetery was more than doubled when they transferred this land to the Jay Family Cemetery on February 8th of the same year.[51] Today, the cemetery is still used and cared for by members of the Jay family.

Above: The Jay Family Cemetery on August 19, 1908.

Center Right: The Jay Family Cemetery in 1947. The monument at the grave of John Jay is visible at far right. The third and fourth tombstones from left in the front row mark the graves of John Jay's brother, Peter Jay (1734-1815), and his wife, Mary (1736-1821), respectively. The flat stone which is partially shaded by the bush at bottom right marks the interments which were removed from the family's vault in Manhattan in 1807.

Bottom Right: In 1946 the Jay family expanded their cemetery to its present size. This 1947 map shows the original cemetery lot in relation to the full size of the present cemetery.

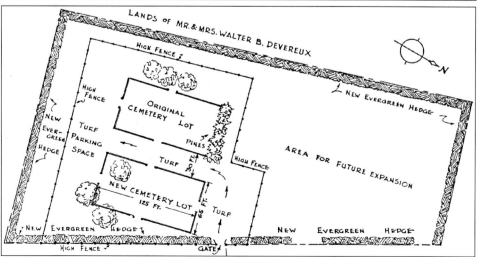

Miriam Osborn Memorial Cemetery
Rye City

Location: Between the New England Thruway (I-95) and the New Haven Line of Metro North Railroad. The cemetery (A) can be accessed by a tunnel which begins at the southeast corner of the intersection of Theodore Fremd Avenue and Garver Drive.

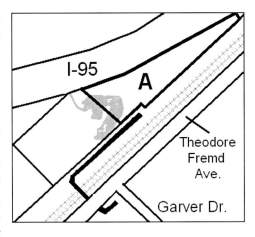

Dates of Activity: 1913 – Present.

Notes: The Miriam Osborn Memorial Home Association was established by Miriam Adelaide Trowbridge Osborn, widow of a wealthy Wall Street broker, when she bequeathed $675,000 "to establish a home for 'respectable women in needy circumstances.'"[52] The association purchased land at Theall's Hill for the home, which was formally opened on April 21, 1908.[53] In 1911 the Osborn Home began acquiring land between Greenwood Union Cemetery and the New York New Haven and Hartford Railroad to establish a burial ground for its residents. This property was later transferred to the Miriam Osborn Memorial Cemetery Association, an organization which had been incorporated on May 4, 1911.[54] The following description of the cemetery was provided by Helen C. Adams, a former executive superintendent of the home, and was included in a booklet published on the occasion of the institution's 50th anniversary:

The present cemetery was established west of the railroad, reached by an underpass, in 1913. Chauncey B. Garver, President of the Home since 1940, was one of the incorporators of the original cemetery. Mr. [John William] Sterling engaged the Presbrey-Leland Company to erect a shaft of one solid piece of Barre granite, one of the tallest monoliths in the country. The shaft is 50 ½ feet high, and bears the inscription secured by Mr. Sterling from Anson Phelps Stokes of Yale, who suggested: "In Loving Memory of the Founder and Beneficiaries of the Miriam Osborn Memorial Home."[55]

The first burial in the cemetery, that of Isabella Irwin, was made on January 7, 1916. The cemetery's size was significantly reduced when the Osborn Home sold a portion of it to Westchester County for the Pelham-Port Chester Parkway right-of-way. Although that roadway was not constructed, the New England Thruway was later built on that land. As a result, the cemetery is now wedged in between the highway and the New Haven Line of the Metro North Railroad. The cemetery is still occasionally used by the Osborn Home.

Left: The monument at the Miriam Osborn Memorial Cemetery in 2007. The New England Thruway is visible on the other side of the fence. The original monument "slipped from the rigging" and "broke into several pieces" while being put into place. At the time of its construction, the replacement was the "second-tallest cemetery monument...in the country."[56]

145

Purdy Family Burial Ground
Rye City

Above: The tombstone of Joshua Purdy (1721-1800) in the foreground is located next to a number of fieldstones which mark the earliest interments in the Purdy Family Burial Ground.

Location: Alongside Blind Brook at the northeast corner of Disbrow Park.

Dates of Activity: c.1768 – 1847.

Inscriptions: *WCHS* Book #17 (p.72).

Notes: Joseph Purdy (c.1652-1709), a native of Fairfield, CT, settled in Rye in the late 17th century. There he served in the governmental posts of justice of the peace, supervisor of the Town of Rye, and member of the New York General Assembly. In his will, Joseph's son, Daniel (c.1685-1768), one of the patentees of Budd's Neck, reserved a burial ground for his family: "I will and order that the Burying Place on the neck shall be and remain as a burying place for ever for the use of our family and relations, with full liberty to go [to] and from the same, to bury their dead."[57] Throughout the 18th and 19th centuries, the Purdy family maintained ownership of their ancestral estate, a parcel of land bounded roughly by present-day Playland Parkway, Oakland Beach Avenue, Boston Post Road, and Blind Brook. However, the family ceased using their burial ground after the interment of 62-year-old Jonathan Purdy in 1847. In 1848 the Reverend Robert Bolton mentioned the Purdy Family Burial Ground in his history of Westchester County:

> The Purdy estate is situated upon the eastern shore of Rye neck bordering the Blind Brook. A short distance from the house is the burial place of the Purdy family. Among other memorials is the

146

following: In Memory of JOSHUA PURDY who departed this Life March 4th, 1800 in the 79th Year of his age.

By the time the Reverend Charles W. Baird visited the Purdy Family Burial Ground in 1871, many of the older inscriptions had already been lost to the elements:

> The Purdy family have a burying-ground on the western bank of Blind Brook Creek, opposite the public cemetery. This is probably one of the oldest places of interment in Rye. It contains many antique memorials of past generations; but the imperfect records of their names have been worn away by time, and none prior to the present century are now legible.[58]

The oldest inscribed tombstone in the cemetery, a sandstone which marks the grave of Daniel Purdy's son Joshua, dates from 1800. However, the plot contains a number of simple fieldstones which mark the graves of the earliest members of the Purdy family. Unfortunately, maintenance of the Purdy cemetery lapsed, as *The Daily Record* noted in 1981:

> Rye City officials take good care of the Rye Public Cemetery on Milton Road at Mayfield Street, but purposely do not trim the dozen-grave Purdy family cemetery across Blind Brook, in Disbrow Park. "It's just a strategy," said Harold Cook, Rye parks and trees foreman. Since the Purdy cemetery is out of view and away from homes, it attracts vandals and teen-age beer parties. This would be truer if the cemetery were kept up, Cook said. Many of the cemetery's stones have been knocked over or damaged, Cook said.[59]

This policy of neglect has since changed, and today, the Purdy Family Burial Ground is kept free of overgrowth and can be accessed by the bridge at the rear of the Blind Brook Burial Ground or through Disbrow Park. Several small stone markers containing the names and dates of birth and death of the deceased have been placed by the Rye Historical Society at the identifiable graves in the Purdy Family Burial Ground.

Above: Looking north from the entrance to the Purdy Family Burial Ground in 2007. The plaque on the stone in the left foreground was placed by Purdy family descendant Louis Haight in 1969.[60] The plaque reads:

THE PURDY BURYING GROUND
PRE-REVOLUTIONARY PLACE OF INTERMENT
OF ONE OF RYE'S EARLY FAMILIES.
THIS TRACT OF LAND WAS PURCHASED
BY JOSEPH PURDY FROM JOHN BUDD
IN 1685.

Rye Presbyterian Churchyard

Rye City

Location: The churchyard, which consisted of two family vaults and a single grave, was established behind the 1841 church (visible on lot A on the map at right). Today, the churchyard, which contains no above ground markers, is located on the lawn between the present 1872 church and Boston Post Road.

Dates of Activity: 1834 – 1909.

Notes: A Presbyterian congregation had existed in Rye before the Revolutionary War. However, "at the close of that conflict," the members of this congregation "were very few and feeble."[61]   In 1793 the Presbyterians acquired a quarter-acre parcel on the Boston Post Road, and they constructed a church, although the congregation was so limited that this edifice was primarily used by a Methodist society from 1811 to 1828.[62]   This situation changed "by the efforts of Mr. Ebenezer Clark, a merchant of New York who came to Rye in 1821" and reclaimed the church building for the Presbyterians.[63]   In 1841 the congregation constructed a new church at the corner of the Boston Post Road and Parsons Street.   This

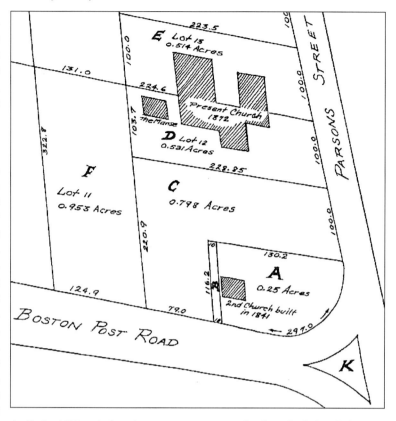

building was used until the present church was built in 1872.   A few interments were made directly behind the 1841 building, as Ellen Cotton McKay noted in her 1957 history of the church:

> [Ebenezer Clark] was buried in the Clark family vault. On the church grounds, between the present church and the street, are two family vaults, one of the Clark family and one of the Parsons family (Catherine Ann Clark married Arthur Wellesley Parsons in 1840), and the grave of David Remington. These were back of the church built in 1841, which stood close to the street. The remains of a member of the Clark family (probably Annie Knower Clark) were removed and buried in the plot in [Greenwood] Union Cemetery in November, 1896. These are all the known interments in the church yard.[64]

These vaults may have been established about the time that the 1841 church was constructed. Two interments in the Clark vault, those of Ebenezer's children Daniel (1799-1803) and Catherine Ann (1809), predate the construction of that church. Therefore, it is likely that their remains were removed from another resting place.[65] The Reverend David Remington (1797-1834), who had had charge of the Rye Presbyterian Church for "about twenty months" at the time of his death, was interred near the Clark and Parsons vaults. According to Mrs. McKay:

> …[Remington] died suddenly [on] January 24, 1834. He was buried in the church yard and his is the only single grave there. It cannot now be located, but is in front of the present church. "His remains now repose, awaiting a joyful Resurrection near the site of the pulpit in which he so faithfully labored." The inscription read:

> THE GRAVE OF
> DAVID REMINGTON
> WHO DIED JANUARY 25, 1834
> THE 39TH YEAR OF HIS LIFE
> THE 2ND OF HIS PASTORAL CHARGE
> OF THIS CHURCH

> EXAMPLE IN WORD, IN CONVERSATION, IN CHAIRTY
> IN SPIRIT, IN FAITH, IN PURITY.[66]

Saint Mary's Cemetery
Rye City

Above: This monument, which contains a stained glassed window depicting the risen Christ, is located in the southeast portion of Saint Mary's Cemetery.

Location: Northeast corner of the intersection of South Ridge and High streets.

Dates of Activity: 1870 – Present.

Other Names: Rye Catholic Cemetery.

Mailing Address: 1 High Street, Rye Brook, NY 10573.

Notes: Saint Mary's Cemetery was founded as the burial ground of Our Lady of Mercy Church in Port Chester. The origins of this church were discussed by the Reverend Charles Baird in Scharf's *History of Westchester County, New York*:

> In 1834 the few Roman Catholics of Port Chester congregated for the first time, for religious purposes, in a private house. This they continued to do for several years, visited occasionally by priests from Harlem, Westchester and New Rochelle. About the year 1846 they purchased a small frame building on Main Street, which they used as a church until 1852...[when] the old church, which had become too small, was sold, [and] a new site was bought and the present church, named "Our Lady of Mercy," was built upon it.[67]

To provide a suitable cemetery for the growing Catholic population of Port Chester, Archbishop John McCloskey purchased 10 acres on Ridge Street from Martin Dowling on December 14, 1870.[68] As with most Catholic graveyards in Westchester County, the earliest interments here were of Irish and Italian immigrants. By the early 1940s, the Catholic population of the Port Chester area had grown to the point that more burial space was needed. The Church of Our Lady of Mercy acquired a parcel on the east side of the cemetery on August 1, 1945, and that enabled the parish to nearly double the size of their burial ground.[69] As most of the plots in the cemetery have been sold, a large mausoleum has been opened at the northwest corner of the burial ground. Among the local notables interred at Saint Mary's is Nicholas Fox, a member of the 28th Connecticut Infantry who was awarded the Medal of Honor for "making two trips across an open space, in the face of the enemy's concentrated fire," to "secure water for the sick and wounded" at the Siege of Port Hudson during the Civil War.[70]

Theall Family Burial Ground
Rye City

Right: Most of the removals from the Theall Family Burial Ground were reinterred in Greenwood Union Cemetery. The tombstones were laid flat on the ground in the open area next to the monument in the foreground, and are now covered by grass and soil.

Location: Formerly in the vicinity of the intersection of Boston Post Road (Route 1) and Old Post Road.

Dates of Activity: c.1803 – 1855.

Removed: To Greenwood Union Cemetery (Section A, Lots 339-341) in the City of Rye sometime after 1871. Two other Theall plots are located in Greenwood Union Cemetery. Thomas Theall's son, Billa, and his descendants are buried in Section A, Lot 183, while several other Thealls who lived in Rye during the early 1800s are buried in Section A, Lot 257. It is not known whether or not the Thealls interred in these plots were removed to Greenwood Union from the Theall Family Burying Ground.

Notes: This burial ground is only briefly mentioned by the Reverend Charles Baird in his 1871 history of Rye: "The THEALL burying-ground is on the property of Mr. Abraham Theall."[71] Maps and land records indicate that the Theall family owned a large amount of property on either side of the split of Boston Post Road and Old Post Road, with the home of Mr. Theall being located about where the present driveway to the Osborn Home turns off from the latter street. The Theall property was considered quite valuable, as it is said that Joseph Bonaparte, the former King of Spain and brother of Napoleon, considered purchasing the land when he came to America in 1815.[72] The first written mention of this burial place is found in the will of Thomas Theall, a document which was probated on February 1, 1832. In passing his land to his children, Mr. Theall "reserve[ed] nevertheless for the purposes of Interment the Burying Ground for my Family and their Descendents forever."[73] The interments and tombstones in the Theall Family Burial Ground were removed to Greenwood Union Cemetery for reasons unknown sometime in the late 19th century. A significant portion of Thomas Theall's property presently comprises the land on which the Osborn Home is located.

Town Field Burying Ground
Rye City

Location: Formerly in the vicinity of the northeast corner of the intersection of Milton Road and Apawamis Avenue.

Dates of Activity: pre-1860.

Notes: According to the Reverend Charles Baird, this burial ground was still in existence in 1871:

> In olden times the colored people of Rye had a place of interment in the Town Field, on the property now owned by Mr. Anderson…. [This plot] contains a number of humble, unchronicled graves."[74]

The Town Field comprised "all the space between Grace Church Street on the north and Milton Road on the south" and served as "the common pasture ground where cattle were permitted to run at large."[75] In 1867 the Anderson property was located on the east side of Milton Road on the north side of present-day Apawamis Avenue.[76] Traces of the burial ground remained into the early 20th century, as John Quirk, a "Rye post office employee [and] life[long] resident" of the area, told historian Allison Albee that "a lone grave used to be seen at the south side of Midland Ave. in Rye a few hundred feet east of the junction with Apawamis Ave."[77] The Town Field Burying Ground was abandoned after the Rye African Cemetery opened, and was apparently destroyed during the development of this area into a residential neighborhood.

Town of Rye

Above: The tombstones in these two plots in Greenwood Union Cemetery in the City of Rye were removed from their original locations in small family burial grounds. The plot in the top photo contains the removals from the Merritt Family Burial Ground on Hog Pen Ridge. The large monument at the left commemorates Daniel and Rebecca Merritt, while the smaller monument at the far right marks the graves of Daniel E. and Emma Merritt. The bottom photo depicts the headstones of Mary (1776-1849), Caleb (1850-1827) and Hannah Sniffen (1747-1829), which were originally located in the Sniffen Family Burial Ground.

Brown-Sands Family Burial Ground	152	Merritt Family Burial Ground, Hog Pen Ridge	163
Brundage Family Burial Ground	153	Merritt Family Burial Ground, Lyon's Point	164
Gedney Family Burial Ground	156	Merritt-Pine Family Burial Ground	165
Griffen-Rogers Family Burial Ground	158	Port Chester Presbyterian Church Cemetery	166
Guion Family Burial Ground	160	Sniffin Family Burial Ground	168

Prior to 1942, the present City of Rye was part of the Town of Rye. Therefore, the town's community cemetery, the Blind Brook Burial Ground, is no longer within the limits of the municipality. Three of the family burial grounds in the town belonged to the Merritt family, all of whom were descendants of Thomas Merritt (b.c.1630). Unfortunately, few of the town's cemeteries are in their original locations. All of the Merritt burial grounds, as well as the Port Chester Presbyterian Church Cemetery and the Sniffin Family Burial Ground, were removed to Greenwood Union Cemetery between 1866 and 1931, while the Brundage Family Burial Ground was relocated a few hundred feet west of its original location in 1965 to make room for Port Chester Middle School's baseball field. Additionally, the town's four burial grounds which are still in their original location have suffered from neglect and vandalism. Many of the tombstones in the Gedney Family Burial Ground have been broken and removed from their original locations, while all of the headstones in the Griffen-Rogers Family Burial Ground were stolen in the mid-20th century.

Brown-Sands Family Burial Ground

Rye Town (Port Chester)

Location: On the north side of Indian Road at its intersection with Puritan Drive. Please note that the cemetery is surrounded by private property.

Dates of Activity: 1808 – 1906.

Other Names: Sands-Brown Burying Ground.

Inscriptions: *WCHS* Book #15 (p.58-59), #17 (p.81-82), #33 (p.243-244) and #34 (p.351-353).

Notes: Brothers Hachaliah and Deliverance Brown arrived in the Town of Rye from Stamford, Connecticut, sometime after 1715.[1] The Browns built a house in 1740, which still stands today on the east side of Browndale Place about 400 feet south of Indian Road.[2] Samuel Brown (1722-1811), a grandson of Deliverance Brown, founded the graveyard when he buried his wife, Amy (1730-1808), on the family's farm in a plot about 800 feet west of King Street. Samuel's son, Nehemiah (1771-1851), set out the boundaries for this cemetery in his will:

> At the death of my said wife Ann I order the said homestead or farm to be sold at the discretion of my executors (reserving a place for a burial spot for my family and the descendants of my father of eighty feet in an easterly and westerly direction and sixty feet Northerly and Southerly where the bodies of my father and mother are laid).[3]

The cemetery is generally referred to as the Brown-Sands Family Burial Ground, as Samuel Brown's granddaughter Hannah (1801-1885) is buried here alongside her husband, Elisha Sands (1792-1860), and three of their children. The Brown family used the cemetery until they sold their estate to the Clark & Palmer Realty Company for subdivision in 1906.[4] An article which appeared in the *Westchester County Magazine* during the early 20th century told the story of Cuff Brown, who is buried here along with his wife, Ann, and an unnamed daughter:

> In the old Brown burying ground just off of King street, in the Village of Port Chester, is to be found a series of headstones bearing unusual inscriptions…. Among them is one to a negro slave reared in the family of John Brown and known as Cuff Brown. The full inscription follows:

> CUFF BROWN
> Born
> November, 1799,
> Died
> March 4, 1872.
> Bred in the family of the late
> JOHN BROWN.

> The grave may easily be found near the south wall of the family burying ground, which is now included in the tract known as Colonial Ridge, recently developed as a residential section for high-class homesites. Beautiful views of Long Island Sound may be had from the adjacent property.[5]

The Brown-Sands Family Burial Ground appeared in the news when a trio of Boy Scouts sought to clean up the cemetery in 2004. By that time, the neglected graveyard was much in need of repair, as the *New York Times* noted:

> It was hidden behind four houses and buried under a jumble of weeds and vines. Trees felled by storms and old age had toppled tombstones, their inscriptions faded by centuries of wind and rain.[6]

The scouts were permitted to clean up the cemetery after some legal wrangling. Although the cemetery is visible from Indian Road, it is located on private property and cannot be accessed without permission.

Brundage Family Burial Ground
Rye Town (Rye Brook)

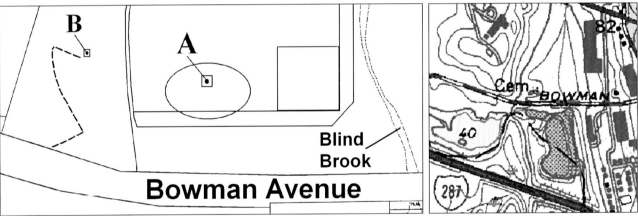

Top: Looking east at the enclosure which contains the tombstones from the Brundage Family Burial Ground in 2008.

Location: The Brundage Family Burial Ground was originally located (A) about 110 yards west of Blind Brook and 40 yards north of Bowman Avenue on a ridge that was excavated to create the playing fields for Port Chester Middle School. This site is now occupied by the left field area of the baseball field. In 1965 the cemetery was removed to a plot (B) on the ridge which overlooks the field. This plot can be accessed by a path denoted by the dotted line. The topographical map at right indicates the location of the cemetery prior to its removal.

Dates of Activity: Pre-1741 – c.1801.

Other Names: Bowman Cemetery.

Inscriptions: *WCHS* Book #33 (p.241) and #34 (p.285).

Notes: John Brundage (or Brundige), who was "referred to as 'Stout Old John,'" came to Rye from Massachusetts in the late 17th century. "One of the original founders of Rye," John served his municipality from 1678 to 1693 as its first town clerk.[7] Upon his death, he was interred in a plot on his property just west of Blind Brook. His land was then split among four of his sons. His youngest son, Joshua, apparently received the land on which the family burial plot was located. Joshua's son, also named Joshua, retained the use of this burial place when he sold his land in 1741. This transaction was mentioned by the Reverend Charles W. Baird in his description of the cemetery as he saw it in 1871:

The earliest allusion in our records to a family burying-ground is in a deed of 1741, from Joshua Brundige, conveying his house and farm of thirty acres, on the corner of the Ridge Road and the road to Bloomer's mill.... The deed in question excepts and reserves:

The liberty of a burying place at the southwesterly corner of said premises for the burying of my family, where some persons are already buried.

This plot was to be two rods square. It lies on the north side of the road, nearly opposite Park's mill, and contains a number of graves, with dilapidated head-stones, upon most of which only here and there a letter can be made out. One half-buried slab bears the inscription: "R.B. 1771." This was probably Robert Bloomer, the third of that name, who lived in this neighborhood about the year 1765. Members of the Merrit[t] family are known to have been buried here, and many others. One well-preserved inscription is:

In
memory of
Nathaniel Brown,
who departed this life
April 10th 1801
in the 70th year of his age.[8]

Top Right: In this 1963 photo a newsman examines the headstone of Nathaniel Brown at the original site of the Brundage Family Burial Ground.

Bottom Right: The tombstone of Nathaniel Brown in 2008. Nathaniel Brown appears to have been the grandson of Hachaliah Brown, who, with his brother Deliverance, was the first of the Brown family to settle in Rye.[9]

The state of the burial ground greatly declined over the next 50 years after the Reverend Baird wrote his account. When the surrounding land was sold in 1920, the accompanying deed excepted "the unfenced graves and what *may* be an old cemetery plot."[10] Genealogist Francis Ferdinand Spies visited the plot on April 14, 1922, at which time he found Nathaniel Brown's headstone and a "rough field stone" marked "S.M. 1772," as well as "about 50 rough field stones all illegible."[11] Several years later, the Works Progress Administration survey of veterans' graves found the interment of John Merritt, a soldier of the American Revolution, buried among 10 identifiable graves in the graveyard. In 1963 the Board of Education of the Union Free School District #4 acquired a large parcel of land including the burial ground between Bowman and Westchester avenues for the site of a new middle school. Unfortunately, the board's plans for the site included the leveling of the small ridge on which the cemetery was located so that playing fields could be laid out.[12] After two years of legal maneuvering, the New York State Supreme Court granted permission to the Port Chester District 4 School Board to move the cemetery to its present location atop a ridge to the west of the Port Chester Middle School's baseball field.[13] Shortly before the removal, the Port Chester *Daily Item* reported on the status of the neglected burial ground:

The area is hard to recognize as a cemetery, due to acts of both nature and man. It is completely overgrown with weeds, trees and brush. Several graves have been dug open, and grave markers, dating back to the late 18th and early 19th centuries and badly weathered by time, have been broken and scattered over the wooded hillside, the work of unknown vandals over the years.[14]

In February 1966 work crews removed the grave markers to a small plot located about 50 yards west of the cemetery. The crews dug seven feet deep in the cemetery, but did not come across any bones. Two months later, however, a "dozen skulls and a few other bones" were uncovered about 150 feet from the cemetery site. These remains were reinterred beneath the relocated grave markers.[15] Today, the small burial ground is accessed by an often-overgrown trail marked by wood chips. The site contains a few fieldstones, Nathaniel Brown's sandstone marker, and a plaque that was placed at the site in 1966.

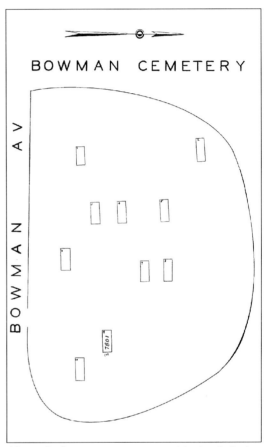

BOWMAN CEMETERY

Above: The tombstone of Nathaniel Brown stands at the head of a circle of fieldstones in the plot which contains the removals from the Brundage Family Burial Ground. The plaque at right reads: "HERE LIES THE REMAINS OF ROBERT BLOOMER "1771" NATHANIEL BROWN "1801" AND JOSHUA BRUNDIGE. THESE REMAINS WERE MOVED TO THIS SITE IN 1965 FROM ANOTHER LOCATION ON THE MIDDLE SCHOOL PROPERTY."

Above Left: This image appeared in the *Daily Item* on October 7, 1965. The caption read: "Final resting place for a tomb dating to the late 1700's is this vandalized grave in an old burial ground in Rye Town. Members of early Rye area families were buried in this hilltop site, now overgrown by brush and laid bare by vandals. Reporter Ron Patafio examines the nearly illegible inscription on the soft headstone."

Above Right: This map of the Brundage Family Burial Ground was made by the Works Progress Administration in the 1930s. Each rectangle denotes an identifiable grave, although there were probably many more that were not counted in this survey. The rectangle with the number 7801 at bottom center denotes the grave of Revolutionary War veteran John Merritt.

155

Gedney Family Burial Ground
Rye Town (Mamaroneck Village)

Above: The Gedney Family Burial Ground from the northwest corner in 2008. The F.E. Bellows Elementary School is visible behind the cemetery.

Right: The Gedney Family Burial Ground is marked "Cem" just above the center of this 1867 map. The property of the Hains family, who were related to Solomon Gedney, is marked on the east side of the cemetery.

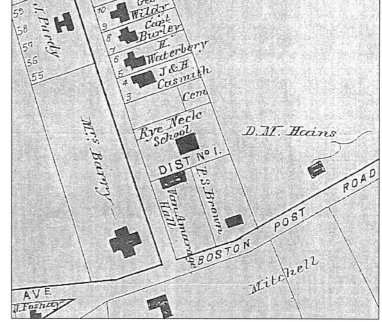

Location: Behind the F.E. Bellows Elementary School. The cemetery can be accessed by a driveway off of Barry Avenue (east side of the street about 440 feet north of the Boston Post Road). Please note that only foot access to the cemetery is available through this driveway.

Dates of Activity: c.1817 – 1947.

Other Names: Burying-ground east of Barry Avenue.

Inscriptions: *WCHS* Book #17 (p.48-49) and #78.

Notes: The first known interment in this cemetery was made in 1817 when Solomon Gedney (1769-1836), a great-grandson of Eleazar Gedney (founder of the Gedney Cemetery in the Town of Mamaroneck), allowed for the burial of Phebe Hains, the wife of his friend Peter Hains, in his family plot.[16] Although Solomon referred to members of the Hains family as his "friends" in the deed for this burial ground, they were probably relatives of his mother, Elizabeth Hains (1742-1801).[17] Additionally, the number of fieldstones in the southeast portion of the burial ground indicates that the cemetery may date from the 18th century. The land on which the graveyard is located was purchased by Solomon's grandfather, James (1702-

1764), in 1760.[18] Solomon and his wife, Amy Haight (d.1836), had a large and apparently upstanding family, as their son Jonathan noted: "I have seen Father, Mother, twelve children, and an uncle sit around the table at one time…. Another remarkable fact is that the twelve children were all temperate people."[19] Solomon reserved this burial ground from the sale of his 40-acre estate to his son David on June 1, 1824. On March 4, 1835, Solomon formally deeded the cemetery to his friends and descendants:

> I, SOLOMON GEDNEY, of the Town of Rye, in the County of Westchester, and State of New York, inconsideration of the NATURAL LOVE AND AFFECTION I bear toward the persons hereinafter named and for the securing to them and their heirs, the right of a place to bury their dead…forever quit-claim unto my sons Jonathan H. Gedney, Nicholas H. Gedney, David H. Gedney, Solomon Gedney, Alexander Gedney, Peter Gedney, William Gedney, and Benjamin Gedney, my daughters Charlotte Marshall, Elizabeth Fletcher and Sally Ann Rowles and to my friends George Hains, Elijah Haines, James Hains, Nicholas Hains and Alexander Seely and to their heirs forever…all that certain piece or parcel of land now made use of as a burial ground…to the above named persons and their heirs, to be made use of by them as a burial ground and for no other purpose. TOGETHER with a right of way from the Turnpike road to and from said Burial place for horses, carriages and footmen at all times and seasons whenever it may please any of the above named persons to visit said burial place or to carry any of their dead there to be buried without any let, suit, hindrance, or molestation.[20]

At least 37 persons were buried in this cemetery, including Solomon and Amy Haight Gedney, and their children Solomon (1806-1900), Alexander (1816-1843), Peter (c.1813-1835), William (1818-1846), Charlotte (1796-1870), Sally (or Sarah) Ann (1810-1895), and Susan (1808-1830), as well as their spouses and descendants. The cemetery was actively used by the Gedneys until the mid-20th century. Unfortunately, a number of the headstones in the burial ground have been damaged, broken, or removed from their original location in the six decades that have passed since the last interment.

Above: The broken headstone of Hester C. Gedney (1804-1847), wife of Nicholas H. Gedney, leans against the north wall of the Gedney Family Burial Ground and depicts a woman mourning at a grave between two weeping willows.

Right: The headstone of William H. Hains contains the symbol of a heart with an eye as well as three linked bands, the symbol of the Independent Order of Odd Fellows.

IN MEMORY
OF
WILLIAM H. HAINS
WHO DIED
March 21, 1851:
AGED
31 Years 7 Mo. & 26 Days.

Griffen-Rogers Family Burial Ground
Rye Town (Mamaroneck Village)

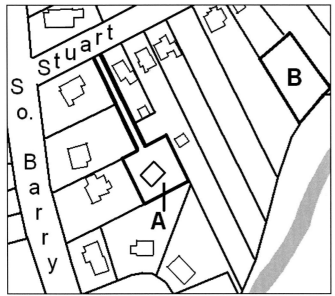

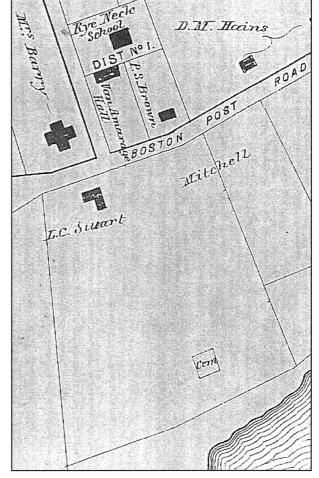

Right: The Griffen-Rogers Family Burial Ground is marked near the bottom of this 1868 map.

Location: The right-of-way to the Griffen-Rogers Family Burial Ground begins on the southern side of Stuart Avenue about 150 feet east of its intersection with South Barry Avenue, and is now used as a driveway for a number of neighboring homes. The parcel reserved for the cemetery (A) is 100 feet square. The small box within the burial ground marks the place where the interments are located. The cemetery is about 350 feet southwest of the Guion Family Burial Ground (B).

Dates of Activity: 1752 – 1853.

Inscriptions: *WCHS* Book #17 (p.50).

Notes: The Griffen family can be traced to the earliest days of the Town of Mamaroneck when Edward Griffen, a native of South Wales and resident of Oyster Bay, served as "an interpreter between the Indians and John Richbell in the purchase of the land" that presently comprises that municipality. Edward's grandson Benjamin moved to Mamaroneck from Flushing about the year 1711, at which place he married Mary Disbrow.[21] The first known burial in this cemetery, that of Sarah Horton, was made in 1752, while the first legal mention of this burial ground was made by Benjamin Griffen's grandson, John (1761-1797), in his will:

> I do also in addition to my said Will give and devise to my brother Benjamin Griffen Esquire and to his Heirs and Assigns forever in trust for all the family of my late Father Benjamin Griffen deceased one quarter of an Acre of Land situate in the corner of the old Orchard about the spot of ground where my son Jeremiah was intered for a burying place for the purpose of my brethren being all my Fathers family to Inter their dead in forever and also a priveledge of going to and from the said burying ground through my other lands in such place or places as shall be most convenient from Time to Time for the purpose of carrying their dead to be intered. Which said quarter of an Acre of ground I order my Executors first mentioned in my Will to measure out and set off for the purpose aforesaid as they shall think most convenient to my Estate and to my bretheren.[22]

Mr. Griffen's will bequeathed 30 acres of land to his sister, the widow Deborah Horton (1755-1833). This parcel comprised much of the land between the Boston Post Road and the body of water presently known as Guion Creek.[23] Mrs. Horton's daughter Esther married Dr. David Rogers, Jr. (c.1773-1841), who purchased his mother-in-law's estate for $4,000 in 1821, at which time the family cemetery was again mentioned:

...reserve of the use of a burying ground which is on said farm, with the full privilege of going to and from the same for the purpose of burying the dead of the family of the said Deborah Horton, her heirs and descendants forever and it is understood and agreed that said burying ground is not to be extended more than the one fourth of an acre.[24]

Above: A scattering of trees at the end of a driveway marks the location of the interments in the Griffen-Rogers Family Burial Ground.

Dr. David Rogers, Jr., was the son of David Rogers, Sr., a surgeon in the American army during the Revolutionary War who was "at the side of Generals Wooster and Gould when they fell at the battle of Ridgefield in the year 1777." According to Mamaroneck Village Historian Gloria P. Pritts, Dr. David Rogers, Jr. "aided in founding the Medical Society of Westchester County and was president of the society from 1817-1820. In March 1822 he was admitted to the Medical Society of the County of New York and served as treasurer, 1824-1825, and as president, 1835-36."[25] David L. Rogers, the son of David, Jr., served as Inspector-General of Hospitals during the Civil War. In this burial ground, David, Jr., interred the remains of his 28-year-old son Gilbert, who died in New York City from yellow fever in 1822. Catharine Wright Rogers, the wife of David L., was buried in this cemetery upon her death in 1852.[26] Dr. David Rogers, Jr., was interred here upon his death, and the burial of his widow, Esther Horton (c.1774-1853), was the last to be made in this cemetery.

On March 28, 1913, genealogist Evelyn Briggs Baldwin found 10 fully inscribed tombstones during a visit to this burial ground.[27] During the time that has elapsed since Mr. Baldwin made his list of inscriptions, the Griffen-Rogers cemetery has been all but completely lost to history. On September 23, 1942, the minutes of the Mamaroneck Historical Society noted that vandalism had occurred at the cemetery. When the society met again on the same day in the following year, they noted that "there was no evidence of any markers to be found."[28] In December 1991 Gloria P. Pritts found that "the following footstones were still in the cemetery: S.H., U.H., J.H.R., and G.H.R."[29] By 2000 none of these stones could be found. Today the northern half of the cemetery, as well as its right-of-way, are used as a driveway and parking area, while the southern portion, which is apparently where the interments were made, is largely overgrown and gives no evidence of having been used as a burial ground.

Guion Family Burial Ground
Rye Town (Mamaroneck Village)

Above: Looking southeast toward Guion Creek in the Guion Family Burial Ground in 2008.

Location: The cemetery (A) is located on the shore of Guion Creek behind 733 and 805 Stuart Avenue. It can be accessed by walking along Guion Creek from the parking lot (B) for the Continental View Apartments (1035 East Boston Post Road).

Dates of Activity: 1808 – 1908.

Inscriptions: *WCHS* Book #17 (p.62-64) and #81 (p.76-82).

Notes: The first member of the Guion family to reside in Rye Neck was John Guion, Sr. (1723-1792), a grandson of Huguenot immigrant Louis Guion.[30]

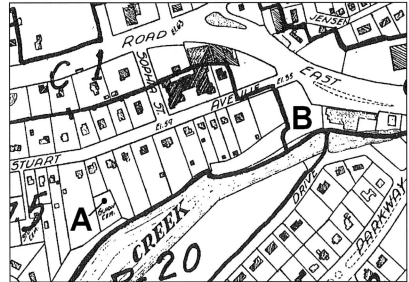

Although John was interred at the Huguenot Burying Ground in New Rochelle, his wife and descendants founded a shorefront burial ground on their property 16 years after his death. John, Sr.'s son, John Guion, Jr. (1762-1823), reserved this burying ground in his will:

> I do will order and direct my Executors & Executrix whenever they shall sell my landed `Estate to reserve a certain piece of ground which I have laid out for a burial ground bounded as the stone fence at this time stands on the east as wide as the bars above thence running a strait [sic] course or line to the fence of Deborah Horton which piece as above described I give and bequest unto my heirs forever as a burial ground for them and their heirs forever, with a right of passing and repassing to the same for the purpose of burying their dead.[31]

160

Above and Right: The c.1910 photo at right was taken looking west from the shore of Guion Creek at the Guion Family Burial Ground. The photo above, taken in 2008, depicts the cemetery from the southeast.

A portion of the area surrounding the cemetery remained in the hands of the Guion family until the executors of the will of Thomas Guion sold this land on June 6, 1896, reserving a "right of way over the said premises" so that the cemetery could be accessed.[32] As with many of the family cemeteries in Westchester County, the Guion Family Burial Ground was neglected as the descendants of those who were buried there moved away and became detached from their family history. The location of the burial ground overlooking Guion Creek, a setting which probably provided friends and relatives of the deceased an ideal view as they paid their respects at the graves of their loved ones, proved to be a mixed blessing, as overgrowth and an isolated situation contributed to the decline of the graveyard in the latter half of the 20th century. Mamaroneck Historical Society President Donald March described the condition of this cemetery as it appeared in 1987:

> It lacks even the most basic attention in terms of care. Overgrowth, a swamp bog, mosquitoes, debris, previously dumped cut limbs from trees, rotten vegetation, poison ivy, poison oak, tangled vines, weeds, litter, and rampant vandalism are what welcomes a visitor. Accessibility is next to impossible from any direction. Only with effort and patience can one negotiate any direction. Upon entry, however, one almost wishes they had not made the attempt in the first place. Upon close inspection, the stark reality of the amount of vandalism takes hold…. Head stones are scattered at random and some so badly shattered they probably cannot even be repaired or erected anew. A fence encircles the cemetery and appears to have likewise been allowed to fall victim to the deteriorating influences of negligence, time, and vandalism.[33]

The condition of the Guion Family Burial Ground has improved since Mr. March presented his report to the Mamaroneck Historical Society and various government officials, and the cemetery can now be accessed by following the wall along Guion Creek southwest from the parking lot at 1035 East Boston Post Road.

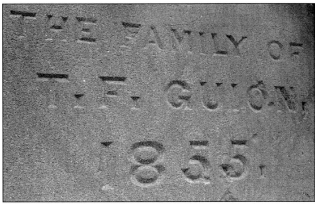

Above and Right: The 2008 photo at the top of the page depicts the northeast corner of the Guion Family Burial Ground. An inscription at the top of the vault (bottom left) notes that it was built in 1855 and contains the remains of the family of T.F. Guion. The monument at right is a cenotaph which reads:

TO THE
MEMORY OF
MARY F. NORTH
WIFE OF
J.H. NORTH,
AND ONLY DAUGHTER OF
T.F. & MARIA GUION,
DECEASED AT BELLAGIO,
LAKE OF COMO, ON THE
28TH OF SEPT. 1863,
IN THE 23RD YEAR OF
HER AGE
AND HER REMAINS THERE
BURIED.
ALSO TO THOSE OF HER
INFANT DAUGHTER
DECEASED AND INTERED
AT DRESDEN, SAXONEY.

Merritt Family Burial Ground, Hog Pen Ridge
Rye Town (Rye Brook)

Location: The cemetery (A) was formerly located on the west side of North Ridge Street just north of its intersection with West Ridge Drive. Its location is presently occupied by 274 and 278 Ridge Street.

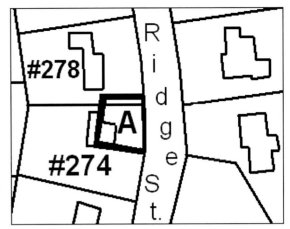

Bottom Right: Marked "Cem," the location of the Merritt Family Burial Ground can be seen near the bottom of this 1868 map. The house marked "D Merritt" just south of the cemetery no longer stands today. However, a circa 1750 saltbox house that once belonged to the family and is not depicted on the map still stands at 129 North Ridge Street.

Dates of Activity: 1836 – 1914.

Removed: To Greenwood Union Cemetery in the City of Rye (Terrace Acre Lots 36-39) in 1930. See photo on page 151.

Other Names: Daniel Merritt Cemetery, Ridge Street Cemetery.

Inscriptions: *WCHS* Book #15 (p.78), #17 (p.83), #33 (p.242) and #34 (p.287).

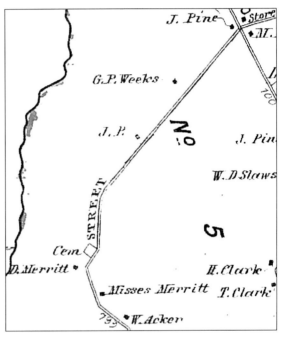

Notes: The first member of his family to settle in Westchester County, Thomas Merritt arrived in Rye in 1673 and purchased a piece of land on Hog Pen Ridge seven years later.[34] Present-day Ridge Street takes its name from Hog Pen Ridge, a geographical feature between that road and Lincoln Avenue "where settlers penned hogs to keep them out of town."[35] The Merritt family founded a burial ground on Hog Pen Ridge in 1836 when Thomas's great-great-grandson Daniel (b.1764) was laid to rest in a small plot on his farm. Over the next 78 years, Daniel Merritt was followed to the grave by his wife, Rebecca, his brothers Jotham and Nehemiah, at least seven of his children, and several other relatives. The area surrounding the cemetery remained in the hands of the Merritt family throughout its entire existence, and as a result, the burial ground was always well cared for. Genealogist William Eardeley found the burial ground to be "well kept" and "finely situated on high ground" during his visit to the plot about 1910.[36] The last burial in the cemetery occurred in 1914 following the death of Daniel E. Merritt (b.1846), a grandson of Daniel Merritt. Daniel E. Merritt wished that his family plot would be developed into a larger public cemetery, as the *New York Times* noted:

> The will of Daniel E. Merritt of Port Chester directed that upon the death of his sister, as a memorial, his large fortune be used to establish a public cemetery for the village. Mr. Merritt for nearly half a century lived practically as a recluse with his aged and incompetent sister, Emma.... Miss Merritt is 75 years old and has been an incompetent since she was about 20 years old.... [Mr. Merritt's will] directs that John S. Lyon, Sr., and John S. Lyon, Jr., who are named as executors, on the death of the sister must turn over to a Board of Trustees the residue of and income from the estate, which is estimated to be worth about $3,000,000, to establish and maintain "The Merritt Public Cemetery" on the Ridge Street farm.... People of Port Chester and vicinity may be buried there free of charge. If this cannot be done legally, Mr. Merritt directs that an act of Legislature be had to enable the Trustees to carry out his wishes.[37]

The board of trustees for this proposed cemetery was to be comprised of "the President of the Village of Port Chester and the pastors of the Methodist Episcopal, the Roman Catholic, Congregational and Baptist Churches."[38] This cemetery was not established, as a judge found that Mr. Merritt's estate only amounted to $11,000.[39] The individuals assigned as guardians for Emma Merritt purchased a plot in Greenwood Union Cemetery on November 3, 1930, to which the interments and headstones in the burial ground on Hog Pen Ridge were removed. This action was apparently taken to avoid any problems stemming from the construction of the Hutchinson River Parkway.[40]

Merritt Family Burial Ground, Lyon's Point

Rye Town (Port Chester)

Location: Formerly on the north side of the intersection of Traverse and Westchester avenues. The burial ground is marked "Cem" near the center of the 1867 map at right (just above the "S" in "Lyons Point").

Dates of Activity: c.1726 – 1847.

Removed: To Christ Church Cemetery in the City of Rye (Lot 36) in 1898.

Inscriptions: *WCHS* Book #15 (p.77).

Notes: John Merritt (1657-1726), the son of Thomas Merritt, purchased land on Lyon's Point in 1687. By the time of his death, John's property "extend[ed] on both sides of Grace Church St. to below Port Chester."[41] John's son Andrew (1689-1782) founded a family cemetery on this land when he buried his father in a plot overlooking the Byram River on what was then called Merritt's Point. In his will, Andrew set out the boundaries of this cemetery, which he willed to his son, Robert (1735-1817):

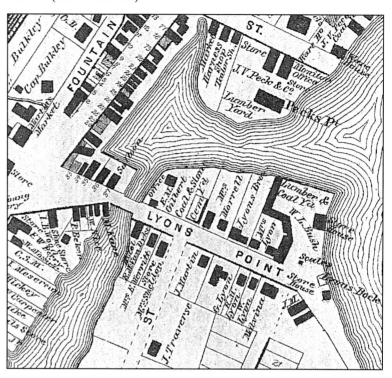

> Unto my son Robert…four rods square of my land about the graves on the north part of my land to go to him, about where the graves of my father and mother and former wife Rachel are buried; to be a burying place for myself, family and other relatives.[42]

In 1871 the Reverend Charles W. Baird of the Rye Presbyterian Church stated that "some of our older inhabitants remember[ed]" Robert Merritt, and "[spoke] of him as a man of sincere and consistent piety."[43] On August 21, 1801, Robert Merritt transferred an acre of land surrounding the cemetery to John Merritt, "deducting out of the said bounds four rods Square which is reserved for a burin' ground by my Father Andrew Merritt disceast."[44] Four years later, John Merritt sold the entire 54-acre Merritt estate to David Rogers, "excepting out of said bounds sixteen square rods for a Burying Place & for no other purpose to be used."[45]

When the Reverend Baird visited the cemetery in 1871, he found that "only the more recent names and dates in the cemetery [were] decipherable," with the "tomb of John Merritt, who died in 1759" being the oldest stone that could be read.[46] The last burial in the cemetery occurred in 1847, when Sarah Carpenter was interred there. By then, ownership of the cemetery appears to have passed to the Carpenter family. The area surrounding the Merritt Family Burial Ground began to feel the effects of development as the rural hamlet of Saw Pit became the thriving community of Port Chester in the

latter half of the 19th century. By the 1890s, the burial ground was surrounded on three sides by Congressman William Ryan's coal and wood company. After removing the interments to Christ's Church Cemetery, the descendants of Isaac Carpenter sold the burial plot to Congressman Ryan on April 9, 1898.[47] Unfortunately, the few remaining old tombstones that were brought to Christ's Church Cemetery have since sunk into the ground and are barely discernable, much less legible.

Right: The interments from the Merritt Family Burial Ground on Lyon's Point were removed to the empty space on the left side of this photo next to the Price family plot. The Prices were among those who sold the old cemetery to William Ryan in 1898. The location of several buried tombstones can be discerned at the plot.

Merritt-Pine Family Burial Ground
Rye Town (Rye Brook)

Above: The interments from the Merritt-Pine Family Burial Ground were removed to this plot in Greenwood Union Cemetery in the early 20th century. The two rows of rectangular markers on the ground behind the large monument mark these graves.

Location: Formerly on the west side of King Street at its intersection with Glenville Street.

Dates of Activity: Pre-1753 – 1890.

Removed: To Greenwood Union Cemetery in the City of Rye (New Addition Section, Lot #13) circa 1907.

Inscriptions: *WCHS* Book #15 (p.79).

Notes: John Merritt, a grandson of Thomas Merritt and an owner of property on both sides of the New York and Connecticut border, founded this cemetery in his will written in 1753: "Reserving ½ of an acre at the corner of the south half [of the land], joining to King street road and Stephen Stockholm's land, and to be square, to remain for a burying place for myself and family, and where some children are already buried."[48] Two of John's daughters, Sarah (b.1720) and Hannah (b.1725), married James and Samuel Pine, respectively. Both of these couples and several of their descendants were interred here.[49] The cemetery was used by the Pine family throughout the remainder of the 19th century. However, the interments in the graveyard were removed to Greenwood Union Cemetery about the time that Sullivan M. Pine sold the surrounding land to William W. Cook in 1907.[50] Unfortunately, none of the tombstones from the burial ground were removed to Greenwood Union Cemetery, and the re-interments are marked by flat, rectangular markers. Today, the site of the Pine-Merritt Family Burial Ground is occupied by the entrance to the Blind Brook High School campus.

Right: Identical, low rectangular stones such as this one at the grave of Samuel Pine (1722-1798) mark the interments of the persons whose remains were taken to Greenwood Union Cemetery from the Merritt-Pine Family Burial Ground.

Port Chester Presbyterian Church Cemetery
Rye Town (Port Chester)

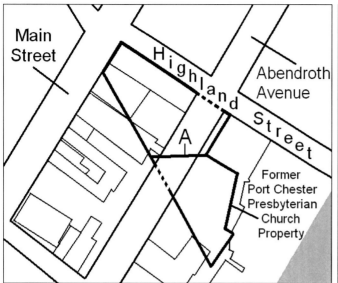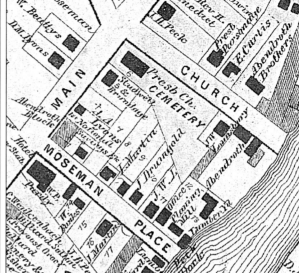

Above Right: The Port Chester Presbyterian Church and Cemetery are marked on this 1868 map.

Right: Looking east from Main Street at the Port Chester Presbyterian Church. The driveway in the foreground led to the cemetery.

Location: The Port Chester Presbyterian Church was located at the southeast corner of the intersection of Main and Highland streets. The portion of the church property on the south side of the line marked "A" was where the cemetery was located.

Dates of Activity: Pre-1808 – 1863.

Removed: To Greenwood Union Cemetery in the City of Rye (Vista Acre Lots 127 to 133 and 145 to 151) in 1931.

Inscriptions: *WCHS* Book #15 (p.59-60), #33 (p.245-246) and #34 (p.355-357).

Notes: This cemetery appears to have begun as a public burying ground for the residents of Saw Pit, a small community that has since become the Village of Port Chester. The oldest tombstone in this graveyard dated from 1810, although the county's land records indicate that this burial place was in use as early as 1808.[51] In 1830 the Presbyterian Church of the Town of Rye established a meeting house on the west side of this cemetery. On January 18, 1842, the land on which the church stood, as well as the cemetery, were formally donated to the Presbyterian Church of Port Chester by William Adee, who stipulated that the cemetery should be kept as a "burial ground for public use free from charge."[52]

The burial ground was seldom used after the opening of Greenwood Union Cemetery in 1854. As the number of burials declined around the mid-1800s, so did the condition of the cemetery. Genealogist William Eardeley noted that the "Church Yard had not been used for many years, and many bodies and stones had been removed" to other burial grounds by the time of his visit there in the beginning of the 20th century.[53] In April 1922 Francis Ferdinand Spies found a mere 22 marked burials in the cemetery, which he noted was "in bad condition."[54] The eastern half of the Presbyterian Church property on which the cemetery was located was "sold to the village [of Port Chester] to permit construction of Abendroth Avenue" in 1930, and the remains and headstones from this burial ground were removed to a plot in Greenwood Union Cemetery, which the congregation purchased on January 7, 1931.[55] Unfortunately, the relocated stones were laid flat on the ground in this new plot, and most of their inscriptions have since faded. The church which adjoined the cemetery was sold and demolished in 1957.[56]

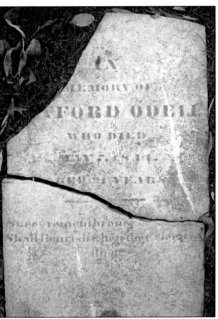

Above: Now lying on the ground in Greenwood Union Cemetery, these four tombstones once stood upright in the Port Chester Presbyterian Church Cemetery.

Top Left:	**Bottom Left:**		**Top Right:**	**Bottom Right:**
In memory of GEORGE W. SEABERRY died Nov. 13 1833 AE 34 yrs. A native of Little Compton, Rhode Island.	JOB MERRITT BORN Jan. 15th, 1761 DIED Apr. 23d, 1857	MARY MERRITT BORN Nov. 2nd, 1775 DIED March 6th, 1858	In Memory of WILLIAM BUCKLEY who died Dec. 21, 1842 Aged 29 Yrs. 4 Mos. & 24 Dys.	IN MEMORY OF HANFORD ODELL WHO DIED MAY 7, 1844, AGED 21 YEARS,

Top Right continued:

When we at death must part,
How keen how deep the pain
But we shall still be join'd
      in heart,
And hope to meet again

Bottom Right continued:

Sweet remembrance of the just,
Shall flourish when they sleep in
dust.

Sniffin Family Burial Ground
Rye Town (Port Chester)

Location: The cemetery (A) was formerly located on the west side of the Boston Post Road (Route 1) about 150 feet west of its intersection with Olivia Street (B). As of 2008, the site was occupied by the parking lot of a bank.

Dates of Activity: Pre-1866.

Removed: To Greenwood Union Cemetery (Section A, Lots 272-273) in 1866. See photo on page 151.

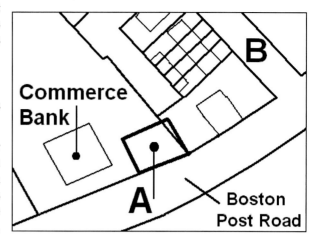

Notes: The Kniffen family, who sometimes spelled their surname Kniffin, Sniffen, and Sniffin, came to Rye from Stratford, Connecticut, about the year 1666, when George Kniffen (c.1632-1694) purchased land from John Budd. One of George's descendants, Jonathan Kniffin, owned property south of the present-day Village of Port Chester, as the Reverend Charles W. Baird noted:

> JONATHAN KNIFFIN's farm in 1770 bordered upon the post-road above Regent Street, and extended northward to Purchase Avenue. Regent Street was then called "Kniffin's lane." It led to his house, which stood on the west side of the lane, opposite Mrs. A. Sherwood's barn.... It was Jonathan Kniffin's daughter who was so cruelly murdered on the highway near Rye, in 1777.[57]

The murder of Miss Mary Kniffen occurred during the Revolutionary War in the vicinity of the intersection of the Boston Post Road and Harrison Avenue and was described by her cousin Nehemiah Brown:

> She was going to New York with a party of five or six who were driving cattle below and had not gone as far as the bridge at Rye Neck over Stoney Brook when they were fired upon by a party [of men], and she was killed.... It was said she was going down to be married to Jacob Tier, a very respectable butcher. Her death was considered an accident by all except her relatives. Maynard's party said they didn't know there was a woman with the party.[58]

It is likely that Mary Kniffin was interred in a burial plot that was located on her family's farm. In 1871 the Reverend Charles W. Baird mentioned this burial plot, which had been removed a few years before:

> The burying-place of a portion of the KNIFFIN family was a plot of ground by the road-side, on the land now owned by Mr. [George W.] Quintard. This property, a century ago, belonged to Jonathan Kniffin. A few years since some graves could be distinguished from the road at the top of the hill south of Mr. Quintard's gate. They have been removed in order to the grading of the land.[59]

George Quintard purchased the former Sniffin property in 1865, and his driveway was eventually transformed into present-day Olivia Street.[60] On November 1, 1866, Mr. Quintard concluded an agreement with members of the Sniffin family whereby he promised "at his own cost and expense to have the remains of any person buried or deposited" in the burial ground to be "removed in a careful manner" and reinterred in Greenwood Union Cemetery. In return, the Sniffins agreed that "after the disinterment of the remains," the cemetery would "cease to be a burial place of the dead and may be occupied and used by Quintard in his way as if it had never been used as a Grave Yard."[61] At the time of this land transfer, the cemetery was described as "containing about eighty feet on [the] Turnpike in length and about fifty four feet in depth."[62]

Town/Village of Scarsdale

Griffin-Cornell Family Burial Ground   170

Saint James the Less Episcopal Church Cemetery   172

Above: Looking west inside the Griffin-Cornell Family Burial Ground in 2008. Several headstones are visible lying flat on the ground. The one near the bottom right corner of the photo marks the grave of Ruth Merritt, and is the oldest inscribed tombstone in the cemetery, while the headstone with the white flowers closer to the center of the photo marks the grave of Anna Brown, wife of Scarsdale Town Supervisor Nathaniel Brown, whose moss-covered headstone can be seen on the ground at the far left. The fieldstones in the western portion of the burial ground mark the earliest interments in the cemetery. The open space beyond belongs to the Quaker Ridge Country Club.

Left: Leonora R. Schuyler was the daughter of Colonel Samuel St. George Rogers, a native of Tennessee who served in both the Army and Congress of the Confederate States of America during the Civil War. Mrs. Schuyler served as President General of the United Daughters of the Confederacy from 1921 to 1923 and was interred in the cemetery which surrounds the Episcopal Church of Saint James the Less.

     Only two burial places are located in the Town/Village of Scarsdale. The Griffin-Cornell Family Burial Ground, a private graveyard that was founded in the 18th century, is located next to the Quaker Ridge Country Club in the Colonial Acres neighborhood. The cemetery which adjoins Saint James the Less Episcopal Church off of Crane Road has been used by that congregation since 1847.

Griffin-Cornell Family Burial Ground
Scarsdale

Above: The southeast corner of the Griffin-Cornell Family Burial Ground in 2007.

Location: Southwest corner of the intersection of Colonial and Continental roads.

Dates of Activity: c.1795 – 1878.

Other Names: Burying Ground on Old Benjamin Archer Farm, Colonial Acres Cemetery, Quaker Ridge Cemetery.

Inscriptions: *WCHS* Book #17 (p.51-52).

Notes: John Griffen/Griffin (1660-1743), a native of Flushing, Queens, moved to Westchester and purchased land in Heathcote Manor in 1711.[1] Although it is impossible to tell exactly when the Griffin family founded this burial ground, it is known that John's grandson, William Griffin, was interred here upon his death in 1795.[2] On June 26, 1795, William Griffin's son, William, Jr., sold 125 acres of the Griffin estate to Samuel Titus, at which time a family burial ground was reserved:

> Excepting and reserving at the same time a square of land containing one quarter of an acre for burying ground where William Griffen deceased is interred for the purpose of Interring the deceased hereafter of the family of said William Griffen deceased and others and also a privilege of going to and from the same through the lands hereby conveyed to bury the dead and to fence and enclose the same without any unnecessary waste in said land being omitted.[3]

The "others" mentioned in the deed included the neighboring Cornell and Morell families. The Griffin farm was later acquired by Nathaniel Brown (c.1767-1844), who served as Supervisor of the Town of Scarsdale for two years. Mr. Brown also used this burial ground and mentioned the cemetery in his will:

> All the residue of my personal Estate I give and bequeath to my said wife Ann...reserving out of my lands in Scarsdale where I now reside a Burying Ground to the extent of twenty square rods for the interment of the relatives of persons already intered [sic] there with a free and uninterrupted passage to and from the said Burying Ground to the public High way leading to Mamaroneck Landing and my

Executors are hereby directed to cause said Burying Ground to be enclosed with a good and sufficient Stone Wall.[4]

The last burials made in this cemetery were of members of the Cornell family, who may have been related to the Griffin family by marriage. Today, the cemetery is surrounded on three sides by the Colonial Acres neighborhood, and its western frontage borders the Quaker Ridge Country Club. Unfortunately, years of neglect have resulted in damage to most of the tombstones. However, the homes of the families who set aside the cemetery are in much better condition. The house built by William Griffin's father, Benjamin, still stands on Old Mamaroneck Road, while Nathaniel Brown's home is located at 400 Mamaroneck Road.[5]

Above: The headstone of Ruth Merritt, who died on at the age of 85 on January 2, 1822, is the oldest inscribed tombstone in the Griffen-Cornell Family Burial Ground. Today, it lies cracked on the ground next to its accompanying footstone.

Left: These two headstones lie on the ground in the Griffin-Cornell Family Burial Ground. The tombstone depicted in the top photo marks the grave of Anna Brown, who was born on June 20, 1766, and died on September 7, 1854. The bottom photo depicts the tombstone of Anna's husband, Nathaniel Brown, who died on December 1, 1844, at the age of 77.

171

Saint James the Less Episcopal Church Cemetery
Scarsdale

Above: Saint James the Less Episcopal Church and Cemetery in 2008. The stones in the foreground mark the graves of slaves who died while escaping through Scarsdale on their way to Canada. The plaque on the large boulder in the center of the photo was placed in 1980.

Location: Southeast corner of the intersection of Crane Road and Church Lane.

Dates of Activity: 1847 – Present.

Inscriptions: WCHS Book #8 (p.59-67). A microfilm copy of the cemetery records is held by WCHS (Reel #117).

Mailing Address: 10 Church Lane, Scarsdale, NY 10583.

Notes: The Church of Saint James the Less is located on property that was once owned by the Popham family. Major William Popham (1752-1847) was a native of County Cork, Ireland. He immigrated to America as a child and served the patriot cause with distinction during the Revolutionary War.[6] At the end of the war, Major Popham settled in Scarsdale and later served as President-General of the Cincinnati Society, an organization of "commissioned Revolutionary Officers."[7] Major Popham's son, William Sherbrooke Popham (1793-1885), sought to establish a parish for the Episcopal residents of Scarsdale, a municipality which at that time was ministered to from White Plains.[8] As a result of Mr. Popham's efforts, the Church of Saint James the Less was established in 1849, and the church building itself was constructed on the Popham property.[9]

William S. Popham leased the land surrounding the church to the parish with the "right or privilege of burying therein" on June 28, 1851. [10] It appears that Major Popham, who died four years prior to this transaction, was the first person interred in this cemetery. Dr. Allan M. Butler gave the following account of the churchyard in 1886 for Scharf's *History of Westchester County, New York*:

> The interments in the parish graveyard number one hundred and ten. To the southwest of the church are the vaults of the Bleecker, McFarlan and Popham families, and in the last-named repose the remains of the late William Popham, of Revolutionary fame, and his son, William Sherbrooke Popham. In

172

this churchyard lie the remains of several unknown persons who died within the town limits, and so were given burial here. The following curious epitaph—the only peculiar one in the little burying-ground—appears on the tombstone of James Bell. The stone was prepared by him and the lines were presumably of his own composition—"All you friends who are gathered here to weep, / Behold the grave wherein I sleep; / Prepare for death while you are well-- / You'll be entombed as well as Bell." [11]

Above: A marker which notes the Revolutionary War service of Major William Popham stands at the entrance to the Popham family vault.

The vaults of the Bleecker and Popham families are located about 75 feet southwest of the west end of the church building. Although these two vaults are located entirely underground, the McFarlan vault was built into the hillside near the southwest corner of the cemetery. The church has made use of the unused southern half of the McFarlan vault by establishing a walk-in columbarium. Visitors to Saint James the Less will notice a small cluster of uninscribed fieldstones situated in the northern half of the burial ground. These simple markers identify the "unknown persons" mentioned by Dr. Butler in the previous passage. Several of the persons who lie in these anonymous graves were not indigents or transients but rather escapees from slavery. A small plaque placed at this site in 1980 reads: "This and adjoining gravestones mark the final resting places of those unfortunate slaves who despite help given them and many others in Scarsdale did not survive in their flight to freedom in Canada prior to our Civil War."[12]

As of 2001, more than 60 men who served in seven of America's wars were buried or honored in this churchyard. A total of 16 of these servicemen were killed in action during World War II and the Korean War.[13] Lieutenant Snowden

Haywood (1922-1944) was killed in action in Luxembourg during World War II. Beside his grave is a cenotaph for his brother, naval Ensign Alfred Williams Haywood, Jr., who was killed aboard a motor torpedo boat off of New Britain during that same conflict. Not far from these memorials is a cenotaph for Henry C. Ballinger, a member of the Royal Canadian Air Force, who was lost in action in 1942. Two simple crosses mark the adjoining graves of Dwight B. Eldred, Jr., and Bruce K. Stowell, both of whom were killed in action during World War II. The cemetery is still occasionally used as a place of interment.

Left: The graves of Dwight B. Eldred, Jr., (left) and Bruce K. Stowell (right) in the Saint James the Less Episcopal Church Cemetery in 2007.

173

Top: The cenotaph at left commemorates Alfred Williams Haywood (1921-1944), an ensign in the US Navy who was killed in action off of New Britain in the South Pacific during World War II. The tombstone at right marks the grave of Snowden Haywood (b.1922), a lieutenant in the US Army who was killed in action in Luxembourg on December 26th, 1944. Lieutenant Haywood was posthumously awarded the Distinguished Service Cross "for extraordinary heroism in connection with military operations against an armed enemy...at the cost of his life."[14]

Center: The two markers in the foreground at left stand at the graves of two brothers, Lieutenant Warren B. Corwin (1922-1944) and Sergeant Nuel D. Corwin (1924-1944), both of whom were killed while serving in the US Army Air Force during World War II. The two markers at right stand at the graves of their parents, Raymond W. (1895-1977) and Ruth B. Corwin (1897-1985). Raymond W. Corwin served as a Chief Pharmacist's Mate in the US Navy during World War I.

Left: This broken decoration was placed at the grave of Charles R. Carmer (1838-1917) by Farnsworth Post 170 of the Grand Army of the Republic. The GAR was the fraternal organization established by Union veterans of the Civil War. Mr. Carmer is buried beside his wife, Emma.

City of Yonkers

Above: Richard Penfold Berrian and his wife, Elizabeth Vanderbeeck, saw three of their sons join the 5th New York Volunteer Infantry Regiment, also known as Duryea's Zouaves, following the onset of the Civil War. Today, Stephen (d.1876), William (d.1871), and Richard Berrian (d.1871) lie side by side in Saint John's Cemetery

Asbury Methodist Church Cemetery	176	Sacred Heart Friars' Cemetery	193
Congregation People of Righteousness Cemetery	181	Saint John's Cemetery	194
Oakland Cemetery	187	Saint John's Episcopal Church Cemetery	198
Philipsbugh Manor Potter's Field	190	Saint Joseph's Cemetery	200
Philipsbugh Manor Slave Burying Ground	190	Saint Mary's Cemetery	203
Rich Family Burial Ground	191	Tuckahoe Road Burial Ground	206
Sherwood Park Cemetery	191		

> The plow has obliterated traces of most of the farm and neighborhood burial places.... Over many a plot in Yonkers the citizen of to-day walks, unconscious that he is treading where "Each in his narrow cell, forever laid, the rude forefathers of the hamlet sleep." It has been well observed that men gain immortality, not so much by what others do for them, as by what they do for others. Among the uncounted multitudes who sleep in St. John's, Oakland, St. Mary's and St. Joseph's Cemeteries, are those who rendered this and all coming generations large service by periling their lives for the Republic. Year after year on Decoration Days, their mounds are gratefully marked with the flag they loved, and embroidered with flowers.[1] – The Reverend Charles E. Allison, 1896.

As it did not develop into a sizable community until the early 19th century, Yonkers does not boast a large Colonial burial ground. Several denominational cemeteries sprang up after the close of the Revolutionary War, including Saint John's Cemetery on Saw Mill River Road, Saint John's Episcopal Church Cemetery in present-day Colonial Heights, and the Asbury Methodist Church Cemetery. As space in these burial grounds became scarce during the mid-19th century, the non-denominational Oakland Cemetery was established in 1867. The industry and commerce that developed in Yonkers during the mid to late 1800s brought with it a number of immigrants who created their own burial grounds. The Roman Catholics of Yonkers established Saint Mary's Cemetery and Saint Joseph's Cemetery in 1855 and 1877, respectively. The Jewish residents of the city founded the Sherwood Park Cemetery and the Congregation People of Righteousness Cemetery in 1895 and 1899, respectively. The former is one of Westchester's most unique graveyards as it was originally established in the 18th century as the burial ground of a German Protestant family, while the latter is best known for the controversy that surrounded its removal in 1989 for the creation of a shopping center.

Asbury Methodist Church Cemetery

Yonkers

Above: The Asbury Methodist Church and Cemetery on April 16, 1910.

Right: This marble tombstone reads:

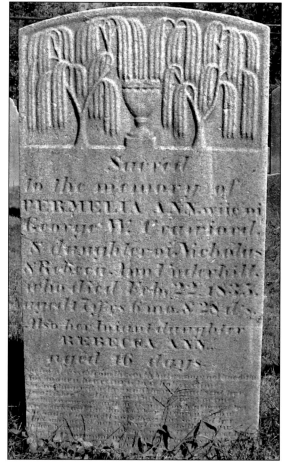

Sacred
to the memory of
PERMELIA ANN, wife of
George W. Crawford,
& daughter of Nicholas
& Rebecca Ann Underhill,
who died Feb. 22, 1835,
aged 17 y'rs 6 mo. & 28 d's.
Also her infant daughter
REBECCA ANN,
aged 16 days.

She hath passed from the earth, but we may not lament her,
Nor mourn her return to a holier clime;
She but lingered below, until He who had sent her,
Recalled her to Eden in morning's sweet prime.
Ere the sorrows of earth or its passions had moved her;
Ere darkened the light of her innocent brow;
She bade a farewell unto those who so loved her,
And whispered, my father, I come to thee now.
In her beauty she sleeps, but we will not regret her,
Our tears may not moisten the flowers on her tomb,
For the smiles of her Saviour In mercy have met her,
Oh death thou art vanquished, and past is thy gloom.

Location: 167 Scarsdale Road (west side of the street between Park View Avenue and Underhill Street).

Dates of Activity: 1800 – 1972. A columbarium that is actively used by the congregation is located next to the cemetery.

176

Other Names: First Methodist Episcopal Church of Yonkers Cemetery, Tuckahoe Methodist Church Cemetery.

Inscriptions: *WCHS* Book #17 (p.145-153), #49, and #87 (p.15-25). A microfilm copy of the cemetery records is held by WCHS (Reel #112).

Notes: A Methodist Society at Tuckahoe formed in 1771 around the time that the renowned Francis Asbury preached at the hamlet, which was then located on the west side of the Bronx River. [2] Asbury visited Tuckahoe again 26 years later to dedicate the newly-constructed Methodist church there. "Being too feeble to walk," Asbury was "carried in a chair...to the church, and performed the ceremony seated in a chair." [3] Many of the church members who attended this dedication were later buried in a small churchyard on the north side of the meeting house, as Mrs. John G. Anderson noted in a historical sketch written for the church's 175th anniversary in 1946:

> Adjacent to the church is a burying ground which contains the mortal remains of most of the church and community pioneers...many of whose names are still legible on the tombstones.... For many years a charge of five dollars was made to church members, and a charge of seven dollars was made to strangers and non-members for burial in the church yard. [4]

The churchyard was briefly mentioned by Frances G. Mead in her 1935 article on the Asbury Methodist Church, including an amusing anecdote of a "haunting" in this burial ground:

> In the churchyard adjacent to the building, many familiar names meet curious scrutiny and keep alive the memory of the founders. The oldest stone on which the inscription may be read bears the date of 1800. It marks the grave of Elizabeth (Betsy), wife of Jonathan Sherwood—or Shearwood. The name of John Bonnett draws attention for he was the son of John Bonnett of New Rochelle and the grandson of Peter Bonnett. The name of Daniel Odell conjures up a picture of that man as he appears in a reminiscent tale of an old Tuckahoe resident.
>
> Daniel Odell was a shoemaker and had an apprentice who stayed out until long after dark when delivering the wares of his employer. With the intention of scaring the fellow out of this habit, Daniel enlisted the assistance of a group of friends. Dressed in white sheets they seated themselves in the old burying ground one night to wait for the unsuspecting culprit. But unknown to Daniel Odell and protected from discovery by darkness, his neighbor, Abe Vermilyea, had wrapped himself in a black rubber sheet. As the apprentice approached, the white figure of Odell glided forth and directly behind him came the rustling rubber sheet and Abe Vermilyea. Startled by the unexpected sound and apparition, Odell did not wait for explanations. In unquestionable fright he ran for home with the black ghost apparently following. Jumping up and down with excitement, the apprentice shouted after them, "Run, white devil! For the black devil will catch you!" [5]

Nearly all of the older stones in the churchyard face to the west, away from Underhill Street. Although the churchyard has been closed to burials for nearly half a century, a columbarium has been constructed on the south side of the cemetery, allowing the church property to continue to serve as a final resting place for members of the congregation.

Right: The inscription on this sandstone reads.

In
Memory of
Steashey Brown, daughter
of Robert and Mary Brown
she departed this life Feb'y 24th,
AD : 1826. Aged 52 Years
4 Months and 15 days.

All weary travelers that pass by,
Behold the place wherein I lie;
As you are now so once was I,
As I am now so you must be,
Prepare for death and follow me.

Above Left: The tombstones of Benjamin and Hannah Huestis read:

BENJAMIN HUESTIS
BORN FEB. 18TH, 1765
DIED SEP. 20TH, 1853

Look down upon this sacred spot and see
What death can do to you as well as me
Dear bosom friends, your falling sand is nigh
Children prepare tis' God that calls on high

HANNAH.
WIFE OF
BENJAMIN HUESTIS.
BORN JUNE 16TH, 1771.
DIED MAY 19TH, 1855.
AGED
83 Y'RS 11 MO'S & 3 DAYS.

In calm repose a Mother's dust lies here
We view the spot and drop affection's tear
Her weary spirits now no more oppressed
Has reached the mansions of eternal rest.

Above Right: This damaged sandstone was sealed in concrete in 1935. The only remaining portion of the face reads:

Repent in time while time you have,
there's no repentance in the grave.

Right: This small marble tombstone marks the grave of Bishop L. Underhill, the son of Gilbert and Eliza Underhill, who died in 1832 at the age of 13. The verse at the bottom of the stone reads:

Lord he is thine
And not my own
Thou hast not done me wrong
I thank thee for the precious loan
Afforded me so long.

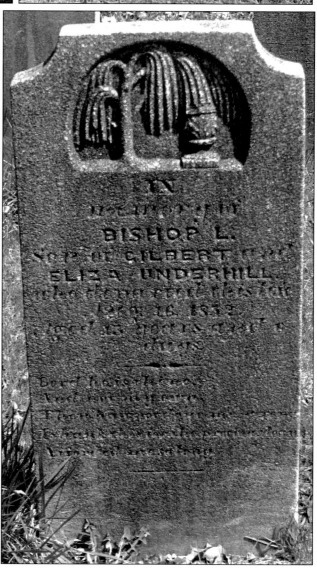

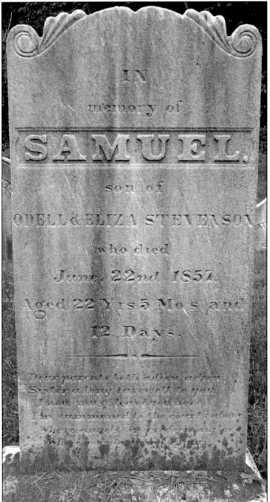

Above Left: A child's tombstone in the Asbury Methodist Church Cemetery. According to cemetery historian Gray Williams, "the design of a rose branch with a broken, dangling bud was a popular symbol of early death during the 19th century, and was sometimes accompanied by the epitaph, 'A bud on earth, to bloom in heaven.'" The inscription is given at right.

Frances Augusta
Daughter of Daniel K.
and Frances Underhill
who died Aug. 3, 1845,
aged 5 Mo's.

O, dear Saviour, to thee I trust
This precious part of mortal dust,
O, keep it safe in sacred tomb
Till a mother asks for room.

Above Right: Eliza Stevenson (1811-1872) was the mother of Samuel Stevenson, whose tombstone is depicted at bottom left. The top line of this headstone reads: "MY WORK IS DONE THE REST REMAINETH." The remainder of the tombstone reads:

ELIZA,
Wife of
ODELL STEVENSON
DIED
SEPT. 13TH, 1872
AGED 61 Y'RS 1 MO'
& 1 DAY.

Rest, sweetly rest on Jesus' dear breast
Thou who hast fled to the land of the blest
Glorified spirits has borne thee above
Blest in the keeping of infinite love.

Left: As is indicated by his tombstone, Samuel Stevenson (1835-1857) predeceased his parents, Odell and Eliza, as well as his sister. The first five lines of Samuel's epitaph read:

Dear parents both, adieu, adieu
Sister a long farewell to you
I now must leave you here
I'm summoned to the courts above
Where angels sing redeeming love

179

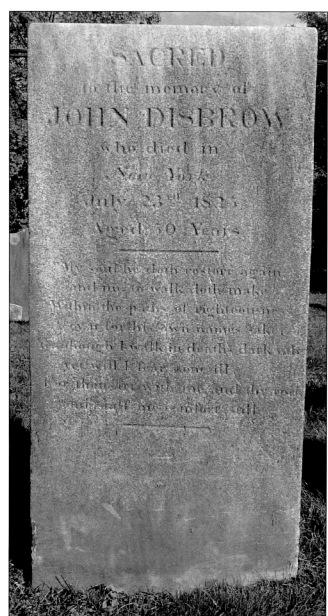
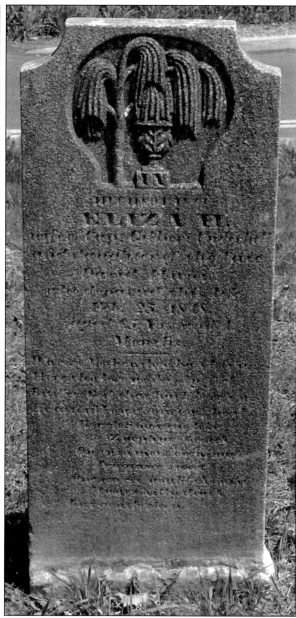

Above: Two marble headstones in the Asbury Methodist Church Cemetery. The epitaph on the tombstone at left is taken from Psalm 23:3-4.

SACRED
to the memory of
JOHN DISBROW,
who died in
New York
July 23rd, 1825
Aged 50 Years

"My soul he doth restore again
    and me to walk doth make
Within the path of righteousness
    even for his own name's sake.
Yea, though I walk in death's dark vale
    yet will I fear no ill;
For thou art with me; and thy rod
    and staff my comfort still."

IN
Memory of
ELIZA H.
wife of Capt. Gilbert Underhill
and daughter of the late
David Hunt,
who departed this life
Feb 3rd . 25, 1848,
aged 65 Yrs. And 4
Months

Dearest mother thou hast left us
Here thy loss we deeply feel
But 'tis God that has bereft us
He can all our sorrows heal.
    Her closing scene like
        Zyephyr's breath
    On summer's evening's
        Fragrance sweet
    One scarce would thought
        T'was chilly death
    But gentle sleep.

Congregation People of Righteousness Cemetery
Yonkers

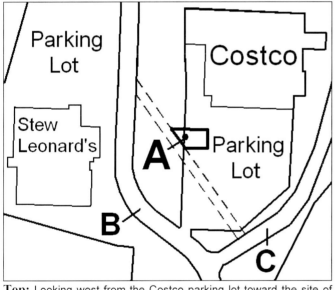

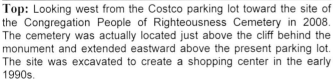

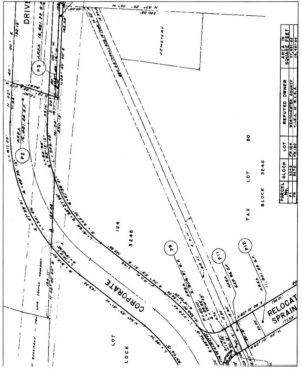

Top: Looking west from the Costco parking lot toward the site of the Congregation People of Righteousness Cemetery in 2008. The cemetery was actually located just above the cliff behind the monument and extended eastward above the present parking lot. The site was excavated to create a shopping center in the early 1990s.

Location: The cemetery (marked "A" on the map at left) was formerly located on the grounds of a shopping center. The plan at right shows the location of the cemetery shortly before it was removed. The cemetery was accessed on its west side by a road which ran between the present Stew Leonard Drive (B) and Austin Avenue (C). Today, the cemetery site is marked by a monument on the west side of the Costco parking lot about 350 feet north of Stew Leonard Drive.

Dates of Activity: 1899 – 1969.

Right: Tombstones in the Congregation People of Righteousness Cemetery in the mid-1970s. Photo courtesy Harvey Wolchan.

Removed: In 1989 to make way for the construction of a shopping center. Twenty of the identified removals were claimed by family members and reburied in the Sharon Gardens Cemetery in Mount Pleasant, Mount Hope Cemetery in Greenburgh, and a cemetery in Moshav Merchavia, Israel. The remaining 74 were re-interred at the Eretz HaChaim Cemetery in Israel.[6]

Notes: An orthodox synagogue that was also known as "the Ingram Street Shul," the Congregation People of Righteousness was formed in the late 19th century by immigrants from the Russian Empire.[7] On May 31, 1899, the congregation purchased a half-acre plot from William H. Varian for $1,350 to use as a burial ground.[8] Interestingly, the congregation founded their cemetery several years before their synagogue was formally dedicated in 1906. Membership fees to the synagogue "included burial in the congregation's cemetery."[9]

The congregation disbanded in 1969 with the exception of five directors who remained as the proprietors of the cemetery. By 1974 the majority of the headstones in the cemetery had been knocked over by vandals.[10] Rather than reset the tombstones and make them targets for future vandalism, the directors decided to leave the memorials flat on the ground.[11] The cemetery and its access road also became a dumping ground. In 1980 the *Herald Statesman* reported that "two DPW trucks [had] carted debris from the area, which mostly consisted of building materials such as stones, concrete and wood," and even included "an abandoned car."[12]

The remaining directors of the congregation were mostly in their 80s when they agreed to transfer the burial ground to Morris Industrial Builders on September 15, 1989, in exchange for "up to $350,000 to relocate the remains in accordance with Jewish law" at Eretz HaChaim Cemetery in Jerusalem.[13] Morris Industrial Builders planned to turn the hillside overlooking the New York State Thruway into a large shopping center, and the cemetery was situated on a slope that the company hoped to excavate in order to build a parking lot. The rabbi who consulted for the exhumation project remarked that the deplorable state of the burial ground was "a source of scandal to Jews everywhere."[14]

Top: The entrance to the Congregation People of Righteousness Cemetery in the mid-1970s. Photo courtesy Harvey Wolchan.

Bottom: Debris litters the access road to the Congregation People of Righteousness Cemetery in this 1980 photo. Note the entrance to the cemetery at right as well as the abandoned car at left.

183

Unfortunately, the removal of the cemetery was not the final chapter in the history of the burial ground. In 2003 Allan and Sherrie Turkheimer attempted to visit the burial ground where Mrs. Turkheimer's maternal grandparents had been interred, only to find a "sea of concrete" at the site.[15] The Turkheimers requested an investigation by the New York State Attorney General's office, which concluded that Morris Industrial Builders neglected to remove the remains of 135 of the 147 children who had been interred in the cemetery.[16] The *New York Times* reported on the exhumations:

> The funeral official responsible for the transfer declared to the court in 1989 that "all known human remains" had been removed." But Morris Builders made no mention of the failure to find the remains of many children listed in the cemetery.... Officials of the attorney general's office said he had told them he dug up all of the remains he located, but found none of children, even where a 1930 map of the cemetery said they should be.... He said he sent two bags of dirt to the Jerusalem cemetery on the advice of rabbis.[17]

Further questions about the exhumation were raised when an anonymous tipster alerted the *Journal News* to two gravestones from the cemetery in an overgrown area north of Stew Leonard's parking lot.[18] In January 2005 a settlement was reached in which Morris Industrial Builders paid $100,000 "to erect a monument on the [cemetery] site and pay for research into the number of people who were buried there."[19]

Right: Three views of the northeast portion of the Congregation People of Righteousness Cemetery in the mid-1970s. The large tombstone in the foreground of the center photo may be seen at right in the bottom photo. The New York State Thruway is faintly visible through the trees at right in the bottom photo. Photos courtesy Harvey Wolchan.

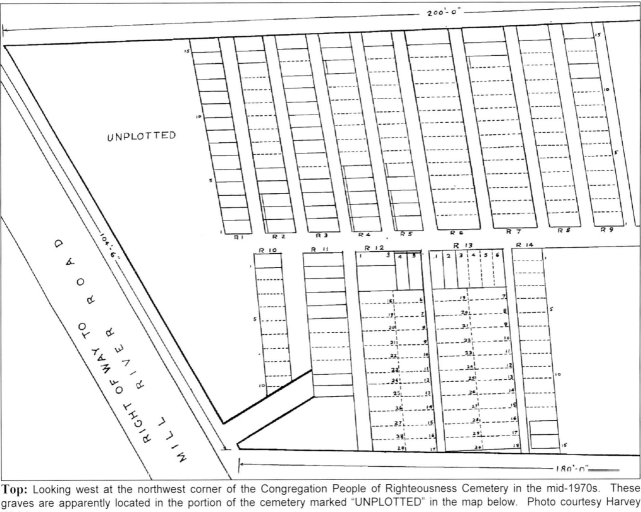

Top: Looking west at the northwest corner of the Congregation People of Righteousness Cemetery in the mid-1970s. These graves are apparently located in the portion of the cemetery marked "UNPLOTTED" in the map below. Photo courtesy Harvey Wolchan.

Bottom: The Works Progress Administration drew this map of the Congregation People of Righteousness Cemetery in 1930. It is not known if the dotted lines on this map represent actual burials or unused plots.

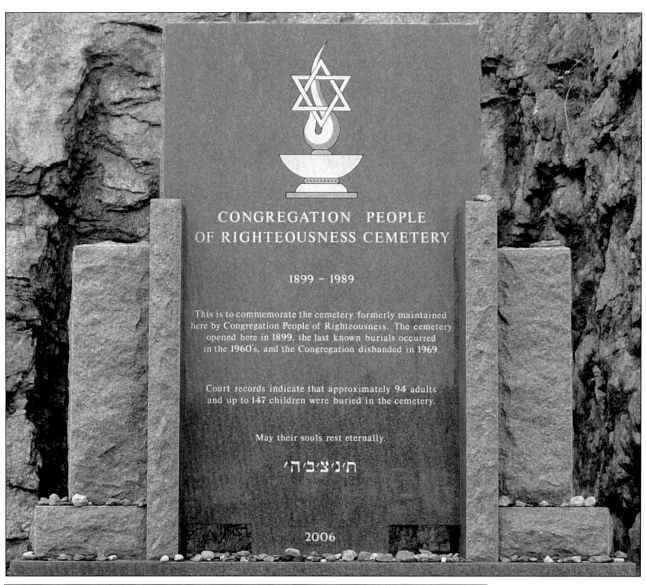

CONGREGATION PEOPLE
OF RIGHTEOUSNESS CEMETERY

1899 - 1989

This is to commemorate the cemetery formerly maintained
here by Congregation People of Righteousness. The cemetery
opened here in 1899, the last known burials occurred
in the 1960's, and the Congregation disbanded in 1969.

Court records indicate that approximately 94 adults
and up to 147 children were buried in the cemetery.

May their souls rest eternally.

תנצב״ה׳

2006

Above: The monument at the site of the Congregation People of Righteousness Cemetery in 2008.

Left: The northeast corner of the cemetery in the mid-1970s. Photo courtesy Harvey Wolchan.

Oakland Cemetery

Yonkers

Right: This monument marks the grave of elevator magnate Elisha Otis. The north (left) face of the monument reads:

ELISHA G. OTIS
BORN
HALIFAX, V.T.
AUG. 3, 1811
DIED
YONKERS, N.Y.
APRIL 8, 1861
FATHER
INVENTOR AND ORIGINAL
MANUFACTURER OF THE
OTIS SAFETY ELEVATOR

Location: Northeast corner of the intersection of Saw Mill River Road (Route 9A) and Ashburton Avenue. The cemetery entrance is located on the east side of Saw Mill River Road at that intersection.

Dates of Activity: 1867 – Present.

Other Names: Yonkers Cemetery (official name, 1867-1882).

Mailing Address: 2 Saw Mill River Road, Yonkers, NY, 10701.

Notes: As discussed more fully in the entry for Saint John's Cemetery on page 194, the land at the northwest corner of Saw Mill River Road and Ashburton Avenue was donated to the Episcopal Church by the Philipse family in 1751 for use as a glebe. It is fitting, therefore, that another burial place would be established on that parcel. Writing for Scharf's *History of Westchester County, New York*, the Reverend David Cole described the founding of the cemetery:

> The cemetery was first established by the Yonkers Cemetery Association on the 3rd of December, 1866.... The [cemetery] land covers what had once been in three farms, - the Seymour farm, the Biggs farm and the Beebe farm, - together comprising about one hundred acres. All this land, just before the company obtained it, was in the hands of Leonard W. Jerome, who conveyed it to the company for certificates, to the redemption of which one-half the receipts for the sale of lots was pledged. The aggregate amount of these certificates was two hundred thousand dollars. In 1870 a settlement was effected with Mr. Jerome, in which he surrendered all certificates remaining in his hands in exchange for the Biggs farm, containing about forty acres and valued at eighty-one thousand dollars. This settlement left the cemetery with an area of sixty-five acres.[20]

Unfortunately, the cemetery association would soon encounter financial difficulties which resulted in the present name of the cemetery, as the Reverend Cole noted:

> The construction of roads, a receiving vault and other improvements were provided for by the issue of seven percent bonds. The amount of these bonds that had been issued in 1880 was sixteen thousand five hundred dollars and the interest had fallen in arrears. In 1882 the association was reorganized under the name of the "Oakland Cemetery Association," and the former bondholders became stockholders to an equal amount.... From the valley of the Nepperhan the land rises gradually to the east, culminating in a considerably extensive plateau, covered with groves, containing some of the finest old forest-trees growing in this part of the State. The level ground is admirably adapted for burial-plots, while the hillside affords ready facilities for the construction of vaults and tombs. Abundant springs of water gush forth at several points among the rocks, which add much to the life of the ground.... A

receiving vault, built in the side of the hill, about a quarter of a mile back from the entrance, is of gray stone and cost about eight thousand dollars. The entrance to the cemetery is a particularly easy one, at the southwest corner of the grounds.[21]

Above Left: Across from the grave of Elisha Otis is the final resting place of Dr. Charles Augustus Leale (1842-1932). Dr. Leale was in the audience at Ford's Theater on the night of April 14, 1865, when John Wilkes Booth fatally shot President Abraham Lincoln. Moments after the shooting, Dr. Leale reached the presidential box and was able to revive Lincoln. After pronouncing that the President's wound was mortal, Dr. Leale ordered that Lincoln be carried out of the theater and into a house across the street so that he could spend his last hours in relative comfort. Later, the doctor served as an Honor Guard at the services for the President in the East Room of the White House and the Capitol Rotunda. The Leale plot is located just inside Oakland Cemetery next to its border with Saint John's Cemetery. The large vault behind the Leale plot is located in Saint John's Cemetery and belongs to the Copcutt family, of which Dr. Leale's wife Rebecca was a member. One of the other two doctors who assisted Dr. Leale at Ford's Theater, Dr. Charles Taft, is interred at Saint Paul's Episcopal Church Cemetery in Mount Vernon.

Above Right: This monument marks the grave of Rear Admiral Benjamin F. Isherwood (1822-1915), who served as engineer-in-chief of the US Navy during the Civil War. At the time of his death, Admiral Isherwood was the last surviving flag officer of the Civil War.

Right: This Hungarian-inscribed tombstone marks the grave of György Gönczi. Hungarian tradition places the surname before a person's first name.

188

Top Left: The monument in Collison family plot.

Top Right: Although Oakland Cemetery is a non-denominational burial ground, many Orthodox Christians have purchased plots in the southern portion of the cemetery in the shadow of Holy Trinity Russian Orthodox Church.

Center Right: The grave of Captain William Heermance (1837-1903) in his family's plot at Oakland Cemetery. Captain Heermance was awarded the Medal of Honor for his actions on April 30, 1863, at the beginning of the Battle of Chancellorsville. His citation reads: "Took command of the regiment as its senior officer when surrounded by Stuart's Cavalry. The regiment cut its way through the enemy's line and escaped but Capt. Heermance was desperately wounded, left for dead on the field and was taken prisoner."[22]

Bottom Left: This statue of a fireman from the turn of the 20th century stands atop the Yonkers Volunteer Fire Department plot, which is located at the entrance to the cemetery. Yonkers was served by a number of volunteer companies before the first professional firefighters were hired in 1896.

Shortly before World War I the cemetery began construction of a large mausoleum in the southwest portion of the grounds. Although this project was abandoned, the concrete platform on which the structure was to have been built can still be seen today.[23] Oakland Cemetery is still actively used today, and there is much unused space in the burial ground's eastern portion, which is situated atop a ridge overlooking downtown Yonkers.

Philipsburgh Manor Potter's Field
Philipsburgh Manor Slave Burying Ground
Yonkers

Right: This circa 1843 map of southwest Yonkers indicates the city's old shoreline. Part of the large orchard along the Hudson River north of the pier was planted over the Philipsburgh Manor Potter's Field. The manor's slave burying ground was located on the small peninsula between the glebe of Saint John's Episcopal Church and the Hudson River.

Location: The Philipsburgh Manor Potter's Field, which was destroyed about 1765, was formerly located about 40 yards south and 500 feet west of the intersection of Warburton Avenue and Quincy Place. The Philipsburgh Manor Slave Burying Ground, which was destroyed sometime after 1783, was located approximately in the block bounded by Larkin Plaza to the north, Market Place to the east, Main Street to the south, and Buena Vista Avenue to the west.

Dates of Activity: Philipsburgh Manor Potter's Field, pre-1765; Philipsburgh Manor Slave Burying Ground, pre-1783.

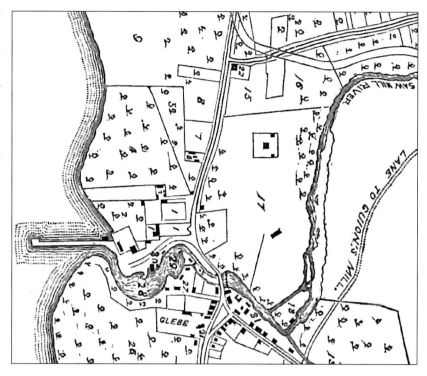

Notes: While discussing the improvements made by Frederick Philipse III to the area surrounding his manor house in Yonkers in the mid-1700s, the Reverend Charles E. Allison mentioned the existence of this burial ground:

> Anthony Archer (who was born in 1746 and died about 1837, aged nearly ninety-two years) when he was about eighteen years old worked for Colonel Philipse nearly a year making terraces west of the manor-house and its garden.... It was a very stony place. There was an old burying-ground under the new sections, which was covered up.[1]

These "new sections" were apparently part of an extensive orchard and garden complex to the west and north of Philipse Manor Hall. The Reverend Allison indicated that this burial place may have served as a potter's field:

> Near the foot of the present Locust Street was a cove into which sometimes the bodies of drowned persons were washed by the tide. These, and other bodies, were buried at that point.[2]

It is difficult to reconcile the above descriptions of 19th-century Yonkers with the city of the present day due to the landfill which has changed the shoreline and the construction which has eradicated the Locust Street. The cove mentioned by the Reverend Allison is reflected by the route of the Hudson Line of Metro-North Railroad, which curves to the east between Getty Square and Glenwood. The railroad right-of-way, which was established in the late 1840s, roughly follows the 19th century shoreline. Locust Street ran westerly from Warburton Avenue and began about 40 yards south of Quincy Place. Therefore, the site of this burial ground was most likely about 500 feet west of Warburton Avenue. The Westchester County Historical Society is in possession of a typescript written by an unknown person regarding the history of Saint John's Cemetery, which puts forth the theory that this burial ground was, in fact, the cemetery for the slaves of the Philipse family. However, the author believes that the statements made by the Reverend Allison are indeed correct.[3]

The Philipsburgh Manor Potter's Field was not the only Colonial burial ground near the Philipse manor house. According to the Reverend Charles E. Allison, "it is said that the Philipses buried their negroes on what was then a high bank, east of the present Hudson River Railroad Station."[4] In the 18th century, the Saw Mill River, which has since been covered over by urban development, formed a small peninsula as it wound its way eastward from the Hudson River. The site of this peninsula is now occupied by the Yonkers Post Office, which encompasses the entire city block described above. No records of removals from this burial ground exist.

Rich Family Burial Ground
Sherwood Park Cemetery
Yonkers

Above: Looking southwest past the tombstones of Hannah (1765-1834), Stephen (1804-1828) and Lewis Rich (1765-1833) toward Sherwood Park Cemetery in 2007. Stephen was the son of Lewis and Hannah Rich.

Location: Sherwood Park Cemetery is located on the west side of Bronx River Road between Reyer Avenue and Charles Place. The Rich Family Burial Ground is located in the northeast corner of Sherwood Park Cemetery.

Dates of Activity: Rich Family Cemetery, 18th century – 1881; Sherwood Park Cemetery, 1895 – Present.

Inscriptions: *WCHS* Book #87 (p.14, Rich Family Burial Ground only).

Notes: Balthasar Ryche, a native of the Palatinate in present-day Germany, settled in Yonkers sometime before 1717. His grandson, Thomas Rich, settled in Mile Square before the outbreak of the Revolutionary War, and was living in a house on the west side of Bronx River Road about 150 yards north of his family's burial ground. During the war, a group of 200 to 300 patriots en route to Mile Square fired into the Rich house while a party was going on, wounding Joshua DeVoe and making six holes "in one woman's petticoats and three in another." One of these ladies was identified as "the widow Rich."[5] Thomas Strang, the leader of the patriot force, later apologized for this action, saying that he "thought the house full of Refugees," a name given to the Tories who had fled to Morrisania.[6]

Although the oldest inscribed tombstone in the Rich Family Burial Ground dates from 1824, the unmarked fieldstones in the graveyard indicate that the founding of the cemetery most likely predates this year. The following passage is excerpted from an article which appeared in *The Westchester Record* in 1889:

> A quaint and desolate family burying ground, which shows long years of neglect, lies on the road to Yonkers, a short distance from West Mount Vernon. It was originally a part of the old Rich farm, and is now owned by a widow, who some time ago offered it for sale. But it is believed by the neighbors that it is a consecrated piece of ground, set apart by the original owners for a burial place, and not to be disposed of. The widow has been unfortunate of recent years, and she has disposed of the farm, little by little, until this quarter acre is all that is left of it. The farm was originally a large one and belonged to the Rich family, but the march of improvements has encroached upon it, leaving only the forlorn looking

burial spot. The crowded graves prove that the family was a numerous one, the inscriptions on the head stones dating back more than a century to say nothing of those where the inscriptions have been entirely obliterated by the storms and the winds…. The last male member of the family was John Rich, who died twenty years ago, and left the place to his wife, who is now living.[7]

As is referenced in the above article, John Rich left 100 acres of land on the west side of Bronx River Road to his widow, Anna Maria. In 1866 and 1867, Mrs. Rich sold off all of this land, with the exception of the family cemetery, in four separate parcels.[8] The final burial at the Rich cemetery occurred on December 11, 1881, when Thomas L. Rich (1803-1881) was interred there.[9] On November 14, 1882, Abigail Rich had the remains of seven people exhumed and reinterred at Saint Paul's Episcopal Church Cemetery in Mount Vernon.[10] In order to preserve what was left of her family's burial ground and at the same time receive financial support for her last years, Anna Maria Rich decided to sell the quarter-acre burial ground in 1894 to two Jewish benevolent societies, Mount Vernon Lodge No. 67 and Yonkers Lodge No. 77 of the Independent Order B'rith of Abraham, for the creation of a cemetery to serve the residents of that faith who lived in Mount Vernon and Yonkers.[11] As part of this arrangement, the burials of the Rich family were not disturbed and remain in place on the north side of the cemetery.[12] Among those graves that are still identifiable within the Rich plot are those of Lewis Rich, a great-grandson of Bathasar Ryche; Hannah, the wife of Lewis Rich; Lewis' daughter, Sarah; and the latter's husband, Daniel Devoe.[13] In 1923 there were also "about 25 illegible stones, mostly field stones" in the burial ground.[14] These anonymous interments were occasionally unearthed by the Sherwood Park Cemetery caretaker, who would catch "a fleeting glimpse of a hand or a face while digging a grave, but the bones would disintegrate when the air hit them."[15]

The Yonkers and Mount Vernon lodges of the Independent Order B'rith of Abraham purchased the "lot of land commonly known as the Old Rich Burying Ground" on July 5, 1894, "for the purpose of having some exclusive ground in which to inter their deceased members."[16] On March 7, 1895, the two organizations transferred the plot to Sherwood Park Cemetery, an association that had been incorporated on October 10, 1894.[17] This approval was granted on January 14, 1895, and the cemetery was formally dedicated on June 9th of that year.[18] By 1966 there were only "six or seven" empty burial spots remaining in the cemetery, all of which were for "people who have families there."[19] The cemetery is now full.

Above: The headstone of Bella Levine, who died on July 2, 1922, at the age of 46, features a small image of the deceased. Although the embedding of photos in tombstones was a practice adopted primarily by Italian Americans, several Jewish headstones from the early 20th century in Westchester County also contain this feature.

Left: The English portion of this tombstone reads: "In memory of my beloved Husband and our dear Father LOUIS SUBITZKY Died July 15, 1904 Age 60 Years." The hands at the top of the tombstone symbolize a priestly blessing, and indicate that Louis was a *Kohen*, a descendant of Aaron. The small enclosure for planting in front of the headstone can be found in front of many Jewish headstones from the 20th century.

192

Sacred Heart Friars' Cemetery

Yonkers

Above: The southeast section of the Sacred Heart Friars' Cemetery in 2008.

Location: West side of Voss Avenue about 200 feet south of its intersection with Shonnard Place.

Dates of Activity: 1891 – Present.

Notes: The Reverend Bonaventure Frey, a Swiss Roman Catholic priest who was the founder of the first province of the Order of Friars Minor Capuchin in the United States, acquired land for the establishment of a monastery and parish in northwest Yonkers on May 25, 1891.[20] The Capuchin order was formed in the 16th century and is an order of mendicants who have taken vows of poverty and rely solely on the charity of others. As they follow the example set by Saint Francis of Assisi, they are more commonly known as the Franciscans. The church that the friars operate in Yonkers is relatively unique in that it is among the few Catholic parishes in Westchester County that are not run by diocesan priests.

Shortly after the Capuchins established themselves in Yonkers, they created a small cemetery at the northeast corner of their property for deceased members of their order at the northeast corner of their property. Several interments in the cemetery predate the acquisition of this property, and were likely moved to this graveyard from other burial grounds. Today, there are three sections in the Friars' cemetery: the original western plot, the adjoining, full southeast plot, and the currently active northeast plot, which contains a statue of two friars in mourning. In addition to the burials themselves, the cemetery has a small memorial garden with cenotaphs which honor the friars who have been buried elsewhere, including places far from Yonkers, such as Japan and Guam. At the end of the garden is a memorial which reads:

> Linger here in this garden,
> If only for a moment,
> To reflect on the goodness
> Of the God who calls us.
> And in your musing and prayer,
> Remember us, your brothers
> Who rest here and elsewhere
> Who have found in Him our peace.

Right: A typical tombstone in the Sacred Heart Friars' Cemetery. The number next to the letters "REL" denote the number of years that the deceased was a member of the order, while the number next to the letters "SAC" denotes the number of years that the deceased served as an ordained priest.

FR. MARTIN COOHILL, O.F.M. CAP.
DIED DEC. 27, 1993
AGE 84
REL 58
SAC. 50

193

Saint John's Cemetery

Yonkers

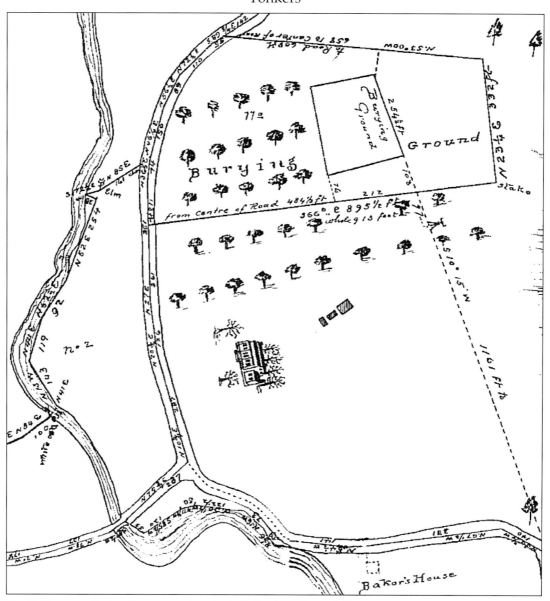

Above: This 1842 map indicates the boundaries of Saint John's Cemetery. The smaller of the two parcels marked "Burying Ground" indicates the older portion of the cemetery. The parsonage is depicted just south of the burial ground on land which presently comprises Oakland Cemetery. Westchester County Clerk Map #306.

Right: This c.1980 photo depicts an interesting soul effigy that was carved on a sandstone in Saint John's Cemetery. Unfortunately, this tombstone has since been broken into pieces.

Location: East side of Saw Mill River Road (Route 9A) about 1000 feet north of its intersection with Ashburton Avenue (adjoining the north side of Oakland Cemetery). The burial ground is best accessed through Oakland Cemetery.

Dates of Activity: 1783 – Present.

Inscriptions: *WCHS* Book #86.

Notes: Frederick Philipse II, the second Lord of the Manor of Philipsburgh, bequeathed a 250-acre farm on the east side of the Saw Mill River to the Church of England upon his death in 1751.[21] Although Frederick's son, Frederick Philipse III, built a house of worship for members of the Church of England near the Hudson River about 1753, the farm was used as a glebe as well as the location of the parsonage.[22] The area around the church itself was not used as a burial ground "on account of its rocky situation."[23]

In 1783 a cemetery was established on the glebe land when Richard Archer, "whose home stood a short distance south and west" of the parsonage lot, was interred there. The story is told that "Mr. Archer, while sitting on the porch of his house, often viewed the hill on the Glebe and expressed his wish that he be buried on its summit."[24] At first, burials were made "in long lines across the hill" nearer to the center of the present cemetery, and "families were grouped together but it was only in a few cases that plot fences were erected."[25] The oldest stone ever recorded in the cemetery read: "Here Lyes The Body of Daniel William Thate Dyed 10 Day of March 1760 Aged 50 years."[26] This stone was apparently moved to Saint John's from another burial ground.

In 1845 a new parsonage was built closer to the church itself, and the portion of the glebe that was not being used as a cemetery was sold to Charles Archer.[27] Shortly after this sale, the unused space in the burial ground was formally laid out and plotted. The cemetery was described by the Reverend David Cole for Scharf's *History of Westchester County, New York*, in 1886:

> The ground is on a high and beautiful elevation [and] comprises 7.6 acres, and is still the property of St. John's Church and under its control. The carriage entrance to it from the Saw-Mill River road is on the northwest corner of the grounds. The foot entrance, further to the south, is by sixteen steps of very abrupt ascent. On the grounds, are several family vaults, some of which are very old, and several quite imposing obelisks and other monuments.... The ground is now becoming very closely filled with graves. There must be a time, and it cannot be far distant, when its room will be wholly taken up.[28]

Ironically, some of the most well-known burials in the cemetery are actually those of unidentified and unclaimed persons whose resting place is marked by a marble column with an inscription that faded many years ago. Eight of the 72 persons who lost their lives on July 28, 1852, in the wreck of the *Henry Clay* on the shore of the Hudson River near Ludlow were buried in Saint John's after that disaster.[29] A.W. Mandeville noted the poor state of this monument in his 1908 article for *Westchester County Magazine*:

Above: The monument which marks the graves of the victims of the wreck of the *Henry Clay*. The inscription, which was illegible as long as 100 years ago, once read.

HERE LIE THE BODIES OF
MRS. ANNE HULL, and her sister
MRS. ELIZA A. SMITH, both of Phila
ELIZA JOHNSON of Albany
BRIDGET BRODERICK. WM. MC
CLUSKEY and two women
and one man whose names
are unknown all of whom
were lost from the HENRY CLAY
on the burning of that
steam boat 2 1-2 miles below
the village of Yonkers on
her passage from Albany
to New York July 28th 1852

A marble monument was placed in St. John's Cemetery, Yonkers, to mark the place where a number of victims of this disaster are buried. The monument, in a state of decay, its inscription no longer readable, stands a little way north of the walk which leads one easterly from the stone steps of the gateway opening into the cemetery. Few beholding that crumbling marble realize that there sleeps those who came to such an untimely death on that fatal summer afternoon.[30]

The opening of adjoining Oakland Cemetery in 1867, coupled with the sale of nearly all of the available burial plots by the end of the 19th century, led to a decline in the use of the cemetery in the late 1800s. Nevertheless, interments are still occasionally made in what little available space remains in the cemetery.

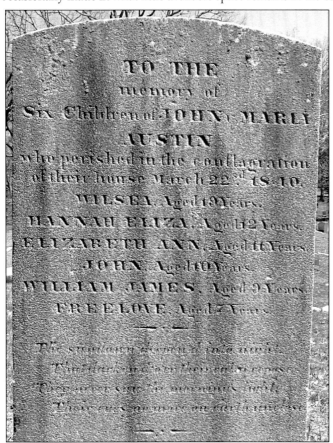

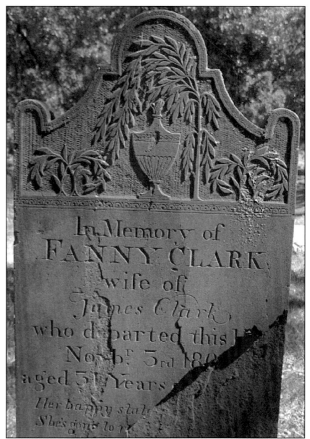

Above Left:

TO THE
memory of
Six Children of JOHN & MARIA
AUSTIN
who perished in the conflagration
of their house March 22nd, 1840.
WILSEA, Aged 19 Years.
HANNAH ELIZA, Aged 12 Years.
ELIZABETH ANN, Aged 11 Years.
JOHN, Aged 10 Years.
WILLIAM JAMES, Aged 9 Years.
FREELOVE, Aged 7 Years.

The sundown deepen'd into night,
That darken'd o'er their calm repose
They never saw the morning's light;
Their eyes, no more on earth unclose.

Above Right:

In Memory of
FANNY CLARK
wife of
James Clark
who departed this life
Novbr. 3rd 1805
aged 31 Years & 4 Mos.

Right:

GEORGE S.
SON OF
S.D. & O.J. ROCKWELL
BORN MAR. 26, 1840
KILLED AT THE BATTLE OF
STONE RIVER, TENN.
JAN. 2, 1863.

196

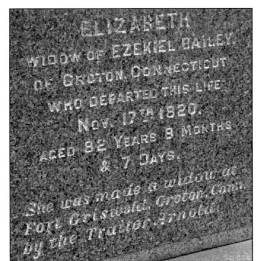

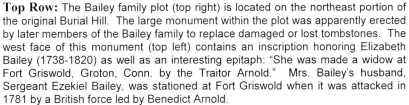

Top Row: The Bailey family plot (top right) is located on the northeast portion of the original Burial Hill. The large monument within the plot was apparently erected by later members of the Bailey family to replace damaged or lost tombstones. The west face of this monument (top left) contains an inscription honoring Elizabeth Bailey (1738-1820) as well as an interesting epitaph: "She was made a widow at Fort Griswold, Groton, Conn. by the Traitor Arnold." Mrs. Bailey's husband, Sergeant Ezekiel Bailey, was stationed at Fort Griswold when it was attacked in 1781 by a British force led by Benedict Arnold.

Bottom Left: This c.1984 photo depicts the sandstone which marks the grave of twin siblings John and Rachel Oakley. John died on January 31, 1791, at the age of one year, three months and 10 days. Rachel died on February 12th of the same year. This tombstone has since been broken into several pieces. Photo courtesy Gray Williams

Bottom Right: This interesting monument, which is visible in the photo at bottom left, marks the graves of Timothy C. (c.1806-1875) and Catherine E. Dwight (c.1809-1877), as well as their son, Albert Sutherland Dwight (c.1842-1864). The inscription for the latter notes that he was "Killed near Petersburg, Va. June 22nd 1864" during the Civil War while serving as a 2nd Lieutenant in the 55th New York Volunteer Infantry Regiment.

Saint John's Episcopal Church Cemetery
Yonkers

Above: The east side of Saint John's Episcopal Church Cemetery in 2008.

Location: Northwest corner of the intersection of Underhill Street and Bradford Boulevard.

Dates of Activity: 1800 – Present.

Inscriptions: *WCHS* Book #87 (p.1-13).

Notes: Writing on the occasion of the 150th anniversary of Saint John's Church, David H. Killeffer commented on the beginnings of this parish, which was founded as a satellite of the church of the same name near Getty Square:

> On the other side of the hills to the east of Yonkers was a little settlement made up of nineteen buildings, sixteen of them small houses. The other buildings were a public house known as Underhill's Tavern, a blacksmith shop, and a schoolhouse. This was Turkey Hoe (or Turkeyhoe or Turkeyho), or "Turkey Hill", so named because wild turkeys abounded all through the woods. To this little hamlet in 1789 came the energetic and determined young rector of St. John's, Elias Cooper, to bring the Gospel. He was then in his 31st year...[and] was a man of great energy, and he commanded respect in a rough country. Out of his efforts came the building of the new chapel.[31]

The Reverend Cooper founded not only a house of worship for the small community, but a burial place as well. The oldest tombstone in the burial ground, which borders the church on three sides, dates from 1800. At the annual meeting of the vestry in April 1866, "burial fees were fixed at $7 for persons residing in the neighborhood and $15 for others," while "a year later the fee for all burials was set at $15."[32] Although its burial space is limited, the graveyard at Saint John's is one of the few churchyards in lower Westchester that still serves as an active cemetery. A columbarium is located on the west side of the church.

198

Above: The space adjoining the southeast corner of the church contains the oldest tombstones in the cemetery, nearly all of which still have their accompanying footstones.

Above: The headstone of Hannah Smith (c.1726-1805) is one of the oldest tombstones in the cemetery and shows the kind of damage that can occur to sandstones.

Right: This tombstone was "erected by Nelson & Mary Oliver in memory of their daughter[s]" Mary (1836-1838) and Adeline (1837-1838). Mary died on November 6, 1838, while her sister passed away four days later.

Saint Joseph's Cemetery
Yonkers

Above and Right: The tombstone of Francesco (1866-1927) and Maria Chiaro (1870-1962) is typical of those which mark the graves of many early 20th-century Italian-Americans in Westchester County. It features a statue of an angel or religious figure, is inscribed in the Italian language, and contains a portrait of the deceased.

Location: South side of Tompkins Avenue about 450 feet west of Nepperhan Avenue.

Dates of Activity: 1877 – Present.

Mailing Address: Saint Joseph's Cemetery, 209 Truman Avenue, Yonkers, NY 10703.

Notes: Prior to 1871, there was but one parish and cemetery, Saint Mary's, to serve the Roman Catholic residents of Yonkers. This situation changed in May of that year when "the parish of St. Joseph was set off from St. Mary's."[33] Masses were held in Public School No. 6 until the present church on Ashburton Avenue was opened in December 1871.[34] As the Catholic population in Yonkers grew, so did the need for additional burial space. To meet this need, the first pastor of Saint Joseph's, Father Albert A. Lings (1844-1915), purchased a 20-acre plot near the Greenburgh border on July 5, 1877, for $12,000.[35] One month later Father Lings took out an ad in the *Yonkers Statesman*:

> The Saint Joseph's Church New Cemetery, of twenty acres, is now ready. Plots are ready for sale, as well as single graves. It is being artistically laid out, so that it will be an ornament to the city, while securing respect to our dead. The Cemetery is situated on the old pickle farm, in the Third Ward…. All business connected with the Cemetery must be transacted with Rev. A.A. Lings. [36]

Several impressive memorials mark the graves of some of the longtime pastors of Yonkers' Catholic churches, including Monsignor Joseph P. Caramanno (1905-1990), the Reverend John F. Kelahan (1865-1928), and Father Lings, who had charge of Saint Joseph's from its founding in 1871 to his death in 1915. The cemetery is still used today.

Above and Bottom Left: The east-central section of Saint Joseph's Cemetery is the final resting place for many of the immigrants from southern and eastern Europe who settled in Yonkers around the turn of the 20th century. The marker at top left is inscribed in the Cyrilic alphabet and stands at the grave of a Ukrainian woman named Anastasia, who died on January 21, 1918, at the age of 31.

Bottom Left (Polish):

TU SPOCZYWA
ANNA SZPYTKOWSKA
UMERLA 5. SEPT. 1918

WICZNAJI PAMIAT

PAMIATKA WID
MUZA MIKOLAJA

HERE LIES
ANNA SZPYTKOWSKA
SHE DIED 5. SEPT. 1918

IN ETERNAL MEMORY

FROM THE MEMORY OF
HER HUSBAND MIKOLAJA

Top Right (Italian):

QUI RISIEDE IL DEFUNTO
DOMENICO FULGINITI
NATO 13 MARCO 1866
MORTO 3 GIUGNO 1906
PER MEMORIA DEL SUO CARO
FRATELLO PEPPINO E DI TUTTI
I SUOI PAESANI TORRESI.

HERE LIES THE DECEASED
DOMENICO FULGINITI
BORN 13 MARCH 1866
DIED 3 JUNE 1906
FROM THE MEMORY OF HIS LOVING
BROTHER PEPPINO AND OF ALL
HIS COUNTRYMEN OF TORRES

Above Left: This tombstone stands at the grave of the Gurksnis family. The dates of birth and death for Adela Gurksnis (right) were inscribed in Lithuanian:

CIMUS 31 SPALIU 1923
MIRA 15 VASARA 1927

BORN 31 OCTOBER 1923
DIED 15 FEBRUARY 1927

Above Right: This tombstone stands at the grave of Private Alfred Bruno, who was killed in action on June 17, 1918, during World War I. Alfred's father, Tomaso, was a cobbler who spoke no English. He carried the War Department telegram announcing his son's death to a neighbor, who translated it for him.[37]

Far Right (Polish):

TU SPOCZYWA S.P.	HERE RESTS [IN PEACE]
ROZALIA ROZMYSLOWICZ	ROZALIA ROZMYSLOWICZ
RODZ. W ROKU 1890	BORN IN THE YEAR 1890
UM. DNIA 10 KWIETNIA	DAY OF DEATH 10 APRIL
1926 ROKU	YEAR 1926
POKUJ YEJ DUSZY	PEACE TO HER SOUL

Saint Mary's Cemetery

Yonkers

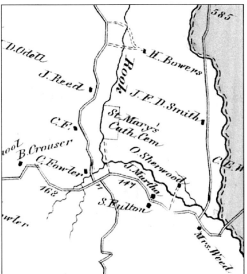 

Left: This 1867 map shows the location of "St. Mary's Cath. Cem" on the east side of Sprain Brook. Note the home of John Murtha (marked "J. Murtha"), the man who donated the land for the cemetery.

Right: Looking northeast from the south entrance of Saint Mary's Cemetery, c.1948. Several years after this photo was taken, the New York State Thruway was constructed along the east side of the cemetery where the tree line is located.

Location: Both sides of Sprain Road about 1,200 feet north of its intersection with Tuckahoe Road.

Dates of Activity: 1855 – Present.

Mailing Address: 114 Sprain Road, Yonkers, NY 10710.

Notes: The first Catholic house of worship in Yonkers was established when a triumvirate of developers deeded a parcel of land on present-day St. Mary's Street to Bishop John Hughes in 1848 for the establishment of the parish of the Immaculate Conception, a congregation comprised largely of Irish immigrants.[38] The following passage regarding the cemetery appeared in a volume written in 1948 on the occasion of the 100th anniversary of the parish:

> "It would be difficult to find a place better suited by nature for a burying ground than this secluded valley, protected by the hills on all sides and framed in superb foliage, the growth of generations." These words written years ago ring true to-day and give in a word picture the setting of St. Mary's Cemetery in the Sprain Valley. It was during the pastorate of Rev. Eugene McGuire, when the Catholic population of Yonkers was only 1200, that the property for the original St. Mary's Cemetery was acquired. Since then the cemetery has been enlarged by degrees to its present size of eleven and one-half acres, including what is now called the New Section. This New Section is a parcel of land, one and a half acres in size, located across Sprain Road from the northwest end of the cemetery proper. The first burial in this section was made in August 1946.
>
> It has ever been the noble ambition of the pastors and people of St. Mary's to give the cemetery the care and attention necessary to maintain it as a sacred shrine to the memory of their beloved dead. The appearance of the cemetery today is indeed pleasing to the eye. One sees a vast, well cared-for, gracefully sloping lawn, dotted with tombstones and lined with trees and shrubbery. To bring the cemetery to its present excellent condition more than ten years of hard work was needed. It was in 1936 that Father Avard, ably assisted by Father McGrath, began to put the cemetery on the "lawn plan." Father McGrath directed the important preliminary work of map drawing and record checking. In this, Mr. Lotzy Proft was of great assistance. When the records had been put in good order and the necessary maps had been drawn the work of leveling and seeding was started. At first there were complaints from people who did not quite understand what was planned; but as the work proceeded and the good results became obvious, the number of complaints became fewer; and today there are no complaints; everyone is well pleased. In 1946 to crown all this work, a large crucifix was erected on the hill and the Holy Sacrifice of the Mass was offered at its base for the repose of the souls of all those whose bodies lie in the cemetery.[39]

As is indicated in the above passage, the original section of Saint Mary's Cemetery was located on the east side of Sprain Brook and was accessed by a lane which led south to Tuckahoe Road. Along the east side of the remnant of this lane is a plot belonging to the Murtha family, from whom the original cemetery land was acquired in 1855. Later, the cemetery could be accessed by a new lane leading eastward from Sprain Road, including a bridge which crossed Sprain Brook. Today, this right-of-way comprises the southern entrance to Saint Mary's. Unfortunately, the peaceful setting of the cemetery was intruded upon by the New York State Thruway when construction of that highway began in the mid-1950s, and more than 170 graves in the eastern portion of the burial ground were relocated in 1954 to accommodate the road.[40]

Above Left: The tombstone of Thomas D. Combs (c.1829-1879) asks visitors to say one Hail Mary.

Above Right: The Murtha plot in Saint Mary's Cemetery in 2007. This photograph shows just how close the New York State Thruway is to the cemetery. The monument in the center of the plot honors John Murtha (1817-1898), "who donated the original and large part of [the] cemetery to the Archbishop of New York by deeds of gift recorded July 17, 1855 and June 22, 1877."

Bottom Right: The inscription of this small monument reads:

W[M] E. CHEEVERS
AUG 1ST 1898,
AGED 24 YEARS
SAN JUAN, CUBA

Private Cheevers served in Company I of the 71st New York Infantry Regiment during the campaign which culminated in the capture of Santiago, Cuba.[41] Sadly, he died from malaria a mere two weeks after the city was taken. The monument features a replica of the regiment's hat. The 71st New York's regimental monument is located in Mount Hope Cemetery in the Town of Greenburgh.

204

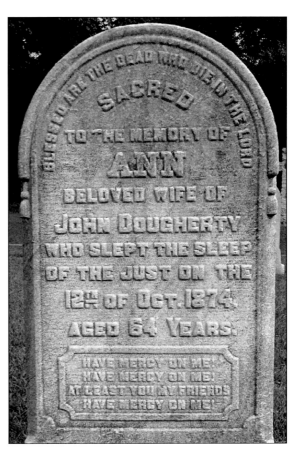

Above Left: One of the oldest memorials in Saint Mary's Cemetery, this tombstone reads:

Sacred
TO THE MEMORY OF
THOMAS REID
A NATIVE OF ------ IRELAND
WHO DEPARTED THIS LIFE
SEPT. 27TH A.D. 1855
AETAT 51 YEARS.
Also his infant children
MARCELLA and THOMAS.
Aged respectively 11 mos. 10 d's and 13 mos. 20 d's
This stone is erected by an affectionate
wife and fond mother to commemorate her
sad bereavement.

Above Right: John Dougherty erected this monument at the grave of his wife, Ann, "who slept the sleep of the just on the 12th of Oct. 1874" at the age of 64. The last four lines on the tombstone read:

HAVE MERCY ON ME!
HAVE MERCY ON ME!
AT LEAST YOU MY FRIENDS
HAVE MERCY ON ME!

Right: This tombstone was "erected by Timothy Monahan" at the graves of his wife, Margaret, and "his five children & mother-in-law, Helen Regan."

Tuckahoe Road Burying Ground

Yonkers

Above: The graves of Vincent Fowler (left, 1744-1813) and his second wife, Elizabeth Brown Merritt (1745-1813), were removed from the Tuckahoe Road Burying Ground to Saint John's Cemetery. Strangely, the tombstone and remains of Vincent's first wife, Dorothy Valentine (right, d.1783), were relocated to neighboring Oakland Cemetery next to the border of Saint John's Cemetery and near the Copcutt vault.

Location: Formerly located at the northeast corner of the intersection of Saw Mill River and Tuckahoe roads.

Dates of Activity: c.1760 – c.1825.

Other Names: Curser Plot.

Removed: to Saint John's Cemetery in 1882.

Notes: Relatively little information is available concerning this cemetery, which was alluded to briefly by the Reverend Charles E. Allison in his 1896 work, *History of Yonkers*:

> One of the oldest burial grounds in Yonkers was near the corner of the Saw Mill Valley and Tuckahoe roads. Some years ago, in order to make way for projected improvements, the bones and the quaint old headstones were removed to the northeast corner of the St. John's Cemetery.[42]

The land which surrounded this burial ground was acquired by Benjamin Fowler (1715-1786) sometime prior to 1756 when he was elected Town Clerk of Yonkers.[43] Benjamin built his home near the present intersection of Tuckahoe Road and Runyon Avenue.[44] An 1806 deed, which transferred the land surrounding the cemetery from Benjamin Fowler's son Josiah to Benjamin Curser, gave the following description of this graveyard, which was apparently no longer in active use at the time:

> Reserving three quarters of an acre of ground more or less within the herein described bounds by four stakes one standing on the southeast corner and another on the southwest corner and another on the northwest corner and the other on the northeast corner, with free passage for those families to go in and come out that formerly used to bury there without hindrance or molestation.[45]

A more detailed historical explanation of the removal of this burial may be found in an unpublished typescript written by an unknown author at the Westchester County Historical Society:

> This plot occupied a small knoll on the northeast corner of Tuckahoe Road and Saw Mill River Road, and served as a burial place for a number of families in the neighborhood. In 1882, this section was developed into building lots and the contents of the burial ground were removed to St. John's. The oldest stone in this group bore the date 1760. There is a tradition that among the bodies removed from the Curser Plot were those of soldiers who died in the vicinity during the Revolutionary War. The number of these soldiers is unknown.[46]

The primary reason for the removal of the cemetery was the development of the Runyon Heights residential neighborhood, a community that was established on the old Curser farm in the 1870s and 1880s.[47]

APPENDIX:
MISCELLANEOUS BURIAL PLACES

Town of Eastchester

Christ Episcopal Church Columbarium

Christ Episcopal Church, located at the intersection of Kensington and Sagamore roads in Bronxville, contains a sizeable outdoor columbarium that was established in the 1960s. Among those whose ashes have been placed here is Ford C. Frick (1894-1978), who served as the Commissioner of Major League Baseball from 1951 to 1965.

Johnson Columbarium at the Village Lutheran Church

The Village Lutheran Church, located at 172 White Plains Road in Bronxville, contains the Johnson Columbarium, an outdoor inurnment space that can hold up to one thousand urns.

Town of Mamaroneck

Edward Merritt Grave

When Mamaroneck High School student Milton Prigoff wrote his study of Mamaroneck's burial places in 1940, he mentioned the existence of an individual grave on the west side of Fenimore Road near Baldwin Place:

> There is only one marked, single grave remaining in the Town of Mamaroneck of which we know today. It stands on a rise off Fenimore Road just back of the Sheldrake River.... It is well hidden in the brush on the side of the hill but it is a clear old redstone and is in good condition.... The inscription reads as follows:

> In memory of Edward Merritt who departed this life
> Novr. 14th 1805 aged 53 yrs, 5 months.
> To honest men with care this stone defend
> For he who lays beneath was once your friend
> By fates decree he moulders in this spot
> Years may roll on, but mer[rits] neer forgot [1]

Edward Merritt owned a substantial amount of land in Mamaroneck, and was elected town supervisor in 1801.[2] It is not known why Edward was interred at this spot. His neighbor, Henry Disbrow, later granted a portion of his own family burial ground on Rockland Avenue to Edward's son, Gilbert.

City of Mount Vernon

Farrington Family Burial Ground

The origins of the Farrington family in Eastchester were described by the Reverend Robert Bolton in his 1848 history of Westchester County:

> [Thomas Farrington] emigrated from Flushing to Eastchester about the year 1750, and became one of the first purchasers of a portion of Long Reach, a district of the town.... Thomas Farrington died about the year 1793, about 90 years of age; his grave and that of his second wife [Margaret Mastin] lies at the junction of a lane called Farrington's Lane, running through his farm with the White Plains Road.[3]

Thomas's will ordered that he be "buried at the discretion of [his] Executors," so the burial place on the Farrington farm was probably founded by his sons, George and Jonas.[4] Long Reach encompassed land along the east side of the Bronx River between Scarsdale and the neighborhood of Williamsbridge in the Bronx. Farrington's Lane is present-day Gramatan Avenue, while the White Plains Road is present-day Lincoln Avenue. Thomas's farm was located on the north side of Lincoln Avenue on both sides of Gramatan Avenue. Thomas left the eastern portion of his farm to his youngest son, George, who sold the land to Thomas Valentine in 1812. George reserved his family's burial ground from this sale:

...with the reservation of one quarter of an acre now in part occupied as a family burial ground & in future to be occupied by the said George Farrington & his heirs & family...& for the special purpose of a burying ground only & no other use.... [5]

Using the descriptions given in the above passages, the cemetery was apparently located at the northeast corner of the intersection of Gramatan and East Lincoln avenues. The burial ground was not mentioned in the next transaction of this portion of the Farrington farm, which occurred in 1845.[6] Most of the immediate descendants of Thomas and Margaret are interred at Saint Paul's Episcopal Church Cemetery in Mount Vernon. In 1859 John A. and Jonas S. Farrington purchased a 16' x 18' plot at Saint Paul's; however, it is not know if the remains of Thomas and Margaret were moved there.[7]

City of New Rochelle

Blessed Sacrament Roman Catholic Church

The remains of Father Thomas McLoughlin (1826-1902) and Monsignor Francis X. Shea (1894-1970) are interred on the south side of Blessed Sacrament Roman Catholic Church (northwest corner of Centre Avenue and Shea Place). Father McLoughlin was installed as the first pastor of Blessed Sacrament in 1853 and served in that post until his death. Per his wishes, he was interred next to his church.[8] Monsignor Shea served as pastor of Blessed Sacrament from 1947 until his death.

Above: The grave of Father Thomas McLoughlin (1826-1902) is located on the south side of Blessed Sacrament Roman Catholic Church in New Rochelle. The inscription on the monument reads:

1826   1902

IN MEMORIAM

REVEREND THOMAS MCLOUGHLIN

FOUNDER OF

CHURCH OF THE BLESSED SACRAMENT

FIFTY YEARS PASTOR OF THIS PARISH

A FAITHFUL PRIEST A TRUE PATRIOT

AN ARDENT DEFENDER OF

THE RIGHTS OF THE PEOPLE

GOD REST HIS SOUL

Bonnett Family Burial Ground

The Bonnett Family Burial Ground, which was located on the family's farm, had disappeared "well over 100 years" before the Daughters of the American Revolution conducted their survey of New Rochelle's cemeteries in 1940. [9]

Church Street Slave Cemetery

A slave cemetery was located on the grounds of present-day 12 Church Street. The only information regarding this burial place is found in the survey of New Rochelle cemeteries conducted by the Daughters of the American Revolution:

> There was another colored cemetery located on Church Street where the City Fire House now stands. It had not been used in 60 years even in 1889 and no removals were ever made. When the Fire House was built many bones were unearthed.[10]

The aforementioned fire house now serves as the home of the French Speaking Baptist Church.

Pell Farm Slave Cemetery

George T. Davis mentioned the existence of a slave cemetery near Cooper's Corners in his 1889 essay:

> The old slave lot is situated on the [Clark] Davis farm near the Seacord farm about 100 yards south of the cider mill of Capt. Davis. It is about 25-50 feet and is marked by an apple tree. No interments have been made here in over 50 years.[11]

The Clark Davis farm was located on the east side of North Avenue in the vicinity of Lovell Road. Land records indicate that the farm on which this plot was located was owned by the Pell family prior to 1794 and by the Toffey family from 1794 to the mid-19th century at which time the estate came into the hands of Clark Davis.[12] The location of the cemetery was lost when the Davis farm was subdivided in the early 20th century.

Willis Family Burial Ground

James Willis, one of the most prominent citizens of New Rochelle during the late 18th century, was interred in a plot on his farm following his death. The only information available concerning this burial ground comes from the pen of George T. Davis, who wrote a sketch of James Willis for *Westchester County Magazine*:

> James Willis, the fifteenth supervisor of New Rochelle, was born on Long Island, where he lived until 1762 when he removed to the main land, and settled on what is now known as the "Hubbard" Farm in Upper New Rochelle. He was a son of Richard Willis, the tenth supervisor of New Rochelle. He was married to Mary Peters, October 18, 1761. He was several times commissioned coroner for the County of Westchester, both by the Crown and Provincial authorities. He was elected supervisor in 1790 and re-elected in 1791-92-93-94-95-96 and 97. He was Town Clerk in 1783-84-85-86-87-88-89-90-91 and 92. Path Master in 1789-90-91-92-93-94-95-96-97-98-99-1800-01. School Inspector in 1801. He was commissioned First Lieutenant in the Army by Congress, his commission dating September 20, 1776. The captain having resigned or being promoted, the command devolved upon him. As captain he started with his company for Quebec, but on arriving at Tarrytown and hearing of the defeat of Montgomery, he stopped. After this time he was mostly occupied as commissary in buying cattle and other supplies for the army until the close of the war. During the war he moved his family to the Highlands that they might be out of the way of the Cowboys and Skinners, but after the war returned to his farm in New Rochelle.
>
> After the war and until his death he followed the occupation of a farmer, although he was a fine worker in wood. He died quite suddenly. He had been ploughing, and feeling tired, he leaned against a fence to rest and died in that position April 23, 1802 and was buried in a family plot on the farm near the boundary line between his farm and that of Peter Bonnett.[13]

The Willis farm was located on the east side of Wilmot Road in the vicinity of its intersection with the Hutchinson River Parkway. Unfortunately, no reservation was made to preserve the plot where Supervisor Willis was buried, and as a result, its exact location has been lost to history.

Wheeler Family Burial Ground

The Wheeler Family Burial Ground, which was located on the family's farm, had disappeared "well over 100 years" before the Daughters of the American Revolution conducted their survey of New Rochelle's cemeteries in 1940. [14]

Town of Pelham

Huguenot Memorial Church Columbarium

Located at the intersection of Boston Post Road and Pelhamdale Avenue, the Huguenot Memorial Church, which is affiliated with the Presbyterian Church (U.S.A.), was founded in 1876. As part of an expansion project that was completed in 1965, the church established an outdoor columbarium that was later dedicated to the memory of Thomas S. Nichols (1950-1967).[15]

Egbert Norton Burial

A single tombstone is located on the grounds of Bolton Priory in Pelham Manor. It reads: "Egbert, son of Egbert and Eliza Norton, died 1813, age 2 years. Suffer the little children to come unto me."[16]

Town of Rye

Anderson Family Burial Ground

A cemetery belonging to the Anderson family was once located near the border between New York and Connecticut. Isaac Anderson, a "Mariner of New York," arrived in Rye in 1707 and "purchased land on the east side of the Byram River from Samuel Lyon" in 1711; two years later, "Captain Anderson was granted permission to build a mill or mills along the Byram River."[17] Captain Anderson died in 1722 and was buried in a plot that he had established in his will: "I order that the burying place on my land, be and remain a burying place for my family forever."[18] The Anderson plot was still intact in 1758, when Daniel and Sarah Hawkhurst sold a parcel of land to Jacobus Roosevelt "reserving a burial place for the heirs of Isaac Anderson."[19]

Fowler Family Burial Ground

William Fowler (c.1687-1747), a native of Eastchester, settled in Rye in 1715. By 1718 William had acquired a sizable farm bordered by the Byram River in Connecticut on the east and by Blind Brook in New York on the west.[20] In 1742 William sold his farm to Adam Seaman, reserving "the burying place to bury those of his own family."[21] William and his wife, Mary, were likely interred in this burial ground following their deaths. Although William's eldest son, Caleb (c.1708-c.1778), was "undoubtedly buried in that plot of ground" that had been reserved by his father, his wife, Ann Miller (1717-1809), was interred at the Mount Zion Methodist Church Cemetery in Somers. Nothing else is known about this burial ground. As William Fowler's farm straddled the border of New York and Connecticut, this graveyard could have been located in either state.

Haviland Family Burial Ground

A Haviland Family Burial Ground was apparently located in the present village of Rye Brook. According to Josephine Frost, Thomas Haviland (1700-1762) was interred "in the burying ground which was on their place in Rye."[22] Thomas' father, Benjamin, acquired a significant amount of land in northeast Harrison and northern Rye. In his family Bible, Thomas wrote that his second wife, Sarah, "was buried by my former wife Hannah [Field] in my own burying-ground." Unfortunately, the location of this burying ground is unknown.

Nathaniel Merritt Burial

Genealogist Grenville C. Mackenzie mentioned the grave of Nathaniel Merritt on Merritt's Point in *Families of the Colonial Town of Philipsburg*:

> In 1732 [John Merritt (1681-1759)] sold 11 ½ acres [on Merritt's Point] to John Morris, excepting one square rod where his son Nathaniel was buried. The deed of John Morris to Samuel Lane in 1741 contains the same exception, mentioning the "grave where Nathaniel Merritt, brother of John Merritt, is buried." The father John was presumably then deceased.[23]

The elder John Merritt was interred at the Merritt Family Burial Ground on Lyon's Point. Unfortunately, the precise location of Nathaniel's grave is unknown.

Mitchell Farm Burials

Evelyn Briggs Baldwin, a genealogist who recorded tombstone inscriptions in many Westchester cemeteries during the early 20th century, found two burials during a visit to Rye on March 31, 1913:

Erasmus Williams, Merchant from New York, D. Sept. 14, 1776. aged 56 years.
Another headstone, by side of large boulder, letters illegible.[24]

According to Baldwin, the property on which the graves were located was occupied at the time by the Asa Lawrence Inn. The Mamaroneck Historical Society notes that this inn, the site of which is presently occupied by the Continental View Apartments (1035 East Boston Post Road), was where the "old Guion farmhouse" was once sited.[25] Unfortunately, the precise location of these graves is unknown.

Slater Family Burial Ground

Above: The Slater family plot in Greenwood Union Cemetery in 2009. The older tombstones in the second and third rows were moved from the Slater Family Burial Ground to Greenwood Union about 1900.

George A. Slater, a member of the New York State Assembly, mentioned this family burial place in a brief history of his family that he wrote for *Ye History of Ye Town of Greenwich*:

The present name of Slater was, prior to the Revolutionary War, known as Slawter, and Slaughter. The family was settled on Hog Pen Ridge, now Ridge Street, in the Town of Rye, N.Y., prior to 1730. The early settler was probably Abraham Slater, who is mentioned in the town records in 1730. He was probably of English descent, and had removed from Long Island, or Virginia.... The early family burial ground was located on the farm, on the west side of Ridge Street, on the side hill...and was only removed about 1900.[26]

Assemblyman Slater's description places the site of the Slater Family Burial Ground near the present intersection of Ridge Street and Betsy Brown Road. The remains and tombstones in the graveyard were removed to Greenwood Union Cemetery in Rye (Section A, Lot 173).

Town of Scarsdale

Phillip and Nancy Washburn Memory Garden at the Scarsdale Congregational Church

The Scarsdale Congregational Church, founded in 1895 and affiliated with the United Church of Christ, established a memory garden on its grounds at 1 Heathcote Road in 2007. The memory garden serves as "both a columbarium and a memorial site for those buried elsewhere." The garden is named for the Reverend Phillip Washburn, minister emeritus of the church, and his wife, Nancy.[27]

Scarsdale Community Baptist Church Columbarium

Founded in 1928, the Scarsdale Community Baptist Church at 51 Popham Road established an indoor columbarium inside the Baptistery Chapel in 2006/2007.[28]

City of Yonkers

Saint Denis Roman Catholic Church

The remains of Mr. and Mrs. Dennis Horgan, who "helped fund the construction" of Saint Denis Roman Catholic Church at 470 Van Cortlandt Park Avenue, are interred in a crypt in the church.[29]

Saint John's Episcopal Church

The Reverend Robert Bolton suggested that the glebe of Saint John's Episcopal Church may have been used as a burial ground prior to the establishment of Saint John's Cemetery on Saw Mill River Road:

> The church yard has been long since abandoned, as a place of sepulture, on account of its rocky situation.... The one now occupied is located on the old parsonage property, bequeathed by Frederick Philipse, with the glebe, in 1751. It is beautifully situated on a rising knoll, in the valley of the Saw Mill. The first interment here on record occurs in 1783.[30]

The glebe on which the church was located extended from South Broadway to a point about 50 feet past the west side of present-day Riverdale Avenue.[31] In his work, *The History of Yonkers*, the Reverend Charles E. Allison mentioned a burial that took place beneath the church:

> Both armies used the church as a hospital. An American soldier of the Revolution, who was killed in the neighborhood, is known to have been interred beneath the floor of the sacred edifice, but no reason has been assigned by history or tradition for the selection of the church as the soldier's sepulcher.[32]

Perhaps it was the remains of this soldier or of a minister that were found not long after the conclusion of the Revolutionary War, as the Reverend Allison continued:

> In May, 1791, a conflagration in Yonkers greatly excited and saddened the people [as] the Episcopal Church [was] partially destroyed. The stone walls remained intact. When the ruins were examined the skeleton of a full-sized man was discovered behind what remained of the pulpit.[33]

Saint John's Church is located at the northwest corner of Palisade Avenue and Hudson Street.

Valentine Family Burial Ground

This burial ground was briefly mentioned in the March 21, 1890, edition of the *Mount Vernon Chronicle*: "On the side of the Mile Square road, is the old Valentine graveyard. The inscriptions on the stones are scarcely legible."[34] The Valentine family settled in present-day Yonkers about 1680. The area on which their farm was located became known as Valentine Hill, and it is now occupied by Saint Joseph's Seminary and College. The fate of the Valentine Family Burial Ground is unknown. Nearly all of the members of the Valentine family are interred at Saint Paul's Episcopal Church Cemetery in Mount Vernon, so it is likely that the remains in this graveyard were moved to Saint Paul's around the turn of the 20th century.

Notes

Pages vi - xii

[1] http://www.nps.gov/archive/sapa/cemetery/RS.html
[2] *Laws of the State of New York Passed at the Seventy-Seventh Sessions of the Legislature.* Albany: Gould, Banks & Co., 1854, 538.

Pages 1 - 10

[1] Richard B. Weir. "Bronxville's Little Cemetery." *The Villager*, March 1992, 5.
[2] "Small Cemetery On City Line Holds Dead of Scotch Religious Sect From New York." *The Daily Argus*, Mount Vernon, NY, 1 July 1931. *Building A Suburban Village: Bronxville, New York, 1898 – 1998.* Bronxville, NY: Bronxville Centennial Celebration, Inc., 1998, 153. *Bronxville: Views and Vignettes.* Bronxville, NY: The Bronxville Diamond Jubilee Committee, 1974, 81.
[3] *Building A Suburban Village*, 153.
[4] Ibid.
[5] *Bronxville: Views and Vignettes*, 82.
[6] Mrs. Harry Leslie Walker and LaMont A. Warner, eds. *A History of the Reformed Church of Bronxville*. Bronxville, NY: The Consistory of the Reformed Church of Bronxville, 1951, 19. Westchester County Land Records Liber 136, 356.
[7] Walker and Warner, 23.
[8] Ibid.
[9] Thomas A. Brennan, Jr. *Church of the Immaculate Conception, Tuckahoe, New York, 1853-2003.* Tuckahoe, NY: Church of the Immaculate Conception, 2003, 58-59. The land on which the cemetery is located was purchased for the parish by Archbishop John McCloskey on December 12, 1882 (Land Records Liber 1020, 11).
[10] Ibid. Westchester County Land Records Liber 1402, 127-128.
[11] Brennan, 58.
[12] A.W. Mandeville. "Were These Revolutionary Soldiers?" *Westchester County Magazine*, Vol. 2, No. 1 (October 1908).
[13] Robert Bolton. *The History of the Several Towns, Manors, and Patents of the County of Westchester, from its First Settlement to the Present Time.* Bowie, MD: Heritage Books, 1996, I, 253-254.
[14] Ibid., I, 160. Bolton found the "remains of a large wolf-pit" in the Winter Burying Ground. A large number of these holes were dug throughout the county in the late 1600s to root out the wolf population, which had caused much loss of livestock.
[15] WCHS Hufeland Scrapbooks – Eastchester.
[16] "Tuckahoe Skeletons." *New York Tribune*, 20 September 1908. "Human Bones Found at Tuckahoe Came From an Old Cemetery There." *The Daily Argus*, Mount Vernon, NY, 13 September 1922.
[17] "Tuckahoe Skeletons." *New York Tribune*, 20 September 1908.
[18] "Colonial Heroes Buried." *The New York Times*, 18 October 1908.
[19] WCHS Hufeland Scrapbooks – Eastchester.
[20] "Tuckahoe Pays Tribute To Revolutionary War Heroes." *The Daily Argus*, Mount Vernon, NY, 23 February 1923. "Unveiling of Wreath in the Memory of Unknown Dead, Historical Event at Tuckahoe." *The Daily Argus*, Mount Vernon, NY, 31 May 1923. "Tuckahoe Honors Boy Hero of 1776." *The New York Times*, 23 February 1923.
[21] WCHS Hufeland Scrapbooks – Eastchester.
[22] "Revolutionary Hero's Grave to Get Tablet." *The Tuckahoe Record*, 25 March 1937.
[23] "Skeleton of Hero Issue in Election." *The New York Times*, 2 March 1937.
[24] Ibid.
[25] "Democrats Want Grave Opened To End 'Bones Mystery.'" *The Herald Statesman*, 4 March 1937. "Mayor's Statement Ends Row Over Bones Of Soldier Of '76." *The Herald Statesman*, 23 March 1937.

Pages 11 - 24

[1] Paula Lippsett. *Mamaroneck Town: A History of "The Gathering Place."* Mamaroneck, NY: Town of Mamaroneck, 1997, 7.
[2] Lippsett, 7.

3 Bolton, I, 482-486.

4 Ibid., 487. The DeLancey house was later moved to the northwest corner of Fenimore and Boston Post roads in 1900.

5 Lippsett, 10. John Peter DeLancey gave the newlyweds use of a home near the northern edge of his property where Cooper wrote *The Spy*. The site of this house is now denoted by a historical marker on the east side of Mamaroneck Road just south of Murray Hill Road.

6 Wills Liber L, 206-217.

7 William G. Fulcher. *Mamaroneck Through the Years*. Larchmont, NY: The Larchmont Times, 1936, 30.

8 Charles Wells Hayes. *The Diocese of Western New York: History and Recollections*. Rochester, NY: Scrantom, Wetmore & Co., 1904, 252. James Grant Wilson. "President Edward F. DeLancey." *The New York Genealogical and Biographical Record*, Vol. XXXVI, No. 3, 170-172.

9 Charles Wells Hayes. "Bishop De Lancey: Address in St. Peter's Memorial Church, Geneva, N.Y., November 2, 1907, on the occasion of the translation of his remains from Mamaroneck." http://anglicanhistory.org/usa/whdelancey/translation.html. "Know Your Westchester." *The Standard Star*, 21 October 1954.

10 Bolton, I, 498.

11 Ibid.

12 Ibid., 499.

13 Fulcher, 37.

14 Bolton, I, 498-499.

15 Westchester County Wills Liber K, 389-392.

16 Westchester County Wills Liber F, 1.

17 Westchester County Land Records Liber 72, 428-429.

18 Ibid., 431-433.

19 "Died." *The Evening Post*, 17 September 1831.

20 Westchester County Land Records Liber 573, 438-440.

21 WCHS Cemetery Inscription Book #81, 6.

22 Westchester County Land Records Liber M, 500-501.

23 Westchester County Land Records Liber 342, 203-206.

24 Westchester County Land Records Liber 186, 75-77.

25 Mrs. Selleck E. Coles. "Mamaroneck, N.Y., Graveyard Inscriptions." *The New York Genealogical and Biographical Record*, Vol. 56 No.1 (January, 1925) 33-41. Mrs. Coles' notes regarding the Gedney family are held by the Westchester County Historical Society (WCHS Gedney Family Vertical File).

26 Westchester County Clerk Map #318.

Pages 25 - 42

1 1790 United States Census, Westchester County.

2 Westchester County Land Records Liber 26, 438.

3 Westchester County Land Records Liber 43, 460. The Winfield Avenue crossing of the Mamaroneck River was known as Hadden's Bridge.

4 *The Underhill Society of America: Annual Report of the Secretary*. Brooklyn: The Underhill Society of America, 1905, 18.

5 Mrs. Selleck E. Coles. "Mamaroneck, N.Y., Graveyard Inscriptions." *The New York Genealogical and Biographical Record*, Vol. 56 No.1 (January, 1925) 33-41.

6 Westchester County Land Records Liber 5495, 131.

7 "29 Graves Too Many? Thruway Displaced Old Cemetery." *The Daily Times*, 19 September 1956.

8 "Westchester Today!: Greenwood Union Cemetery." *The Standard Star*, 11 March 1961.

9 Otto Hufeland. *Westchester County during the American Revolution*. White Plains, NY: Westchester County Historical Society, 1926, 129.

10 Fulcher, 23.

11 Ibid.

12 WCHS McDonald Papers, 23.

13 Ibid., 392.

14 Ibid., 388.

15 Scharf, II, 875.

16 Dunlap, Charles J. "Heathcote Hill." *The Quarterly Bulletin of the Westchester County Historical Society*, Vol. 3 No. 4 (October 1927) 21-22.

17 WCHS Cemetery Inscription Book #81, 7.

[18] Fulcher, 56.

[19] Ibid.

[20] Westchester County Land Records Liber 1689, 462-464.

[21] Alberta R. Tropp. "Methodist Episcopal Church in Mamaroneck." Typescript in WCHS collection.

[22] Westchester County Land Records Liber 1689, 462-464.

[23] David A. Palmer. *William Palmer of Westerfield, Conn. And Westchester, N.Y.* No place: David A. Palmer, c.1994, 27.

[24] Ibid.

[25] Ibid., 29. "Know Your Westchester: Quaker Burying Ground." *The Herald Statesman*, 16 October 1952. Westchester County Land Records Liber C, 318.

[26] Ibid., 35.

[27] Art Dunn. "DAR Shows A Deed For Old Cemeteries." WCHS Vertical Files.

[28] Lippsett, 16.

[29] Mary received the land of her brother Nehemiah upon the latter's death (Wills Liber B, 428).

[30] The persons who are interred in the vault are James Donaldson, his first wife and their children, his second wife, Eliza Barker Swift Donaldson, Cordelia Aston Swift Huntington, and Annie Swift (DAR Cemetery Records, New York State Library).

[31] "Men Working In Village Unearth Skeletons While Digging on the Post Road." *The Larchmont Times*, 13 August 1931. For the sales of pieces of lands for this project, see Land Records Liber 3181, 38 for the Quaker Cemetery, and Land Records Liber 3306, 129 for the Barker-Palmer Cemetery.

[32] Luftig, Victor. "A dump among graves." *The Mamaroneck Daily Times*, 2 July 1974. See also "'56 cleanup recalled," 3 July 1974, and "Cleanup expected for 2 cemeteries," 5 July 1974.

[33] "Notes of the Nelson Family." 1. Typescript in the WCHS Vertical Files.

[34] Ibid. Westchester County Land Records Liber D, 179-180.

[35] "Notes of the Nelson Family," 3.

[36] Scharf, I, 543.

[37] Bolton, I, 306.

[38] Ibid., 305; "Copy of Correction made by Mr. Reginald P. Bolton". WCHS Vertical Files.

[39] Ibid. See Isaiah 8:1-3.

[40] Westchester County Land Records Liber I, 267-268.

[41] J.W. Poucher. *Old Gravestones of Dutchess County, New York.* Poughkeepsie, NY: Dutchess County Historical Society, 1924, 273-274.

[42] Ibid.

[43] http://boards.ancestrylibrary.com/surnames.nelson/5444.1.1.1.1.1/mb.ashx

[44] David W. Hoyt. *A Genealogical History of the Hoyt, Haight and Hight Families.* Somersworth, NH: The New England History Press, 1984, 613-614.

[45] Westchester County Land Records Liber N, 124-127.

[46] Westchester County Land Records Liber Q, 235-236.

[47] Westchester County Land Records Liber S, 274; Liber 118, 190.

[48] Grenville C. Mackenzie. "Families of the Colonial Manor of Philipsburgh." Westport, CT: 1966, 528.

[49] Ibid., 523-528.

[50] Westchester County Land Records Liber 664, 258-259.

[51] Westchster County Land Records Liber 903, 375-376.

[52] Edmund H. Smith. *Reports of Cases Decided in the Court of Appeals of the State of New York.* Vol. 150. Albany: James B. Lyon, 1896, 139-149. Susan A. Dean deeded this plot to Harriet M. Palmer on January 10, 1876 (Westchster County Land Records Liber 906, 294).

[53] Ibid.

[54] WCHS Cemetery Inscription Book #81, 48.

[55] DAR, 65.

[56] Fulcher, William. "Old Palmer Cemetery Emerges After Many Years of Neglect." *The Daily Times*, 26 April 1952.

[57] "Know Your Westchester: John Richbell's Grave." *The Daily Argus*, 14 May 1953.

[58] Lippsett, 3.

[59] Ibid.

[60] Scharf, I, 854.

[61] Mary O'Connor English. *Early Town Records of Mamaroneck, 1697-1881.* Mamaroneck, NY: Town of Mamaroneck, 1979, 192.

[62] Bolton, I, 314.

[63] Scharf, I, 861. Adam Mott, the great-grandfather of Giles Seaman, was the elder brother of James Mott. Mr. Seaman's home appears to have been located on the east side of Orienta Avenue just south of Rushmore Avenue.

[64] Ibid.

[65] Westchester County Wills Liber L, 191-194.

[66] Scharf, I, 861-862.

[67] WCHS Cemetery Inscription Book #17, 34-35.

[68] Fulcher, 11.

[69] Prigoff, 5.

[70] "Know Your Westchester: The Grave of John Richbell." *The Daily Argus*, 22 September 1954

[71] Lippsett, 4.

[72] Bolton, I, 39-43.

[73] Bolton, I, xxix & 306-307. "Know Your Westchester: Gilbert Budd." *The Daily Argus*, 19 December 1952. The Colonel and commander of the regiment was Thomas Thomas, whose family burial ground is located in Harrison.

[74] Westchester County Wills Liber F, 203-208.

[75] WCHS Cemetery Transcription Book #81, 28.

[76] Westchester County Land Records Liber S, 309-311.

[77] English, 223.

[78] Ibid.

[79] Land Records Liber 138, 435-437. It should be noted that the graves of the Budd family have always been in their present location, and were not moved to the Town Burial Ground as some sources have stated.

[80] English, 232 & 309.

Pages 43 - 58

[1] Bolton, I, 223.

[2] William Samuel Coffey. *Commemorative Discourse delivered at the Centennial Anniversary of the Erection and the Sixtieth of the Consecration of St. Paul's Church, East Chester*. New York: Perris & Browne, 1866.

[3] http://www.med.cornell.edu/archives/history/infant_asylum.html?name1=New+York+Infant+Asylum&type1=2Active

[4] "Deserted by its Doctors." *The New York Times*, 19 June 1893. "Fire in an Infant Asylum." *The New York Times*, 17 July 1896.

[5] "Complaint Against Infant Asylum." *The Chronicle*, Mount Vernon, NY, 22 October 1897.

[6] "The New York Infant Asylum." *The Chronicle*, Mount Vernon, NY, 11 July 1890.

[7] "Burial Not Proper, He Says." *The New York Times*, 18 October 1897.

[8] "Infant Asylum Complaint Dismissed." *The Chronicle*, Mount Vernon, NY, 5 November 1897.

[9] "Nine Petrified Bodies Found." *The New York Times*, 19 October 1902.

[10] "Turned to Stone." *The Daily Argus*, 20 October 1902.

[11] "300 Bodies Re-interred." *The Daily Argus*, 9 October 1902.

[12] Bolton, I, 221-222. Reverend Bolton placed the original meeting house closer to present-day South Columbus Avenue on the "Church Green, between the ancient locust trees and burial ground" (Bolton, I, 243). Otto Hufeland believed that the original church was located "probably east or northeast of the present stone structure" (Otto Hufeland. *Early Mount Vernon*. Mount Vernon, NY: Mount Vernon Public Library, 1940, 5).

[13] Bolton, I, 233.

[14] Ibid., 235. A bier is a frame on which a corpse is placed prior to burial.

[15] Ibid., 234.

[16] Ibid.

[17] Ibid., 235. The old meeting house burned "soon after the commencement of the Revolutionary war" (Bolton, I, 223).

[18] Ibid.

[19] "St. Paul's To Be Turned To National Shrine Soon." *The Daily Argus*, 8 September 1934.

[20] David Osborn. "Who Were the Hessians?" *The Westchester Historian*, Vol. 80 No. 1 (Winter 2004), 8.

[21] Bolton, I, 238-239.

[22] Bolton, I, 236-237.

[23] Coffey, 30.

[24] Scharf, II, 726. The Comfort Sands vault was located "in the graveyard of the Middle Dutch Church, Nassau Street, between Cedar and Liberty Streets, New York," and was moved to a vault purchased by Cornelia Prime at St. Paul's "either in 1844 or 1845" (Temple Prime. *Descent of Comfort Sands and of His Children*. New York: The De Vinne Press, 1886, 16-17).

[25] *Records of the Town of Eastchester, New York*. Eastchester, NY: Eastchester Historical Society, 1964-66, IX, 61.

[26] Ibid., 64.

[27] Ibid., 68.

[28] Ibid., 97.

[29] *Fairchild Cemetery Manual*. Brooklyn: Fairchild Sons, 1910, 99.

[30] Ibid.

[31] Carolee R. Inskeep. _*The Graveyard Shift: A Family Historian's Guide to New York City Cemeteries*. Orem, UT: Ancestry, 2000, 198. *Burial Records of Saint Paul's Church*. Eastchester, NY: Eastchester Historical Society, 1973, 322. The three tombstones belong to Anne (1724-1786), Israel (1731-1806), and Nathaniel (1690-1775) Underhill. The Underhill Family Burial Ground was located in the vicinity of Adee and Colden Avenues in the Bronx.

[32] David A. Tompkins. *Eastchester Village, Colonial New York, 1666-1698: Maps & Inhabitants*. Eastchester, NY: Eastchester Historical Society, 1997, 19.

[33] http://www.nps.gov/archive/sapa/cemetery/WB.html

[34] Barr, 144.

[35] *Records of the Town of Eastchester, New York*, IV, 82.

[36] Harry M. Dunkak. "Nurturing Mind, Body and Spirit: the Story of the Wartburg Care Community." *The Westchester Historian*, Volume 85 Number 4 (Fall 2009) 138.

[37] Ibid.

Pages 59 - 98

[1] Morgan H. Seacord. *Biographical Sketches and Index of the Huguenot Settlers of New Rochelle, 1687-1776*. New Rochelle, NY: The Huguenot Historical Association of New Rochelle, 1941, 9.

[2] Ibid.

[3] Ibid.

[4] Ibid.

[5] Westchester County Land Records Liber 523, 109-111. Mr. Allaire had previously purchased this plot from Elias Guion on March 1, 1833 (Westchester County Land Records Liber 86, 389-390).

[6] *New Rochelle Tombstone Inscriptions*. New Rochelle, NY: New Rochelle Chapter, Daughters of the American Revolution, 1940, 55. The bulk of the trust funds were established upon the death of Taulman Allaire in 1905 ("Fund For Huguenot Graves." *The New York Times*, 7 February 1909).

[7] Keyes, Edward. "Group of Trinity Church Men Clean Up Old Cemetery Plot." WCHS Vertical Files.

[8] "Old Burial Plot Sacrificed to Thruway." *The Standard Star*, 9 February 1955. Tait, Jack. "Huguenot Graves to Be Moved." *Herald Tribune*, 11 February 1955.

[9] Scharf, I, 695.

[10] Westchester County Land Records Liber 319, 237.

[11] Beers Atlas 1867. Dr. Smith's home was located on the east side of Beechwood Avenue just north of Main Street.

[12] "New-Rochelle's Tramp Round-Up." *The New York Times*, 17 July 1896.

[13] Charles Barney Whittelsey. *The Roosevelt Genealogy 1649-1902*. Hartford: J.B. Burr & Co., 1902, 42.

[14] "George G. Sickles Buried." *The New York Times*, 21 March 1887.

[15] "Objection to Bo-Bo's Grave." *The New York Times*, 27 August 1905.

[16] Ibid.

[17] "Private Crosby Succumbs to Typhoid." *The New York Times*, 4 September 1898.

[18] "New Rochelle Stricken: Fifteen Residents Killed and Forty Injured in Park Avenue Tunnel Wreck." *The New Rochelle Pioneer*, 11 January 1902.

[19] Westchester County Wills Liber Q, 491-492.

[20] Westchester County Land Records Liber 81, 326-328.

[21] Aaron M. Powell. *Personal Reminiscences of the Anti-Slavery and Other Reforms and Reformers*. New York: Caulon Press, 1899. 161-162. A photo of Mr. Carpenter with the child of "a colored woman whom [he] had befriended" can be found in this book on page 165.

[22] *New Rochelle Tombstone Inscriptions*, 159.

[23] "Mrs. Carrie Gilfelt." *The New Rochelle Pioneer*, 25 April 1896.

[24] Westchester County Land Records Liber 1734, 332-334.

[25] "Bought a Negro Graveyard." *The New York Times*, 21 August 1905.

[26] Westchester County Land Records Liber 1734, 332-334.

[27] Morgan H. Seacord. *Historical Landmarks of New Rochelle*. New Rochelle, NY: New Rochelle Trust Co., 1938, 107.

[28] *New Rochelle Tombstone Inscriptions*, 159.

[29] Westchester County Land Records Liber 81, 328.

[30] Seacord 65-66.

[31] *Christ United Methodist Church, New Rochelle, New York: 200 Years of Service.* New Rochelle, NY: Christ United Methodist Church, 1971, 2.

[32] Ibid., 3-4.

[33] *New Rochelle Tombstone Inscriptions*, 87.

[34] *Christ United Methodist Church, New Rochelle, New York: 200 Years of Service*, 4.

[35] *New Rochelle Tombstone Inscriptions*, 87. Hannah Bonnett of Scarsdale, the wife of John Bonnett, mentioned this vault in her will: "I desire that my body be desantly [sic] deposited in the family vault where the body of my late husband was laid" (Wills Liber 29, 113). According to Morgan Seacord, "John Renoud [c.1745-1837] and his wife [Mary, c.1742-1818] are buried in the cemetery of the First Methodist Church at Upper New Rochelle in an unmarked vault, constructed and owned by their son Stephen Renoud of White Plains, the very existence of which appears to be unknown to the church authorities and known to but very few others" (*The Westchester Historian*, Vol. 43, No. 1, 14).

[36] Westchester County Clerk Map #3882.

[37] *New Rochelle Tombstone Inscriptions*, 87.

[38] *Christ United Methodist Church, New Rochelle, New York: 200 Years of Service*, 13.

[39] Ibid., 14.

[40] Seacord, *Historical Landmarks of New Rochelle*, 52. The Seacord home still stands today at 1337 North Avenue.

[41] *New Rochelle Tombstone Inscriptions*, 87.

[42] Jennifer Medina. "A Temple, 2 Graves and a Headache." *The New York Times*, 5 December 2004. Mrs. Perry was contacted because opponents of the present Temple Israel synagogue hoped to persuade the congregation to build an expansion on the Seacord Family Burial Ground site rather than a new building next to the Wykagyl Country Club.

[43] Seacord, *Biographical Sketches and Index of the Settlers of New Rochelle*, 18.

[44] Seacord, *Historical Landmarks of New Rochelle*, 104. Isaac Coutant's tombstone, which read "Voici le corps de ISAAC COUTANT, Age 50 ans," was stolen from the Huguenot Burying Ground in 1937. Today, Jean Coutant's tombstone lies buried face up in the ground next to the Huguenot Memorial in Trinity Episcopal Church Cemetery.

[45] Seacord, *Historical Landmarks of New Rochelle*, 105-106. Isaac Coutant's tombstone was stolen from the Huguenot Burying Ground in 1937 (Seacord, 104).

[46] Westchester County Land Records Liber 279, 430-431. The trustees were John W. Le Fevre, Prosper Le Fevre, Isaac Coutant, and Lewis J. Coutant.

[47] Ibid.

[48] Westchester County Rural Cemetery Deeds Liber 1, 209-210.

[49] Westchester County Land Records Liber 872, 203; Liber 922, 294 and 296; Liber 936, 332; Liber 1180, 7.

[50] *New Rochelle Tombstone Inscriptions*, 64.

[51] *Fairchild Cemetery Manual*, 36-37.

[52] Ibid. It should be noted that the tablet placed outside the cemetery in 1928 by the well-intentioned Huguenot Heights Association is not entirely accurate. The "falsity of this inscription" was noted by Morgan Seacord: "The homestead of Isaac Coutant stood nowhere near the cemetery. It was two blocks west of it [on the south side of Eastchester Road between Pershing and Rosedale avenues]. Isaac Coutant [Jr.], the owner and occupant of the homestead, was not a French religious refugee. It was his grandfather only who can correctly be termed 'The Huguenot.' The dates 'Circa 1700-1780' have no meaning whatever historically and are [not applicable] to either the person buried [there] or the house, property, or cemetery. Isaac Coutant [Jr.]'s wife was not buried at the time (1776); she lived until 1825. The Mrs. Coutant noted on the inscription was his widowed mother, Catherine Bonnefoy, the wife of the earlier Isaac Coutant...." (Seacord, *Historical Landmarks of New Rochelle*, 106-107)

[53] *New Rochelle Tombstone Inscriptions*, 65.

[54] Westchester County Land Records Liber 1209, 28.

[55] *New Rochelle Tombstone Inscriptions*, 65. The Robinson family settled in Mamaroneck about the year 1740. Gilbert Robinson (c.1738/40-1802) married a member of the Haight family, perhaps explaining the family's connection to the Palmer – Bloomer & Haight Cemetery (Mackenzie, 588).

[56] *Annual Report of the Secretary of War for the Year 1887.* Washington, DC: Government Printing Office, 1887. I, 568.

[57] Thomas F. De Voe. *Genealogy of the DeVeaux Family.* New York: Unknown publisher, 1885, 102-105.

[58] Seacord, *Biographical Sketches and Index of the Settlers of New Rochelle*, 21-22.

[59] *Collections of the New York Historical Society for the Year 1899.* New York: I. Riley, 1899, 299.

[60] De Voe, 128.

[61] Ibid., 127-128.

[62] Westchester County Land Records Liber 224, 234-236.

[63] De Voe, 104-105.

[64] In her will, Mary DeVeau directed her son Andrew to do the following: "I order my executor to bury my body in a decent manner to furnish my tomb with head and foot monument stones and I also order him to furnish the tomb of my husband Daniel Deveau, my daughter Hannah Gales tomb and also the tomb of my daughter Phebe Deveau with monuments head and foot stones all of which I order to be of the same kind of stones." (Wills Liber L, 20).

[65] *Old Wills of New Rochelle*. New Rochelle: New Rochelle Chapter, Daughters of the American Revolution, 1951, 49-51.

[66] Ibid. Kates, Herbert S. and Kates, Jerome S. *A Map of the City of New Rochelle, New York Showing Historic Sites.* 1938.

[67] Westchester County Land Records Liber R, 260.

[68] *New Rochelle Tombstone Inscriptions*, 148.

[69] Ibid., 148.

[70] Ibid.

[71] Ibid., 148-149.

[72] Ibid., 148-150.

[73] Ibid., 150.

[74] Ibid., 149-150. "Harsen Monument Placed on New Cemetery Site." *The Standard Star*, 19 October 1923. The Harsen monument and Flandreau government marker can be seen at Beechwood Cemetery in Section 7 (at the corner of Albert Smith Lane and South Drive).

[75] Robinson, Mary Alice. "Hazelhurst Park Hides Old Flandreau Cemetery." *The Standard Star*, New Rochelle, NY, 30 July 1931.

[76] *Old Wills of New Rochelle*, 49-50.

[77] Jim Cavanaugh. "Children, trash encroach on cemetery." *The Standard Star*, 16 May 1978. J.C. Barden. "An Old Cemetery Plot Is Center of Ongoing Dispute." *The New York Times*, 6 December 1981.

[78] *New Rochelle Tombstone Inscriptions*, 157.

[79] Seacord, *Historical Landmarks of New Rochelle*, 23.

[80] The New Rochelle Pioneer,

[81] "David Harrison's Estate." *The New York Times*, 28 November 1878.

[82] "A Curious Will." *The New York Times*, 26 February 1878.

[83] *New Rochelle Tombstone Inscriptions*, 157.

[84] Westchester County Land Records Liber 1285, 246-247. This sale took place on September 6, 1892. Although the deed "except[ed] Round Island," it does not mention that place as a burial ground.

[85] "Two Harrisons' Tomb Wrecked By Vandals." *The New York Times*, 18 September 1904. "Police at Harrison Tomb." *The New York Times*, 19 September 1904.

[86] *New Rochelle Tombstone Inscriptions*, 157.

[87] Westchester County Land Records Liber 1078, 120.

[88] *New Rochelle Tombstone Inscriptions*, 154-155. *Proceedings of the Board of Supervisors of the County of Westchester, N.Y.*, 1886, 289-291.

[89] Peter P. McLoughlin. *Father Tom: Life and Lectures of Rev. Thomas P. McLoughlin.* New York: The Knickerbocker Press, 1919, 134.

[90] William Quirin. "Under the Apple Tree: The History of Golf in Westchester County." *The Westchester Historian*, Vol. 85 No.3 (Summer 2009) 87.

[91] *New Rochelle Tombstone Inscriptions*, 155.

[92] Ibid.

[93] "Mt. Vernon Loses First Boy In Battle." *The New York Times*, 30 July 1918.

[94] Seacord, *Biographical Sketches and Index of the Huguenot Settlers of New Rochelle*, 42.

[95] Jeanne A. Forbes. *Records of the Town of New Rochelle, 1699-1828.* New Rochelle, NY: Paragraph Press, 1916, xiii-xvi.

[96] *Records of the Town of New Rochelle*, 109.

[97] Seacord, *Historical Landmarks of New Rochelle*, 104.

[98] Ibid.

[99] Bolton, *History of the Protestant Episcopal Church in the County of Westchester*, 480.

[100] *New Rochelle Tombstone Inscriptions*, 10.

[101] Ibid.

[102] Lockwood Barr. *Ancient Town of Pelham, Westchester County, New York*. Richmond, VA: The Dietz Press, Inc., 1946, 92. Alexander Henderson "cohabitated" with "a woman by the name of Betsy," to whom he left $250 in his will (Westchester County Wills Liber A, 30). William was apparently the biological son of Alexander and Betsy. The story goes that a Rajah in India had promised Alexander his favorite daughter (or his favorite Circassian slave girl) as a bride. However, the woman refused to make the voyage from India to America with Captain James Hague, a resident of Pelham whom Alexander had sent to bring her to Hunter's Island. Instead, Captain Hague returned to New York with William Henderson (Scharf, II, 712).

[103] *New Rochelle Tombstone Inscriptions*, 11.

[104] Seacord, *Historical Landmarks of New Rochelle*, 105.

[105] Ibid.

[106] Ibid.

[107] *New Rochelle Tombstone Inscriptions*, 10.

[108] Ibid., 11.

[109] "2nd Burial In 50 Years At Huguenot Cemetery." *The Daily Argus*, 13 April 1950.

[110] Westchester Land Records Liber 5501, 217.

[111] WCHS Cemetery Inscription Book #88, 7. This "only person of the 1st generation" was Fred Archer, a resident of Danbury, CT, who was the son of Benjamin A. Archer.

[112] "Graves Transfer Is Completed." *The Standard Star*, 1 September 1956. "Huguenot's Resting Place Makes Way for High Speed Travel." *The Standard Star*, 19 July 1956. "Know Your Westchester: French Huguenot Burying Ground." *The Citizen Register*, Ossining, NY, 3 September 1953. "Burial Ground Makes Way for Thruway." *The Standard Star*, 24 August 1956. Tait, Jack. "Huguenot Graves to Be Moved." *Herald Tribune*, 11 February 1955.

[113] "Saint Bartholomew's Day." *The Westchester Historian*, Volume 32 Number 4 (Fall, 1956), 111-112. See also "Barbaric Handling of Graves Charged." *The New York Times*, 7 September 1956. Albee, Allison. "Senseless Wisdom." *The Westchester Historian*, Volume 31 Number 2 (Spring, 1955). Roth, Albert. "Bulldozers Respectfully, but Firmly Invade Old Huguenot Burial Grounds." *The Westchester News*, 26 January 1956. "Pre-Revolutionary Graves." *The Standard Star*, 30 August 1956.

[114] "Notice to Bidders." *The New York Times*, 10 August 1956. "Thruway Gets Cemetery Bid." *The Daily Argus*, 22 August 1956.

[115] WCHS Vertical Files – Coutant Family.

Pages 99 - 120

[1] http://www.nysm.nysed.gov/albany/bios/l/anlispenard8081.html

[2] Gray Williams. *Picturing Our Past: National Register Sites in Westchester County*. Elmsford, NY: Westchester County Historical Society, 2003, 19

[3] Ibid., 19.

[4] *New Rochelle Tombstone Inscriptions*, 156.

[5] "Leonard Lispenard in Trinity Vault." *The New York Times*, 9 April 1907.

[6] Ibid.

[7] WCHS Vertical Files – Lispenard Family.

[8] Williams, *Picturing Our Past*, 19.

[9] Bolton, II, 687.

[10] Charles W. Darling. "Antoine L'Espenard, the French Huguenot, and Some of His Descendants." *The New York Genealogical and Biographical Record*, Vol. XXIV No.3 (July 1893), 116.

[11] Ibid., 112-113.

[12] "Leonard Lispenard in Trinity Vault." *The New York Times*, 9 April 1907.

[13] "May Have Huguenot's Bones." *The New York Tribune*, 6 March 1907. See also "Old Huguenot's Bones Found." *The New Rochelle Pioneer*, 9 March 1907.

[14] "Leonard Lispenard in Trinity Vault." *The New York Times*, 9 April 1907.

[15] Abraham Ernest Helffenstein. *Pierre Fauconnier and his descendants with some of the Allied Valleaux*. Philadelphia: S.H. Burbank & Co., 1911, 229.

[16] Seacord, *Historical Landmarks of New Rochelle*, 62.

[17] Ibid., 62.

[18] Ibid., 64.

[19] *New Rochelle Tombstone Inscriptions*, 156.

[20] *First Presbyterian Church, New Rochelle, N.Y.: Yearbook, 1929*. New York: Knickerbocker Press, 1929, 22.

[21] Seacord, *Historical Landmarks of New Rochelle*, 69.

[22] Ibid.

[23] *New Rochelle Tombstone Inscriptions*, 158.

[24] Westchester County Land Records Liber 110, 367. Seacord, *Historical Landmarks of New Rochelle*, 70.

[25] Westchester County Land Records Liber 461, 436-437.

[26] *New Rochelle Tombstone Inscriptions*, 158-159.

[27] Ibid., 158.

[28] Duane Stoltzfus. "Cemetery's existence provokes disagreement." *The Standard Star*, 11 July 1988

[29] Seacord, 108.

[30] Charles Pryer. *Legends, Traditions and Superstitions of Westchester*. New York: The Knickerbocker Press, 1890, 39-42.

[31] Ibid.

[32] Ibid.

[33] Westchester County Wills Liber N, 85-86.

[34] Ibid.

[35] Ibid.

[36] Benson J. Lossing. *The Pictorial Field-Book of the American Revolution*. New York: Harper & Brothers, 1860, II, 614-615. Westchester County Land Records Liber 81, 458-462.

[37] Westchester County Land Records Liber 433, 447-450.

[38] Ibid.

[39] Westchester County Land Records Liber 1589, 332.

[40] Westchester County Land Records Liber 89,531.

[41] *New Rochelle Tombstone Inscriptions*, 131.

[42] Westchester County Land Records Liber 89, 531; Liber 106, 364.

[43] *New Rochelle Tombstone Inscriptions*, 131-132.

[44] *Christ United Methodist Church, New Rochelle, New York: 200 Years of Service*, 13-14.

[45] A plaque placed at the new burial site reads: "Formerly located at Main Street and LeCount Place, New Rochelle, when the church property became a part of the urban renewal area, all remains were reinterred in this cemetery July 1965. Beneath these stones lie buried the remains of the identified and unidentified bodies. All available records may be found in the office of Christ Church and at the New Rochelle Board of Health." The site of Saint John's Church and Cemetery was sold to the City of New Rochelle on July 15, 1965 (Land Records Liber 6527, 48).

[46] Peter Shute Plot Card, Beechwood Cemetery Records.

[47] Mackenzie, 619-620.

[48] Seacord, *Historical Landmarks of New Rochelle*, 55.

[49] *Old Wills of New Rochelle*, 56-59.

[50] Westchester County Land Records Liber 1109, 432-434. Several sources place the Shute Family Lot at the northwest rather than southwest corner of the intersection of Chauncey and North avenues; the former street is most likely being confused with the lane leading to the Shute home, which was in between Chauncey and Coligni avenues. See DAR, 160 and Seacord, *Historical Landmarks of New Rochelle*, 55.

[51] Westchester County Land Records Liber 1109, 432-434.

[52] Henry B. Dawson. *Rambles in Westchester County, New York*. Yonkers, NY: Unknown publisher, 1866, 32-33.

[53] Seacord, *Historical Landmarks of New Rochelle*, 122-123.

[54] Herbert B. Nichols ed. *Thomas Paine Bicentennial Celebrations, 1737-1937*. New Rochelle, NY: Thomas Paine National Historical Association, 1937, 16. In 1937, the house where Paine died in Manhattan was occupied by 59 Grove Street.

[55] http://www.thomaspaine.org/bio/ingersoll1892.html. Moncure Daniel Conway. *The Life of Thomas Paine*. New York: Knickerbocker Press, 1908, II, 449-459.

[56] Ibid., 454-455.

[57] Ibid., 451. It appears that the Quaker cemetery which refused burial to Paine was not located in Westchester, but rather in Manhattan (Conway, 455).

[58] Edward I. Carlyle. *William Cobbett: A Study of His Life as Shown in His Writings*. London: Archibald Constable and Company, 1904, 209-210.

[59] Scharf, I, 689.

[60] *Thomas Paine and New Rochelle, N.Y.* New Rochelle, NY: The Thomas Paine National Historical Association, 1951, 10.

[61] William M. van der Weyde. "Paine's Long Lost Remains Home By Parcel Post." *The New York Times*, 31 May 1914.

[62] Carlyle, 210.

[63] Ibid., 212.

64 Westchester County Land Records Liber U, 125; Land Records Liber Y, 90.

65 G. Vale. *The Life of Thomas Paine*. New York: The Beacon, 1853, 120-121.

66 *New Rochelle Tombstone Inscriptions*, 157.

67 Ibid.

68 James J. Flynn and Charles A. Huguenin. "Where Are the Bones of Thomas Paine?" *The Westchester Historian*, Vol. 37 No. 1 (January-March 1961) 6-12. This article gives an excellent account of the ill-fated journey of the remains of Thomas Paine. The relics purchased from Charles Higham by Dr. Conway were taken from William Cobbett by Benjamin Tilly, a furniture dealer and tailor who helped the latter in his move from London to Normandy. Tilly kept these relics after packing the rest of Paine's bones into a box. After Tilly's death, the relics were taken by his landlord, who later sold them to the Reverend George Reynolds, a Baptist minister. Higham acquired the relics from Reynolds and sold them to Dr. Conway after the latter saw an advertisement for them. The brain fragment was "about two inches by one inch in size, leaden in color, and quite hard in consistency" while the locks were "dark...with a reddish tinge."

69 Ibid. William M. van der Weyde. "Paine's Long Lost Remains Home By Parcel Post." *The New York Times*, 31 May 1914.

70 *Thomas Paine and New Rochelle, N.Y.*, 11.

71 Forbes, xiii.

72 *Trinity Church*. New Rochelle, NY: Trinity Church, 1973, 1.

73 Ibid., 6.

74 Scharf, I, 695.

75 Ibid. According to Morgan Seacord, this "church building extended over the sidewalk onto Division Street. Some of the stones of the foundation of this edifice that were dug up in 1915 were used in the construction of a stone bridge which now stands in the grounds of the Huguenot Historical Association on North Avenue." (Seacord, *Historical Landmarks of New Rochelle*, 60)

76 Robert Bolton. *History of the Protestant Episcopal Church in the County of Westchester*, New York: Stanford & Swards, 1855, 470.

77 C.H. Augur. *New Rochelle Through Seven Generations*. New Rochelle, NY: The National City Bank, 1908, 20.

78 Forbes, 254.

79 Ibid.

80 *Trinity Church, New Rochelle, N.Y., 1688-1938: A Brief Sketch Written on the Occasion of thhe Two Hundred and Fiftieth Anniversary of the Church*. New Rochelle, NY: Trinity Church, 1938, 11.

81 Ibid.

82 Westchester County Land Records Liber 507, 3-5.

83 Evelyn P. Bartow. *Bartow Genealogy*. Baltimore: Innes and Company, 1875, 59-60.

84 Seacord, *Historical Landmarks of New Rochelle*, 61.

85 Scharf, I, 709.

86 Evert A. Duyckinck and George L. Duyckinck. *Cyclopaedia of American Literature*. New York: Charles Scribner, 1856, II, 343.

87 Nichols, 148.

88 Duyckinck and Duyckinck, 343.

89 Nichols, 149.

90 Ibid., 125.

91 Ibid.

92 Seacord, *Historical Landmarks of New Rochelle*, 107.

93 Westchester County Land Records Liber 45, 408.

94 Westchester County Land Records Liber 27, 263-264.

95 Westchester County Wills Liber Q, 491-492.

96 "William Turpin's Will." *The African Repository and Colonial Journal*. Vol. XI No. 3 (March 1835), 80.

97 *New Rochelle Tombstone Inscriptions*, 160.

Pages 121 - 122

1 *Christ Church at Pelham, Pelham Manor, New York*. Pelham Manor, NY: The Vestry of Christ Church, 1943, 15.

2 Westchester County Land Records Liber 421, 179.

3 Westchester County Land Records Liber 372, 275-278.

4 Bolton, *History of the Protestant Episcopal Church in Westchester County*, 699-700.

5 *Christ Church at Pelham, Pelham Manor, New York*, 71.

6 Bolton, I, 99.

[7] Lawrence Bernard Larsen. *A Handbook on the Symbolism of Christ Church at Pelham*. Pelham Manor, NY: Christ Church, 1965, 12.

Pages 123 - 150

[1] Westchester County Land Records Liber 419, 19.

[2] Westchester County Land Records Liber 438, 427.

[3] Ibid.

[4] Gary Kriss. "Volunteers Restore Historic Cemetery." *The New York Times*, 27 May 1984. Mike Meaney. "The cemetery nobody wants." *The Daily Item*, 12 October 1981.

[5] Charles W. Baird. *Chronicle of a Border Town: History of Rye, Westchester County, New York, 1660-1870, Including Harrison and the White Plains till 1788*. Harrison, NY: Harbor Hills Books, 1974, 195-197.

[6] Ibid., 196.

[7] Williams, *Picturing Our Past*, 15.

[8] "Tombstone of 1722 Stands in Ancient Rye Cemetery." *The Daily Argus*, Mount Vernon, NY, 29 September 1934.

[9] Bolton, *The History of the Several Towns ...* , II, 197

[10] Bolton, *The History of the Several Towns ...* , II, 156-159; Mackenzie, 106.

[11] Westchester County Land Records Liber R, 128-130.

[12] *Christ's Church at the Town of Rye in the County of Westchester and the State of New York: A Chronological Historical Review*. Rye, NY: Christ's Church, 1945, 13-15.

[13] Ibid., 15.

[14] Bolton, *History of the Protestant Episcopal Church in the County of Westchester*, 135. In addition to this parish, there were three others created: "in the city of New-York one; the county of Richmond one; in the county of Westchester two; one to have care of Westchester, Eastchester, Yonkers and the manor of Pelham."

[15] Ibid., 347.

[16] *Christ's Church at the Town of Rye in the County of Westchester and the State of New York: A Chronological Historical Review*, 9.

[17] Ibid., 28.

[18] G.H. Van Wagenen. "Inscriptions From Tombstones in a Cemetery at Rye, Westchester County, N.Y." *The New York Genealogical & Biographical Record*, Vol.16 No.3 (July 1885) 137-138.

[19] Bolton, *History of the Protestant Episcopal Church in the County of Westchester*, 349-350.

[20] *Christ's Church at the Town of Rye in the County of Westchester and the State of New York: A Chronological Historical Review*, 18. Interestingly, the Reverend Avery was the stepson of American General Israel Putnam, as the latter, a widower, married the reverend's widowed mother in 1767 (William Farrand Livingston. *Israel Putnam: Pioneer, Ranger, and Major General 1718-1790*. New York: G.P. Putnam's Sons, 1901, 155).

[21] John Reynolds Totten. "Department for Registration of Pedigrees." *The New York Genealogical and Biographical Record*, Vol. LI No. 1 (January 1920), 86.

[22] Westchester County Land Records Liber 113, 315; Liber 116, 18-19.

[23] Bolton, *History of the Protestant Episcopal Church in the County of Westchester*, 349.

[24] Baird, 198.

[25] Westchester County Land Records Liber 1330, 126-127.

[26] *Christ's Church at the Town of Rye in the County of Westchester and the State of New York: A Chronological Historical Review*, 16.

[27] Bolton, *History of the Protestant Episcopal Church in the County of Westchester*, 333.

[28] Westchester County Land Records Liber 87, 143-146.

[29] Ibid.

[30] Ibid.

[31] *Christ's Church at the Town of Rye in the County of Westchester and the State of New York: A Chronological Historical Review*, 24.

[32] Baird, 199. See also Westchester County Land Records Liber 327, 110-113.

[33] Westchester County Rural Cemetery Deeds Liber 1, 302.

[34] Westchester County Incorporation Records Volume 11, 44. Westchester County Land Records Liber 1851, 110; Liber 1674, 31.

[35] *Greenwood Union Cemetery, Rye, Westchester County, New York*. New York: Hill-Matthews Co., Inc., 1912.

[36] Westchester County Rural Cemetery Deeds Liber 7, 51-53.

[37] A monument to Rising which contains a 10-inch shell from the *Maine* is located in Summerfield Park, Port Chester. For an account of the memorial service held for Rising, see WCHS French Scrapbooks Vol. 3, 172-174.

[38] Westchester County Rural Cemetery Deeds Liber 15, 483.

[39] http://www.greenwoodunion.org/Our%20History.htm

[40] Frederick David Bidwell. *History of the Forty-Ninth New York Volunteers.* Albany, NY: J.B. Lyon Company Printers, 1916, 188.

[41] Bolton, *The History of the Several Towns ...* , II, 736.

[42] *Collections of the New York Historical Society for the Year 1903.* New York: I. Riley, 1903, 106; Land Records Liber 39, 453.

[43] Land Records Liber 82, 169.

[44] *The Jay Cemetery, Rye, New York,* Rye, NY: Unknown Publisher, 1947, 5-6.

[45] William S. Thayer et al. *Homes of American Statesmen.* New York: G.P. Putnam and Co., 1853, 202.

[46] Land Records Liber 31, 265-267.

[47] *The Jay Cemetery, Rye, New York,* 8.

[48] Ibid., 13.

[49] Ibid., 14.

[50] Westchester County Land Records Liber 1742, 359.

[51] Westchester County Land Records Liber 4346, 105 & 140.

[52] "Osborn Home: The Need Is A Social One." *The Reporter Dispatch,* 27 August 1963.

[53] Ibid.

[54] Westchester County Land Records Liber 1945, 496; Liber 1950, 64; Liber 2031, 280; Liber 2856, 398; Westchester County Incorporation Records Volume 22, 266.

[55] *Miriam Osborn Memorial Home: 50th Anniversary.* Rye, NY: The Miriam Osborn Memorial Home, 1958, 13-14.

[56] Mark R. Zwerger et al. *Images of America: The Osborn.* Portsmouth, NH: Arcadia Publishing, 2008, 44.

[57] *Collections of the New York Historical Society for the Year 1898.* New York: I. Riley, 1898, 247-248.

[58] Baird, 198.

[59] Mike Meaney. "Cemeteries provide a walk into history." *The Daily Item,* 11 October 1981.

[60] "Purdy Family Burial Ground Is Dedicated." *The Daily Item,* 12 June 1969.

[61] Bolton, *The History of the Several Towns ...* , II, 174.

[62] Ibid.

[63] Ibid.

[64] Ellen Cotton McKay. *A History of the Rye Presbyterian Church.* Rye, NY: Rye Presbyterian Church, 1957. 99.

[65] Ibid., 230.

[66] Ibid., 90-91.

[67] Scharf, II, 700-701.

[68] Westchester County Land Records Liber 760, 134-135.

[69] Westchester County Land Records Liber 4282, 474.

[70] http://www.history.army.mil/html/moh/civwaral.html

[71] Baird, 198.

[72] Ibid., 374.

[73] Westchester County Wills Liber N, 269.

[74] Baird, 199.

[75] *History of Rye.* Rye, NY: Rye Chronicle, 1961.

[76] F.W. Beers. *Atlas of New York and Vicinity.* New York: F.W. Beers, A.D. Ellis & G.G. Soule, 1867.

[77] WCHS Albee Scrapbooks, I, 85.

Pages 151 - 168

[1] Mackenzie, 91-92. *History of the Village of Port Chester, New York.* Port Chester, NY: Village of Port Chester Centennial Historical Book Committee, 1968, 5.

[2] *History of the Village of Port Chester, New York,* 5.

[3] Westchester County Wills Liber 30, 423-425.

[4] Westchester County Land Records Liber 1757, 481.

[5] "Grave of Cuff Brown – Slave." *Westchester County Magazine,* Unknown Issue.

[6] Kirk Semple. "Scout's Good Deed Becomes a Legal Snarl." *The New York Times,* 10 October 2004.

[7] Thomas William Brundage. *A Brundage Family Genealogy.* Paia, HI: T.W. Brundage, 1989, 2-2. Scharf, II, 662.

[8] Baird, 197.

[9] Baird, 399-402.

[10] Westchester County Land Records Liber 2273, 360-363. Author's italics.

[11] WCHS Cemetery Inscription Book #33, 241.

[12] Westchester County Land Records Liber 6374, 17.

[13] "School Gets O.K. To Move Burial Site." *The Daily Item*, 20 November 1965.

[14] "Port Chester Cemetery: Court Action Due." *The Daily Item*, 7 October 1965.

[15] "Human Bones Found, Quietly Reburied at JHS Site." *The Daily Item*, 17 May 1966.

[16] Mackenzie, 279-281.

[17] Ibid., 281.

[18] Helen S. Peck. *A Small History of the Gedney Family of Westchester Co., N.Y. 1603-1896*. Mamaroneck, NY: Curtis G. Peck, 1896, 8-22.

[19] Jonathan H. Gedney. "A remarkable family." Copy of letter in WCHS Vertical Files.

[20] Westchester County Land Records Liber Y, 100; Liber 57, 507-508. Solomon's twelfth child, Susan Caroline, had died in 1830 at the age of 22.

[21] Mackenzie, 290.

[22] Westchester County Wills Liber B, 344.

[23] Westchester County Land Records Liber Z, 97-99.

[24] Ibid. Mackenzie, 333-336.

[25] Mamaroneck Village Historian Files.

[26] Edward Francis Fremaux de Beixedon, Jr. *The Ancestors and Descendants of Dr. David Rogers*. No place, 1921.

[27] Baldwin, 50.

[28] Mamaroneck Village Historian Files.

[29] Ibid.

[30] Natalie M. Seth. *The Guion Family: A Genealogy of the Descendants of Louis Guion of New Rochelle, N.Y.* No place, 1956, 7. Louis Guion (c.1654-c.1726) was the father of Isaac Guion (1692-1783), who in turn was the father of John Guion, Sr. (1723-1792).

[31] Westchester County Wills Liber K, 176.

[32] Westchester County Land Records Liber 605, 106-109.

[33] WCHS Mamaroneck Cemetery Vertical File.

[34] Douglas Merritt. *Revised Merritt Records*. New York: T.A. Wright, 1916, 49.

[35] Richard M. Lederer Jr. *The Place Names of Westchester County, New York*. Harrison, NY: Harbor Hill Books, 1978, 68.

[36] Eardeley, V, 84.

[37] "$3,000,000 for Cemetery." *The New York Times*, 10 June 1914. According to an article which appeared in the *White Plains Daily Record*, it was said that "a romance in life led [Daniel E. Merritt] to retire as much as possible from public."

[38] "A Public Cemetery Provided For." *White Plains Daily Record*, 1914 (found in the WCHS Hufeland Scrapbooks, Volume 20).

[39] "$11,000 to Charity Trust." *The New York Times*, 24 December 1915.

[40] Westchester County Rural Cemetery Deeds Liber 14, 52-55. See also Westchester County Land Records Liber 3002, 3.

[41] Merritt, 49-51.

[42] *Collections of the New York Historical Society for the Year 1903*. New York: I. Riley, 1903, 108-109.

[43] Baird, 346.

[44] Westchester County Land Records Liber N, 504-506.

[45] Ibid., 324-326.

[46] Baird, 198.

[47] Westchester County Land Records Liber 1495, 204-205.

[48] *Collections of the New York Historical Society for the Year 1895*, New York: I. Riley, 1895, 444-445.

[49] Merritt, 57.

[50] Westchester County Land Records Liber 1804, 494.

[51] Westchester County Land Records Liber P, 95.

[52] Baird, 367; Westchester County Land Records Liber 176, 20-21.

[53] Eardeley, XII, 22-23.

[54] WCHS Cemetery Inscription Book #34, 355.

[55] *History of the Village of Port Chester New York*, 39; Westchester County Land Records Liber 3105, 122; Westchester County Rural Cemetery Deeds Liber 14, 92.

[56] Westchester County Land Records Liber 5774, 350.

[57] Baird, 209.

[58] WCHS McDonald Papers, 66-67.

[59] Baird, 197.
[60] Westchester County Land Records Liber 574, 356-358.
[61] Westchester County Land Records Liber 716, 420-422.
[62] Ibid., 716, 421.

Pages 169 - 174

[1] Mackenzie, 290-291.
[2] Helen Lorraine Hultz. *Scarsdale Story*. Morristown, NJ: The Evans Publishing Co., 1987, 257-258.
[3] Ibid.
[4] Westchester County Wills Liber 28, 177-178.
[5] Westchester County Inventory of Historic Places Recommendation Form: Nathaniel Brown House. WCHS Vertical Files.
[6] Hultz, 218.
[7] Ibid., 222.
[8] Bolton, *History of the Protestant Episcopal Church in the County of Westchester*, 708-709.
[9] Ibid., 709.
[10] Westchester County Land Records Liber 180, 400.
[11] Scharf, I, 668.
[12] Eric Nagourney. "Church honors legendary grave of runaway slaves." *The Reporter Dispatch*, 10 August 1980.
[13] "Military graves in St. James the Less Cemetery, Scarsdale, N.Y., copied from the church files by the Scarsdale American Legion." 2001. WCHS Typescript.
[14] http://www.homeofheroes.com/members/02_DSC/citatons/03_wwii-dsc/army_h.html

Pages 175 - 189

[1] Charles Elmer Allison. *History of Yonkers*. New York: Wilber B. Ketcham, 1896, 452-453.
[2] Scharf, II, 60.
[3] Ibid., 61
[4] *The 175th Anniversary of The Asbury Church*. Yonkers: Asbury Methodist Church, 1946, 14.
[5] Frances G. Mead. "The Asbury Methodist Church in Crestwood." *The Westchester Historian*, Vol.11 No.4 (October 1935), 77-78.
[6] Alex Philippidis. "July 23 deadline for arguments in Austin Ave. cemetery case." *Westchester County Business Journal*, 19 July 2004. Valenti, Ken and Castillo, Franziska. "State action may be too late to find graves." *The Journal News*, 11 July 2004.
[7] Baila Round Shargel and Harold L. Drimmer. *The Jews of Westchester: A Social History*. Fleischmanns, NY: Purple Mountain Press, 1994, 124.
[8] Westchester County Land Records Liber 1521, 221-223.
[9] Erin Donar. "Cemetery founders escaped from hate." *The Journal News*, 8 July 2004.
[10] Carolyn Weiner. "Vandals assault Jewish cemetery." *The Herald Statesman*, 15 August 1974.
[11] Jennie Tritten. "Dumping reported at city cemetery." *The Herald Statesman*, 13 March 1980.
[12] Ibid.
[13] Westchester County Land Records Liber 9757, 169. Rick Archer. "Jewish Cemetery Saga." *The Yonkers Current*, 12 July 2004. Desiree Grand. "Groups restore Jewish cemeteries." *The Journal News*, 20 September 2004.
[14] Daniel J. Wakin. "Lost in Yonkers: A Cemetery and 135 of Its Children." *The New York Times*, 7 July 2004.
[15] Ibid.
[16] Alex Philippidis. "July 23 deadline for arguments in Austin Ave. cemetery case." *Westchester County Business Journal*, 19 July 2004.
[17] Daniel J. Wakin. "Lost in Yonkers: A Cemetery and 135 of Its Children." *The New York Times*, 7 July 2004.
[18] Ernie Garcia. "2 gravestones are found near store". The Journal News, 9 July 2004.
[19] Rick Archer. "Developer settles Austin Ave. cemetery dispute." *Westchester County Business Journal*, 31 January 2005. Lipman, Steve. "Cemetery Settlement Praised." *The Jewish Week*, 28 January 2005.
[20] Scharf, II, 150-151.
[21] Ibid., 150.
[22] http://www.history.army.mil/html/moh/civwaral.html
[23] "A Mystery Solved (Maybe)." *The Herald Statesman*, 26 October 1965. "Yonkers: Mysterious Concrete Slab." *The Herald Statesman*, 15 December 1965.

[1] Allison, 64.

[2] Ibid., 452.

[3] "Saint John's: First Public Burial Ground in Yonkers." Unpublished typescript, WCHS Vertical Files.

[4] Allison, 452.

[5] WCHS McDonald Papers, 490-492.

[6] Ibid., 503. Judge MacDonald's interviews with Frederick Rich are in Volume 4, 503-506 and 526-528.

[7] "A Deserted Old Graveyard." *The Westchester Record*, 13 March 1889.

[8] Westchester County Land Records Liber 632, 181; Liber 632, 186; Liber 667, 376; Liber 689, 325.

[9] Davis Funeral Home Ledger, WCHS Manuscript Collection. WCHS Cemetery Inscription Book #13, 259.

[10] WCHS Cemetery Inscription Book #13, 258-259. The persons whose remains were reinterred at Saint Paul's were Charles H. Rich (1854-1861), Elisabeth Rich (d.1807), Frederick Rich (1769-1859), Frederick D. Rich (1808-1866), Hester Rich (c.1773-1861), Phineas Rich (1771-1810) and Thomas L. Rich (1803-1881).

[11] Westchester County Land Records Liber 1358, 470-472.

[12] WCHS Hufeland Scrapbooks, Volume 25.

[13] Mackenzie, 586-587.

[14] WCHS Cemetery Inscription Book #87, 14.

[15] "It's Mount Vernon's Cemetery, But...." *The Herald Statesman*, 7 March 1966.

[16] Westchester County Land Records Liber 1358, 470.

[17] Westchester County Land Records Liber 1387, 291. Westchester County Incorporation Records Volume 5, 271.

[18] *Proceedings of the Board of Supervisors of Westchester County, N.Y.*, 1894, 127127, 155. "City and Vicinity." *The New York Times*, 11 June 1895.

[19] "It's Mount Vernon's Cemetery, But...."

[20] Westchester County Land Records Liber 1236, 188-189.

[21] Bolton, *History of the Protestant Episcopal Church in the County of Westchester*, 488-489.

[22] Ibid., 489-490.

[23] Ibid., 525.

[24] "Saint John's: First Public Burial Ground in Yonkers." Unpublished typescript, WCHS Vertical Files. Richard Archer's tombstone, if it ever existed, disappeared long ago. The oldest remaining tombstone in the cemetery dates from 1790.

[25] Ibid.

[26] *The Underhill Society of America: Annual Report of the Secretary*. Brooklyn: The Underhill Society of America, 1904, 21.

[27] Westchester County Land Records Liber 110, 186. Bolton, *History of the Protestant Episcopal Church in the County of Westchester*, 525.

[28] Scharf, II, 150.

[29] "Saint John's Cemetery Holds Riverboat Victims." *The Reporter Dispatch*, 14 August 1962. "The Henry Clay Catastrophe." *The New York Times*, 2 August 1852. "Know Your Westchester: The Henry Clay Memorial." *The Standard Star*, New Rochelle, NY, 4 February 1954. This plot (Lot 238) was given to the Yonkers Lodge #232 of the Independent Order of Odd Fellows on May 25,1942 (Rural Cemetery Deeds Liber 16, 41).

[30] A.W. Mandeville. "The Burning of the Henry Clay." *Westchester County Magazine*, Vol. II, 86-88.

[31] D.H. Killeffer. *The First 150 Years of St. John's Church 1798-1948*. Tuckahoe, NY: Saint John's Church, 1948.

[32] Killeffer, 38.

[33] Scharf, I, 74.

[34] Ibid.

[35] Westchester County Land Records Liber 934, 311-318.

[36] "The New Catholic Cemetery." *The Yonkers Statesman*, 11 April 1877.

[37] Michelle O'Donnell. "Filling In a Memorial's Blank Space." *The New York Times*, 30 May 2005.

[38] *History of the Parish of the Immaculate Conception, 1848-1948*. Yonkers: Parish of the Immaculate Conception, 1948.

[39] Ibid.

[40] "Thruway To Cut Into Cemetery; Churches Aid Hunt For Owners." *The Herald Statesman*, 5 October 1953. A legal notice listing the names of the transferred remains appeared in *The Herald Statesman* on September 10, 1954. See Westchester County Clerk Map #9038 for a listing of the plots which were disturbed by construction.

[41] *New York and the War with Spain: History of the Empire State Regiments*. Albany, NY: The Argus Company, 1903, 251.

[42] Allison, 452.

[43] Mackenzie, 270.

[44] Ibid.

[45] Westchester County Land Records Liber 1191, 259-261.

[46] "Saint John's: First Public Burial Ground in Yonkers." Typescript in WCHS Vertical Files.

[47] Westchester County Land Records Liber 791, 302.

Pages 207 - 212

[1] WCHS Cemetery Inscription Book #81, 7. Merritt, 63.

[2] Merritt, 63.

[3] Bolton, II, 732.

[4] Westchester County Wills Liber B, 175.

[5] Westchester County Land Records Liber Q, 63-64.

[6] Westchester County Land Records Liber 111, 387.

[7] Westchester County Land Records Liber 537, 143-144.

[8] "Rev. Thomas McLoughlin Dies Suddenly While Celebrating Mass." *The New Rochelle Pioneer*, 13 December 1902.

[9] DAR, 160.

[10] Ibid.

[11] Ibid.

[12] Westchester County Land Records Liber 241, 241.

[13] *Westchester County Magazine*.

[14] DAR, 160.

[15] Edward G. Freehafer. *Huguenot Memorial Church in the Town of Pelham: A Centennial Review*. Pelham, NY: E.G. Freehafer, 1976.

[16] WCHS Cemetery Inscription Book #80, 27.

[17] Donnan, B-1, B-2.

[18] *Collections of the New York Historical Society for the Year 1893*, 279.

[19] Donnan, B-1.

[20] Christine Cecilia Fowlcr. *The History of the Fowlers*. Batavia, NY: Miller-Mac Printing Company Incorporated, 1950, 44-45.

[21] Baird, 466.

[22] Josephine C. Frost. *The Haviland Genealogy*. New York: The Lyons Genealogical Co., 1914, 76.

[23] Mackenzie, 476.

[24] WCHS Cemetery Inscription Book #17, 65.

[25] Anne Miller Hockman. Burial Grounds in the Mamaroneck-Larchmont Area. p.3.

[26] Spencer P. Mead. *Ye History of Ye Town of Greenwich, County of Fairfield and State of Connecticut*. New York: The Knickerbocker Press, 1911, 652-653.

[27] http://www.scc-ucc.org/about-us/our-buildings/memory-garden.html

[28] http://www.scbcny.org/columbarium.html

[29] "Oakland Cemetery." *The Yonkers Historical Society Newsletter*, Volume 1 Number 3 (Fall 1992).

[30] Bolton, *History of the Protestant Episcopal Church in the County of Westchester*, 525. The Parsonage Lot consisted of 107 Acres, including the land on which Oakland Cemetery is now located.

[31] Allison, 161.

[32] Ibid., 112.

[33] Ibid., 134.

[34] "Historic Spots Around Mount Vernon." *The Mount Vernon Chronicle*, 21 March 1890.

Sources

Books

The 175th Anniversary of The Asbury Church. Yonkers: Asbury Methodist Church, 1946.

Allison, Charles Elmer. *History of Yonkers.* New York: Wilber B. Ketcham, 1896.

Annual Report of the Secretary of War for the Year 1887. Washington, DC: Government Printing Office, 1887.

Augus, C.H. *New Rochelle Through Seven Generations.* New Rochelle, NY: The National City Bank, 1908.

Baird, Charles W. *Chronicle of a Border Town: History of Rye, Westchester County, New York, 1660-1870, Including Harrison and the White Plains till 1788.* Harrison, NY: Harbor Hills Books, 1974.

Barr, Lockwood. *Ancient Town of Pelham, Westchester County, New York.* Richmond, VA: The Dietz Press, Inc., 1946.

Bartow, Evelyn P. *Bartow Genealogy.* Baltimore: Innes and Company, 1875.

Bidwell, Frederick David. *History of the Forty-Ninth New York Volunteers.* Albany, NY: J.B. Lyon Company Printers, 1916.

Bolton, Robert. *The History of the Several Towns, Manors, and Patents of the County of Westchester, from its First Settlement to the Present Time.* Bowie, MD: Heritage Books, 1996.

Bolton, Robert. *History of the Protestant Episcopal Church in the County of Westchester.* New York: Stanford & Swards, 1855.

Brennan, Thomas A. Jr. *Church of the Immaculate Conception, Tuckahoe, New York, 1853-2003.* Tuckahoe, NY: Church of the Immaculate Conception, 2003.

Bronxville: Views and Vignettes. Bronxville, NY: The Bronxville Diamond Jubilee Committee, 1974.

Brundage, Thomas William. *A Brundage Family Genealogy.* Paia, HI: T.W. Brundage, 1989.

Building A Suburban Village: Bronxville, New York, 1898 – 1998. Bronxville, NY: Bronxville Centennial Celebration, Inc., 1998.

Burial Records of Saint Paul's Church. Eastchester, NY: Eastchester Historical Society, 1973.

Carlyle, Edward I. *William Cobbett: A Study of His Life as Shown in His Writings.* London: Archibald Constable and Company, 1904.

Christ Church at Pelham, Pelham Manor, New York. Pelham Manor, NY: The Vestry of Christ Church, 1943.

Christ United Methodist Church, New Rochelle, New York: 200 Years of Service. New Rochelle, NY: Christ United Methodist Church, 1971.

Christ's Church at the Town of Rye in the County of Westchester and the State of New York: A Chronological Historical Review. Rye, NY: Christ's Church, 1945.

Coffey, William Samuel. *Commemorative Discourse delivered at the Centennial Anniversary of the Erection and the Sixtieth of the Consecration of St. Paul's Church, East Chester.* New York: Perris & Browne, 1866.

Collections of the New York Historical Society for the Year 1895. New York: I. Riley, 1895.

Collections of the New York Historical Society for the Year 1898. New York: I. Riley, 1898.

Collections of the New York Historical Society for the Year 1899. New York: I. Riley, 1899.

Collections of the New York Historical Society for the Year 1903. New York: I. Riley, 1903.

Conway, Moncure Daniel. *The Life of Thomas Paine.* New York: Knickerbocker Press, 1908.

Dawson, Henry B. *Rambles in Westchester County, New York.* Yonkers, NY: Unknown publisher, 1866.

de Beixedon, Edward Francis Fremaux Jr. *The Ancestors and Descendants of Dr. David Rogers.* No place, 1921.

De Voe, Thomas F. *Genealogy of the DeVeaux Family.* New York: Unknown publisher, 1885.

Duyckinck, Evert A. and Duyckinck, George L. *Cyclopaedia of American Literature.* New York: Charles Scribner, 1856.

Eardeley, William A. *Westchester County, New York, Cemeteries.* Brooklyn: 1914-1917.

English, Mary O'Connor. *Early Town Records of Mamaroneck, 1697-1881.* Mamaroneck, NY: Town of Mamaroneck, 1979.

Fairchild Cemetery Manual. Brooklyn: Fairchild Sons, 1910.

First Presbyterian Church, New Rochelle, N.Y.: Yearbook, 1929. New York: Knickerbocker Press, 1929.

Forbes, Jeanne A. *Records of the Town of New Rochelle, 1699-1828.* New Rochelle, NY: Paragraph Press, 1916.

Fulcher, William G. *Mamaroneck Through the Years.* Larchmont, NY: The Larchmont Times, 1936.

Greenwood Union Cemetery, Rye, Westchester County, New York. New York: Hill Matthews Co., Inc., 1912.

Hayes, Charles Wells. *The Diocese of Western New York: History and Recollections.* Rochester, NY: Scrantom, Wetmore & Co., 1904.

History of the Parish of the Immaculate Conception, 1848-1948. Yonkers: Parish of the Immaculate Conception, 1948.

History of Rye. Rye, NY: Rye Chronicle, 1961.

History of the Village of Port Chester, New York. Port Chester, NY: Village of Port Chester Centennial Historical Book Committee, 1968.

Hoyt, David W. *A Genealogical History of the Hoyt, Haight and Hight Families*. Somersworth, NH: The New England History Press, 1984.

Hufeland, Otto. *Westchester County during the American Revolution*. White Plains, NY: Westchester County Historical Society, 1926.

Hultz, Helen Lorraine. *Scarsdale Story*. Morristown, NJ: The Evans Publishing Co., 1987.

Inskeep, Carolee R. *The Graveyard Shift: A Family Historian's Guide to New York City Cemeteries*. Orem, UT: Ancestry, 2000.

The Jay Cemetery, Rye, New York. Rye, NY: Unknown Publisher, 1947.

Killeffer, D.H. *The First 150 Years of St. John's Church 1798-1948*. Tuckahoe, NY: Saint John's Church, 1948.

Larsen, Lawrence Bernard. *A Handbook on the Symbolism of Christ Church at Pelham*. Pelham Manor, NY: Christ Church, 1965.

Lederer, Richard M. Jr. *The Place Names of Westchester County, New York*. Harrison, NY: Harbor Hill Books, 1978.

Lippsett, Paula. *Mamaroneck Town: A History of "The Gathering Place."* Mamaroneck, NY: Town of Mamaroneck, 1997.

Lossing, Benson J. *The Pictorial Field-Book of the American Revolution*. New York: Harper & Brothers, 1860.

Mackenzie, Grenville C. "Families of the Colonial Manor of Philipsburgh." Westport, CT: 1966.

McKay, Ellen Cotton. *A History of the Rye Presbyterian Church*. Rye, NY: Rye Presbyterian Church, 1957.

McLoughlin, Peter P. *Father Tom: Life and Lectures of Rev. Thomas P. McLoughlin*. New York: The Knickerbocker Press, 1919.

Merritt, Douglas. *Revised Merritt Records*. New York: T.A. Wright, 1916.

Miriam Osborn Memorial Home: 50th Anniversary. Rye, NY: The Miriam Osborn Memorial Home, 1958.

New Rochelle Tombstone Inscriptions. New Rochelle, NY: New Rochelle Chapter, Daughters of the American Revolution, 1940.

New York and the War with Spain: History of the Empire State Regiments. Albany, NY: The Argus Company, 1903.

Nichols, Herbert B. ed. *Thomas Paine Bicentennial Celebrations, 1737-1937*. New Rochelle, NY: Thomas Paine National Historical Association, 1937.

Old Wills of New Rochelle. New Rochelle: New Rochelle Chapter, Daughters of the American Revolution, 1951.

Palmer, David A. *William Palmer of Westerfield, Conn. And Westchester, N.Y.* No place: David A. Palmer, c.1994.

Peck, Helen S. *A Small History of the Gedney Family of Westchester Co., N.Y. 1603-1896*. Mamaroneck, NY: Curtis G. Peck, 1896.

Poucher, J.W. *Old Gravestones of Dutchess County, New York*. Poughkeepsie, NY: Dutchess County Historical Society, 1924.

Powell, Aaron M. *Personal Reminiscences of the Anti-Slavery and Other Reforms and Reformers*. New York: Caulon Press, 1899.

Prime, Temple. *Descent of Comfort Sands and of His Children*. New York: The De Vinne Press, 1886.

Pryer, Charles. *Legends, Traditions and Superstitions of Westchester*. New York: The Knickerbocker Press, 1890.

Records of the Town of Eastchester, New York. Eastchester, NY: Eastchester Historical Society, 1964-66.

Scharf, J. Thomas. *History of Westchester County, New York*. Philadelphia: L.E. Preston & Co., 1886.

Seacord, Morgan H. *Biographical Sketches and Index of the Huguenot Settlers of New Rochelle, 1687-1776*. New Rochelle, NY: The Huguenot Historical Association of New Rochelle, 1941.

Seacord, Morgan H. *Historical Landmarks of New Rochelle*. New Rochelle, NY: New Rochelle Trust Co., 1938.

Seth, Natalie M. *The Guion Family: A Genealogy of the Descendants of Louis Guion of New Rochelle, N.Y.* No place, 1956.

Smith, Edmund H. *Reports of Cases Decided in the Court of Appeals of the State of New York*. Vol. 150. Albany: James B. Lyon, 1896.

Thayer, William S. et al. *Homes of American Statesmen*. New York: G.P. Putnam and Co., 1853.

Thomas Paine and New Rochelle, N.Y. New Rochelle, NY: The Thomas Paine National Historical Association, 1951.

Tompkins, David A. *Eastchester Village, Colonial New York, 1666-1698: Maps & Inhabitants*. Eastchester, NY: Eastchester Historical Society, 1997.

Trinity Church. New Rochelle, NY: Trinity Church, 1973.

Trinity Church, New Rochelle, N.Y., 1688-1938: A Brief Sketch Written on the Occasion of the Two Hundred and Fiftieth Anniversary of the Church. New Rochelle, NY: Trinity Church, 1938.

The Underhill Society of America: Annual Report of the Secretary. Brooklyn: The Underhill Society of America, 1904.

The Underhill Society of America: Annual Report of the Secretary. Brooklyn: The Underhill Society of America, 1905.

Vale, G. *The Life of Thomas Paine*. New York: The Beacon, 1853.

Walker, Mrs. Harry Leslie and LaMont A. Warner, eds. *A History of the Reformed Church of Bronxville*. Bronxville, NY: The Consistory of the Reformed Church of Bronxville, 1951.

Whittelsey, Charles Barney. *The Roosevelt Genealogy 1649-1902*. Hartford: J.B. Burr & Co., 1902.

Williams, Gray. *Picturing Our Past: National Register Sites in Westchester County*. Elmsford, NY: Westchester County Historical Society, 2003.

Zwerger, Mark R. et al. *Images of America: The Osborn*. Portsmouth, NH: Arcadia Publishing, 2008.

Journal and Magazine Articles

Coles, Mrs. Selleck E. "Mamaroneck, N.Y., Graveyard Inscriptions." *The New York Genealogical and Biographical Record*, Vol. 56 No.1 (January, 1925).

Darling, Charles W. "Antoine L'Espenard, the French Huguenot, and Some of His Descendants." *The New York Genealogical and Biographical Record*, Vol. XXIV No.3 (July 1893).

Flynn, James J. and Huguenin, Charles A. "Where Are the Bones of Thomas Paine?" *The Westchester Historian*, Vol. 37 No. 1 (January-March 1961).

"Grave of Cuff Brown – Slave." *Westchester County Magazine*, Vol.II., 86.

Mandeville, A.W. "The Burning of the Henry Clay." *Westchester County Magazine*, Vol. II, 86-88.

Mandeville, A.W. "Were These Revolutionary Soldiers?" *Westchester County Magazine*, Vol. 2, No. 1 (October 1908).

Mead, Frances G.. 'The Asbury Methodist Church in Crestwood." *The Westchester Historian*, Vol.11 No.4 (October 1935), 77-78.

Osborn, David. "Who Were the Hessians?" *The Westchester Historian*, Vol. 80 No. 1 (Winter 2004),

Quirin, William. "Under the Apple Tree: The History of Golf in Westchester County." *The Westchester Historian*, Vol. 85 No.3 (Summer 2009).

"Saint Bartholomew's Day." *The Westchester Historian*, Volume 32 Number 4 (Fall, 1956).

Totten, John Reynolds. "Department for Registration of Pedigrees." *The New York Genealogical and Biographical Record*, Vol. LI No. 1 (January 1920), 86.

Van Wagenen, G.H. "Inscriptions From Tombstones in a Cemetery at Rye, Westchester County, N.Y." *The New York Genealogical & Biographical Record*, Vol.16 No.3 (July 1885).

Weir, Richard B. "Bronxville's Little Cemetery." *The Villager*, March 1992.

Wilson, James Grant. "President Edward F. DeLancey." *The New York Genealogical and Biographical Record*, Vol. XXXVI, No. 3.

New York State Library

Daughters of the American Revolution Cemetery, Church & Town Records

Westchester County Archives

Proceedings of the Board of Supervisors of Westchester County, N.Y.
Westchester County Incorporation Records
Westchester County Rural Cemetery Deeds
Westchester County Wills
Works Progress Administration Cemetery Maps

Westchester County Clerk's Office

Westchester County Clerk Maps
Westchester County Clerk Land Records Libers

Westchester County Historical Society

Cemetery Transcription Books
Davis Funeral Home Ledger
Hufeland Scrapbooks
McDonald Papers

Typescripts

"Military graves in St. James the Less Cemetery, Scarsdale, N.Y., copied from the church files by the Scarsdale American Legion." Typescript in WCHS Collection.

Prigoff, Milton. "A History and detailed lists of the cemeteries in the town of Mamaroneck, N.Y." Typescript in WCHS Collection.

Tropp, Alberta R. "Methodist Episcopal Church in Mamaroneck." Typescript in WCHS Collection.

"Notes of the Nelson Family." Typescript in WCHS Vertical Files.
"The Nelsons of Westchester, Putnam & Dutchess Counties." Typescript in WCHS Vertical Files.

Newspapers

The Daily Argus, Mount Vernon, NY
The Daily Item, Port Chester, NY
The Daily Times, Mamaroneck, NY
The Herald Statesman, Yonkers, NY
The Journal News, White Plains, NY
The Larchmont Times, Larchmont, NY
The New York Times, New York, NY
The New York Tribune, New York, NY
The Reporter Dispatch, White Plains, NY
The Standard Star, New Rochelle, NY
The Westchester Record, Mount Vernon, NY

Websites

www.anglicanhistory.org
www.greenwoodunion.org
www.history.army.mil
www.med.cornell.edu
www.nps.gov
www.nysm.nysed.gov.
www.thomaspaine.org
www.history.army.mil
www.homeofheroes.com

Maps and Atlases

Beers, F.W. *Atlas of New York and Vicinity*. New York: F.W. Beers, A.D. Ellis & G.G. Soule, 1867.
Kates, Herbert S. and Kates, Jerome S. *A Map of the City of New Rochelle, New York Showing Historic Sites*. 1938.

Index

Acheson, Eliza – 2-3
Adams, George Washington – 47
Adams, John Quincy – 47
Adams, Louisa – 47
Adee, William – 166
African Cemetery (Rye) – 123, 124-125
Allaire Family – 89, 92
Allaire Family Burial Ground – 60-63, 117
Allaire, Alexander – 60
Allaire, Alexander (Captain) – 61-62
Allaire, Frances – 62
Allaire, Isaac – 61
Allaire, James McBride – 95
Allaire, Maria – 62
Allaire, Peter Alexander – 60,62
Allaire, Peter Erickson – 63
Allaire, Robert A. – 61
Allaire, Taulman – 61
Andrews, Elisha – 140
Archer Family – 89
Archer, Richard – 194
Asbury Methodist Church Cemetery – 175, 176-180
Austin, Elizabeth – 196
Austin, Freelove – 196
Austin, Hannah Eliza – 196
Austin, John – 196
Austin, William James – 196
Austin, Wilsea – 196
Avery, Ephraim – 134-135
Avery, Hannah – 134-135
Bailey Family – 197
Bailey, Elizabeth – 197
Bailey, Ezekiel – 197
Bain, Agnes – 38-39
Baker, William – 53
Baldwin Family – 102
Ballinger, Henry C. – 173
Banyer, Goldsborough – 143
Banyer, Maria Jay – 143
Barker Family – 31
Barker, Elisabeth A. Bruce – 31
Barker, Laura Ann – 30
Barker, Mary – 31
Barneto, Jacqueline – 50
Bartow, Theodosius – 117
Bayley, Joseph – 118
Bayley, Sarah – 118
Bayley, Susan – 118
Beechwood Cemetery – 59, 64-66, 80-81, 102
Bell, Sarah – 4
Bell, Thomas – 4
Berrian, Richard – 175
Berrian, Stephen – 175

Berrian, William – 175
Bleecker Family – 172
Blessed Sacrament Church Cemetery – 102
Blind Brook Burial Ground – 123, 126-131
Bloomer Family – 35
Bloomer, Robert – 154-155
Bolton, Abby – 122
Bolton, Cornelius Winter – 5
Bolton, Richard Woodhull – 122
Bolton, Robert – 122
Bolton, Robert, Jr. – 122
Bongrand, Louis – 89
Bonnett, Eliza – 67, 69
Bonnett, John – 177
Bonnett, John – 71
Bonnett, T. Cornelius – 67, 69
Boudet, Daniel – 116
Boulle, Augusta – 66
Bouton, Sally Ann – 128
Brevoort Cemetery – 141
Brewer, Solomon – 93
Bridge, Christopher – 133-134
Briggs, Eustatia – 51
Broderick, Bridget – 195
Bronxville Cemetery – 1, 2-4
Bronxville Reformed Church Burying Ground and Vault – 5
Brooks, David – 138
Brown, Amy – 152
Brown, Ann – 170-171
Brown, Cuff – 152
Brown, Hannah – 152
Brown, Jonathan Jr. – 128
Brown, Jonathan Sr. – 110
Brown, Nathaniel (Rye) – 154-155
Brown, Nathaniel (Scarsdale) – 170-171
Brown, Nehemiah – 152
Brown, Samuel – 152
Brown, Steachey – 177
Brown-Sands Family Burial Ground - 152
Brundage Family Burial Ground – 151, 153-155
Brundage, John – 153
Brundage, Joshua – 153-155
Buckley, William – 167
Budd Family Burial Ground (Mamaroneck) – 11, 40-42
Budd Family Burying Ground (Rye City) – 132
Budd, Anne – 130-131
Budd, Elisha – 130-131, 132
Budd, Eme Sutton – 129
Budd, Gilbert (Colonel) – 11, 40-42
Budd, Gilbert (Doctor) – 40-41, 132
Budd, John – 132, 168
Budd, Joseph – 130, 132

Budd, Mary – 40
Budd, Sarah – 41
Budd, Underhill – 40-41, 130, 132
Burns Family – 102
Burying Ground on Old Benjamin Archer Farm – 170
Caramanno, Joseph P. – 200
Carpenter Cemetery – 59, 67-69
Carpenter, Joseph – 67-69
Carpenter, Margaret – 67-69
Carpenter, Sarah – 164
Cashin Family – 104
Cashin, Anne – 104
Cashin, Josie – 104
Cashin, Martin – 104
Cashin, Mary – 104
Cashman, Catherine – 103
Cashman, Hannah – 103
Cashman, John – 105
Cashman, Martin – 105
Cashman, Michael – 105
Cashman, Thomas – 105
Cashman, Timothy – 103
Cemetery Behind Kindergarten – 40
Chiaro, Francesco – 200
Chiaro, Maria – 200
Christ Church Cemetery (Rye City) – 123
Christ Episcopal Church Vaults (Pelham) – 64, 121, 122
Christ Methodist Church Cemetery (New Rochelle) – iv,
    70-73, 109-110
Christ's Church Burial Ground and Tomb – 133-137
Christ's Church Rectors' Burial Ground – 133-137
Christian, Marcus – 46-47
Churchwell, Joseph – 140
City of Rye Cemetery – 126
Clark, Annie Knower – 148
Clark, Catherine Ann – 148
Clark, Daniel – 1468
Clark, Ebenezer – 148
Clark, Elizabeth – 71
Clark, Fanny – 196
Clark, John – 95
Clark, Moses – iv, 71
Clements, Elizabeth – 54
Close, Eloise Allaire – 61
Cobbett, William – 59, 113-115
Cochran Family – 102
Coffey, William S. – 9, 43, 48
Collison Family – 189
Colmbo, L. – 86
Colonial Acres Cemetery – 170
Colored Peoples Burying Ground (Rye) – 124
Combs, Thomas D. – 204
Congregation People of Righteousness Cemetery – 175,
    181-186
Connolly, Emma – viii
Connolly, F. Halcyon – viii

Connolly, Frank H. – xii
Consadene Family – 102
Cooper, James Fenimore – 11, 12
Copcutt Family – 188
Cornell Family – 170-171
Cornell, Margaret – 32
Coutant Cemetery – 74-76
Coutant, Catherine Bonnefoy – 74-75
Coutant, Isaac – 74
Coutant, Isaac Jr. – 75
Coutant, Isaiah – 75
Coutant, Jean – 74, 98
Coutant, Jean Jr. – 74
Coutant, John – 75
Coutant, Sarah Guion – 74
Covenantor Cemetery – 2
Crawford, Permelia Ann – 176
Crosby, Horace Franklin – 66
Crosby, Norman Wilson – 66
Crowther, John J. – 76
Curser Plot – 206
Curtenius, Peter Theobaldus – 121, 122
Cypress Hill National Cemetery – 77
Daniel Merritt Cemetery – 163
Davenport, Elizabeth – 129
Davenprt, Newberry/Newbury – 129
Davids Island Cemetery – 77
DeLancey Family Burial Ground – 11, 12-14
DeLancey, Edward Floyd – 13, 28
DeLancey, Frances Munro – 13
DeLancey, John Peter – 11, 12-13
DeLancey, Josephine Floyd – 13
DeLancey, Thomas James – 13
DeLancey, William Heathcote – 13
DeVeau Family Burial Ground – 78
DeVeau, Abel – 78
DeVeau, Daniel – 78
DeVeau, Magdalen – 78
DeVeau, Mary – 78
DeVoe, Daniel – 192
DeVoe, Joshua – 191
Dillon Family – 102
Dingee Cemetery – 25
Dingee, John – 26
Disbrow Family – 37-38
Disbrow Family Burial Ground – vi, xii, 11, 15-16
Disbrow, Ann – xii
Disbrow, David R. – 6
Disbrow, Henry – xii, 5-6
Disbrow, John – 180
Disbrow, Margaret – 38
Disbrow, Mary – 15, 38
Disbrow, Peter – 15
Dixon, Mary – 21
Donaldson Cemetery – 25
Donaldson, James – 31

Dougherty, Ann – 205
Drake Family – 47
Drake, Cate – 54
Drake, Ellener – 56
Dwight, Albert Sutherland – 197
Dwight, Catherine E. – 197
Dwight, Timothy C. – 197
Eastchester Cemetery – 46
Eastchester Churchyard – 46
Ebelt, William H. – 6
Emma Bizallion Plot – 141
Emmett, Robert Temple – 65
Evans, Elizabeth Rebecca – 122
Evans, William Matthew – 122
Farrell, Edward J. Jr. – 85
First Methodist Church Cemetery (New Rochelle) – 70
First Methodist Episcopal Church of Yonkers Cemetery – 177
Flandreau Family Burial Ground – 59, 79-82
Flandreau, Benjamin (1718-1800) – 79, 81
Flandreau, Benjamin (1762-1807) – 82
Flandreau, Benjamin (1810-1844) – 79
Flandreau, Isabelle – 80
Flandreau, James – 89
Florence, Benjamin – 17
Florence, Elizabeth – 17
Florence, Peter – 17-18
Florence, Sarah – 17
Florence, William J. – 17-18
Florence-Powell Family Burial Ground – 17-18
Foote, David – 137
Forrest Family – 1
Fowler, Benjamin – 206
Fowler, Dorothy Valentine – 206
Fowler, Elizabeth Brown Merritt – 206
Fowler, Jeremiah –54
Fowler, Vincent – 206
Fox, Nicholas – 149
Foy, Eddie – 85
Foy, Madeline – 85
Francis Family – 125
Fulginiti, Domenico – 201
Gedney Family Burial Ground (Solomon, Town of Rye) – 11, 151, 156-157
Gedney Family Cemetery (Eleazar, Town of Mamaroneck) – 19-24, 156
Gedney, Absalom –20
Gedney, Alexander – 157
Gedney, Amy Haight – 157
Gedney, Anna   20 21, 23 24
Gedney, Bartholomew – 23
Gedney, Charlotte – 157
Gedney, Eleazar – 20-11, 23-24, 156
Gedney, Hannah – 23
Gedney, Hester C. – 157
Gedney, James – 21, 156

Gedney, John – 20, 24
Gedney, Jonathan – 157
Gedney, Peter – 157
Gedney, Phebe – 21
Gedney, Sally Ann – 157
Gedney, Silvanus – 20
Gedney, Solomon – 156
Gedney, Solomon Jr. – 157
Gedney, Susan – 157
Gedney, William – 157
Gee, Rachel – 54
Gibbs, Milton – 77
Gönczi, György – 188
Govers Family – 102
Greenwood Union Cemetery – 26, 29, 123, 138-140, 148, 150, 163, 165, 166, 168
Griffen, Benjamin – 158
Griffen, Edward – 158
Griffen, Jeremiah – 158
Griffen, John – 158
Griffen, John – 170
Griffen, William – 170
Griffen, William Jr. – 170
Griffen-Rogers Family Burial Ground – 11, 158-159
Griffin Family – 102
Griffin, Ann – 122
Griffin-Cornell Family Burial Ground – 169, 170-171
Grogan Family – 102
Guion Family – 89
Guion Family Burial Ground – 11, 151, 160-162
Guion, Amon – 96-97, 116
Guion, Elias – 96
Guion, Eliza – 108
Guion, Elizabeth – 92
Guion, John Jr. – 160
Guion, John Sr. – 160
Guion, Louis – 87, 92-93, 160
Guion, Mary – 108
Guion, Thomas – 161
Hadden Family Burial Ground – 11, 25-27
Hadden, Bartholomew – 25
Hadden, Job – 26
Hadden, Lott – 25
Hadden, Ophelia Marie – 26
Hadden, Thomas – 25
Hadden, William – 25
Haight, Anne Bloomer – 35
Haight, Josiah – 35
Hains, Elizabeth – 156
Hains, Martha – 130
Hains, Peter – 156
Hains, Phebe – 156
Hains, Sibbey – 130
Hains, William H. – 157
Halstead, Underhill – 124
Halsted, Ezekiel – 128

Hare, Stanley – 26
Harrison Family Tomb – 83
Harrison, David – 83
Harsen, Elisha – 80
Hart Family Burial Ground – 141
Hart, Eliza – 141
Hart, James – 141
Hart, Jonathan – 141
Hart, Peter G. – 141
Haskell, Mary – 137
Hawser, Lydia – 126
Haywood, Alfred Williams Jr. – 173
Haywood, Snowden – 173
Heady, Lazarus – 25
Heathcote Hill Revolutionary War Burials – 28
Heathcote, Caleb – 11, 12
Heermance, William L. – 189
Henderson Family – 89-91
Henderson, Alexander – 90, 93
Henderson, William – 90, 93
Hoden, Mary – 8
Holohan, Sarah – 7
Holy Mount Cemetery – 1, 6
Holy Sepulchre Cemetery – 59, 84-86, 102, 104
Horstig, Ernst R. – 158-159
Horton, Mary L. – 140
Horton, Sarah – 130
Horton, Sarah – 158
Houdin, Michael – 116
Howell Cemetery – 30
Huestis, Benjamin – 178
Huestis, Hannah – 178
Huguenot Burying Ground – vi, 87-98, 117
Hull, Anne – 195
Hunt Family – 8
Hyer, John – 140
Immaculate Conception Church Burying Ground – 1, 7
Immaculate Conception, Church of – 1, 7
Isherwood, Benjamin F. – 188
Jay Family Cemetery – 123, 142-144
Jay, James – 143
Jay, John – 142-144
Jay, Mary – 144
Jay, Peter [I] – 142, 144
Jay, Peter [II] – 143
Jay, Peter Augustus – 143
Jerome, Leonard W. – 187
John Richbell Burial Ground – 37
Johnson, Eliza – 195
Keirns, Michael – iii
Kelahan, John F. – 200
Kennedy, Ellen – 103
Kennedy, George H. – 3
Kennedy, John – 103
Kniffen, George – 168
Kniffen, Mary – 168

Kniffin, Jonathan – 168
Landrine, Susanne – 87, 92
Lawrence Family – 20
Lawrence, Genevra – 22
Lawrence, William – 20
Lawton, John Warren – 92-93
Leale, Charles Augustus – 188
Leary Family – 1
Leggett, William – 118-119
Leonard Lispenard Tomb – 99-100
Levine, Bella – iii
Lewis, William B. – 65
Lings, Albert A. – 200
Lispenard Family Burial Ground – 99-100
Lispenard, Elizabeth – 99-100
Lispenard, Leonard – 99-100
Lyon, Joseph – 127-128, 130-131
Lyon, Sarah – 128
Lyon, Sarah – 41
Mamaroneck Methodist Church Cemetery – 29
Mamaroneck Quaker Cemetery – 30-32
Marven, Martha – 135, 137
McCluskey, William – 195
McDonald, Charles – 129
McFarlan Family – 172
McLoughlin, Thomas – 84
McLoughlin, Thomas P. – 84
McNamara, Tom – 84-85
Mead Farm Burying Ground (Rye) – 123
Mead, Benjamin – 124
Merritt Family Burial Ground (Hog Pen Ridge) – 151, 163
Merritt Family Burial Ground (Lyon's Point) – 164
Merritt, Andrew – 164
Merritt, Daniel – 151, 163
Merritt, Daniel E. – 151, 163
Merritt, Edward – vi, 16
Merritt, Emma – 151, 163
Merritt, Gilbert – 15-16
Merritt, Job – 167
Merritt, John – 155
Merritt, John – 164
Merritt, John – 165
Merritt, Jotham – 163
Merritt, Mary – 167
Merritt, Nehemiah – 164
Merritt, Rebecca – 151, 163
Merritt, Robert – 164
Merritt, Ruth – 171
Merritt, Thomas – 151, 163, 164
Merritt-Pine Family Burial Ground – 165
Milton Cemetery – 126
Miriam Osborn Memorial Cemetery – 123, 145
Molloy Family – 102
Monahan, Margaret – 205
Monahan, Timothy – 205

Moore, Ann – 136
Morell Family – 170
Morgan Family – 47
Morgan, Abigail – 45
Morgan, Caleb – 45
Morgan, Isabella – 45
Mott Cemetery – 37
Mott, James – 37-38
Mott, Mary Richbell – 38
Muirson, George – 133-134
Mullinex, Joseph – 81
Munro, Peter Jay – 143
Murtha Family – 204
Murtha, John – 204
Nelson Family Burial Ground – 11, 33-34
Nelson, Mahar-shalal-hash-baz – 33
Nelson, Polycarpus – iii, 11, 33-34
Nelson, Samuel – 49
New Rochelle Presbyterian Church Cemetery – 101
New York Infant Asylum Cemetery –43, 44
Nicoll, William – 95
North, Mary F. Guion – 162
O'Gorman, W.H. – 7
Oakland Cemetery – 175, 187-189
Oakley, John – 197
Oakley, Rachel – 197
Odell, Ann – 110
Odell, Daniel – 177
Odell, Hanford – 167
Old Catholic Cemetery (New Rochelle) – 102-106
Old Rye Cemetery – 126
Old Town of Mamaroneck Cemetery – 40
Oliver, Adeline – 199
Oliver, Mary – 199
Osborn Home – 145, 150
Osborn, Miriam Adelaide Trowbridge – 145
Otis, Elisha – 187
Paine, Thomas – 59, 113-115
Palmer, Bloomer & Haight Burial Ground – 35-36, 76
Palmer, Elihu – 35
Palmer, Harriet M. – 35-36
Palmer, John – 35
Palmer, John W. – 35-36
Palmer, Mary – 31
Palmer, Mary – 35
Palmer, Mary Drake – 30
Palmer, Samuel – 30
Palmer, Solomon – 30-31
Palmer-Barker Family Burial Ground – 30-32
Parcot Family   89, 94
Parcot, John – 94
Parcot, John Jr. – 94
Parcot, Pierre – 89, 94
Parsons Family – 148
Parsons, Arthur Wellesley – 148
Pell, Mangle Minthorne – 56

Pell, Philip – 55
Pell, Samuel – 55
Pell's Point, Battle of – 47
Philipsburgh Manor Potter's Field – 190
Philipsburgh Manor Slave Burying Ground – 190
Pine, Hannah Merritt – 165
Pine, James – 165
Pine, Samuel – 165
Pine, Sarah Merritt – 165
Pinkney, Will – 43
Popham Family – 172-173
Popham, William – 172-173
Popham, William Sherbrooke – 172
Port Chester Presbyterian Church Cemetery – 151, 166-167
Powell, Abigail – 17-18
Powell, Thomas – 17-18
Powell, William – 17-18
Pugsley Family Burial Ground – 107-108
Pugsley, Hannah – 107-108
Pugsley, James – 107-108
Punderson, Ebenezer – 136
Purdy Family Burial Ground (Rye) – 146-147
Purdy, Daniel – 147
Purdy, Edwin – 124-125
Purdy, Jonathan – 146
Purdy, Joshua – 146-147
Quaker Ridge Cemetery – 170
Reformed Presbyterian Cemetery (Bronxville) – 1
Reformed Presbyterian Church of Manhattan – 1
Regan, Helen – 205
Reid, Thomas – 205
Remington, David – 148
Renoud, Stephen – 71
Rhineland, Thomas – 49
Rich Family Burial Ground – 191-192
Rich, Anna Maria – 192
Rich, Hannah – 191
Rich, John – 192
Rich, Lewis – 191
Rich, Stephen – 191
Rich, Thomas – 191
Richbell Cemetery – xi, 1, 37-39
Richbell, Ann – 38
Richbell, John – 15, 30, 37-39, 158
Richbell-Williams Cemetery – 37
Ridge Street Cemetery – 163
Riley, Edward – 42
Rising, Newell – 139
Robinson Family Burial Ground – 36, 74-76
Robinson, Elizabeth Palmer – 76
Robinson, Gilbert – 76
Robinson, Israel P. – 76
Robinson, James – 76
Rockwell, George S. – 196
Rogers, Catharine Wright – 159

Rogers, David Jr. (Doctor) – 158-159
Rogers, David L. – 159
Rogers, David Sr. – 159
Rogers, Esther Horton – 158-159
Rogers, Gilbert – 159
Roosevelt, Elbert – 64, 121, 122
Roosevelt, Jane – 122
Roosevelt, Mary Eliza – 122
Roulstone, Clara – 32
Ryche, Balthasar – 191-192
Rye Catholic Cemetery – 149
Rye Colored Cemetery – 124
Rye Presbyterian Churchyard – 148
Rye Public Cemetery – 126
Sacred Heart Friars' Cemetery – 193
Saint James the Less Episcopal Church Cemetery – 169, 172-174
Saint John's Cemetery – xii, 175, 194-197, 206
Saint John's Episcopal Church Cemetery (Colonial Heights) – xi, 175, 198-199
Saint John's Methodist Church Cemetery – 70-71, 73, 109-110
Saint Joseph's Cemetery (New Rochelle) – 102-106
Saint Joseph's Cemetery (Yonkers) – 175, 200-202
Saint Mary's Cemetery (Rye) – 149
Saint Mary's Cemetery (Yonkers) – iii, 175, 203-204
Saint Matthew's Cemetery – 102
Saint Paul's Church Cemetery – iii, 1, 8-9, 43. 45-56
Salter, John B. – 6
Schontag, Christian – 66
Schontag, John – 66
Schureman, Frederick – 78
Schureman, John – 73
Schuyler, Grace Hunter – 122
Schuyler, Harriet – 122
Schuyler, Leonora R. – 169
Scotch Presbyterian Cemetery – 2
Seaberry, George W. – 167
Seacord Family Burial Ground – 70-73
Seacord, Abraham – 72
Seacord, Israel – 71-72
Seacord, James A. – 82
Seacord, Jane – 71
Seaman, Giles – 38
Seaman, Lydia – 38
Secor, Isaac – 32
Sherwood Park Cemetery – iii, 175, 191-192
Sherwood, Elizabeth – 177
Shoemakers Yard – 2
Shute Family Burial Ground – 111-112
Shute, Ann – 111-112
Shute, Elizabeth – 111-112
Shute, Louisa – 112
Shute, Peter – 111-112
Shute, Richard – iii, 48, 52, 111
Sickles, Daniel E. – 64-65

Sickles, George Garrett – 64-65
Sickles, Mary S. – 65
Siegel, Mary E.F. – 84
Smith, Albert – 64-65
Smith, Eliza A. – 195
Smith, Hannah – 199
Smith, Isaac Dyckman – xi
Sniffin Family Burial Ground – 151, 168
Sniffin, Caleb – 151
Sniffin, Hannah – 151
Sniffin, Mary – 151
Soldiers' Burying Ground (Eastchester) – 8
Standard, Thomas – 46
Staple, Elizabeth Lispenard – 99-100
Stevens, Richard – 46
Stevenson, Eliza – 179
Stevenson, Samuel – 179
Stouppe, Pierre – 116
Stowell, Bruce K. – 173
Stowell, Dwight B. Jr. – 173
Stuppe, Magdalene – 116
Szpytkowska, Anna – 201
Taft, Charles Sabin – 56
Taylor, Eliza Cornell – 29
Taylor, Jane Ellenor – 110
Taylor, William – 29
Thate, Daniel William – 195
Theall Family Burial Ground – 150
Theall, Billa – 150
Theall, Jamima – 123
Theall, Thomas – 150
Thomas Paine Burial Plot – 115-115
Titford Family – 143
Town Field Burying Ground (Rye) – 123, 150
Town of Mamaroneck Cemetery – 11, 40-42
Townsend, John – 22
Trinity Episcopal Church African Cemetery – 120
Trinity Episcopal Church Cemetery – 61, 89-90, 98, 116-119
Tuckahoe Methodist Church Cemetery – 177
Tuckahoe Road Burying Ground – 206
Tudor, James – 69
Turnbull, Charles – 51
Turpin, Joseph Thomas – 67, 120
Underhill – Eliza H. – 180
Underhill, Bishop L. – 178
Underhill, Frances Augusta – 179
Underhill, Mary Shute – 112
Valentine Family – 53, 212
Valentine Family Burial Ground – 212
Ward, Stephen – 55
Ward's House Revolutionary War Burials – 1, 8-10
Watkins, Judith Livingston – 143
Webb, Nehemiah – 127
Wetmore, James – 133-135
Weyman, Jonathan – 96

Whittaker, Frederick – 50
Williams, Amos – 125
Winter Hill Burying Ground – 1, 8-10
Wright, Elizabeth – 56
Wright, Thomas – 56

Back Cover, Inside, Top Left: This 2007 photo depicts the monument which marks the graves of the victims of the *Henry Clay* disaster who are buried in Saint John's Cemetery in Yonkers. The inscription, which was illegible as much as 100 years ago, once read:

HERE LIE THE BODIES OF
MRS. ANNE HULL, and her sister
MRS. ELIZA A. SMITH, both of Phila
ELIZA JOHNSON of Albany
BRIDGET BRODERICK. WM. MC
CLUSKEY and two women
and one man whose names
are unknown all of whom
were lost from the HENRY CLAY
on the burning of that
steam boat 2 1-2 miles below
the village of Yonkers on
her passage from Albany
to New York July 28th 1852

Back Cover, Inside, Center Left: This crudely inscribed memorial in Saint Paul's Episcopal Church Cemetery, Mount Vernon, marks the grave of Rachel Gee, who died in 1752.

HER
LIETH · THE
BoDY · OF GE
RECHEl · E
DE · MA · YE
20 1752

Back Cover, Inside, Bottom Left: The headstone of Caleb Morgan was carved by Thomas Brown. Mr. Brown originally carved skulls and bones on his tombstones, but switched to cherubic angels such as this one after the Revolutionary War.

Back Cover, Inside, Top Right: This 1956 photo was taken looking northwest from the southeast corner of the Huguenot Burying Ground shortly before the cemetery was removed for the construction of the New England Thruway. Fieldstones which marked some of the earliest burials in the cemetery can be seen in the foreground. The Henderson family plot is visible at left, while the large building behind the cemetery, the Odell Court Apartments, still stands today.

Back Cover, Inside, Bottom Right: This photo depicts New Rochelle's Flandreau Family Burial Ground in 2005. The tombstone leaning against the tree marks the first interment in the cemetery, that of Benjamin Flandreau. It reads:

In
Memory of
BENJAMIN FLANDRAU,
who departed this life
Feb^ry 19th 1800
Aged 81 Years 5 month
and 15 days

Exult my soul with days that flow
From GOD'S Almighty hand
Whilst here my mouldering body lies
To rise at his command.

The tombstone remnant at the foot of Benjamin's headstone marks the grave of his son, also named Benjamin. The tombstone at left marks the grave of Joseph Mullinex (1724-1807).

Back Cover, Outside: The French-inscribed tombstone of Susanne Landrine (1732-1750) in Trinity Episcopal Church Cemetery, New Rochelle.

VOISI Le
COrP De
SVSanne
LanDrin ag
De · 18 · M · Le · 6
Da · L · 1750